REFLECTIONS ON THE
REVOLUTION IN FRANCE

broadview editions
series editor: Martin R. Boyne

The Right Hon. Edmund Burke, John Jones, 1790. Yale Center for British Art, Yale Art Gallery Collection, The Mabel Brady Garvan Collection.

REFLECTIONS ON THE REVOLUTION IN FRANCE

An Abridgement with Supporting Texts

Edmund Burke

edited by Brian R. Clack

broadview editions

BROADVIEW PRESS – www.broadviewpress.com
Peterborough, Ontario, Canada

Founded in 1985, Broadview Press remains a wholly independent publishing house. Broadview's focus is on academic publishing; our titles are accessible to university and college students as well as scholars and general readers. With over 800 titles in print, Broadview has become a leading international publisher in the humanities, with worldwide distribution. Broadview is committed to environmentally responsible publishing and fair business practices.

© 2022 Brian R. Clack

Library and Archives Canada Cataloguing in Publication

Title: Reflections on the Revolution in France : an abridgement with supporting texts / Edmund Burke ; edited by Brian R. Clack
Names: Burke, Edmund, 1729-1797, author. | Clack, Brian R., editor.
Series: Broadview editions.
Description: Series statement: Broadview editions | Includes bibliographical references.
Identifiers: Canadiana (print) 20210287578 | Canadiana (ebook) 20210287594 | ISBN 9781554814428 (softcover) | ISBN 9781770488304 (PDF) | ISBN 9781460407783 (EPUB)
Subjects: LCSH: France—History—Revolution, 1789-1799—Causes. | LCSH: France—Politics and government—1789-1799.
Classification: LCC DC150 .B857 2021 | DDC 944.04—dc23

Broadview Editions
The Broadview Editions series is an effort to represent the ever-evolving canon of texts in the disciplines of literary studies, history, philosophy, and political theory. A distinguishing feature of the series is the inclusion of primary source documents contemporaneous with the work.

Advisory editor for this volume: Michel Pharand

Broadview Press handles its own distribution in North America:
PO Box 1243, Peterborough, Ontario K9J 7H5, Canada
555 Riverwalk Parkway, Tonawanda, NY 14150, USA
Tel: (705) 743-8990; Fax: (705) 743-8353
email: customerservice@broadviewpress.com

For all territories outside of North America, distribution is handled by Eurospan Group.

Broadview Press acknowledges the financial support of the Government of Canada for our publishing activities.

Canadä

Typesetting: George Kirkpatrick

PRINTED IN CANADA

Contents

Acknowledgements

I am enormously grateful to Don LePan at Broadview for encouraging me to put this edition together, and to Stephen Latta for being a superb (and very patient) editor. Gratitude is also owed to Martin Boyne, Tara Lowes, and Michel Pharand for their careful work on the preparation of the final manuscript. Among the colleagues, friends, and family members who have helped me with this project, I would especially like to acknowledge Keith Bernstein, Derrick Cartwright, Alan Clack, Ann Clack, Beverley Clack, Del Dickson, Steven Ealy, Tyler Hower, Eric Kraft, Robert Lindsey, Felicity McCutcheon, Noelle Norton, Lindy Villa, Lori Watson, and Matt Zwolinski. Highest thanks go to my wife, Sabrina Kaiser, for her love, and for her willingness to let Burke live with us for these past four years.

Introduction

Edmund Burke's *Reflections on the Revolution in France* is a book that, in Russell Kirk's phrase, "set the course" for the conservative tradition in modern politics.[1] Many of the conspicuous themes of that tradition find memorable and eloquent expression in the *Reflections*: a suspicion of abstract theorizing, and a preference for practicality as opposed to idealistic projects; reverence for the past and, accordingly, a stress on political and constitutional continuity; an appeal to prescription as the justification for institutions (namely, that they have existed "time out of mind"); the feeling that society is an organism, upon which reckless experiments should not be made; a preference, therefore, for cautious, gradual, and perhaps even imperceptible reform as opposed to dramatic, innovative, and theory-driven change; an awareness, both of the unintended consequences of theoretically appealing plans, and of the latent functions of extant institutions; a stress on the positive value of custom and prejudice; respect for hierarchies and a disdain for "levelling"; a strong esteem for private property; religion deeply valued, both as the basis of civil society and for its social and personal utility; a recognition of the need for a decent "veiling" of the naked realities of civil life; a condescending attitude toward lavish conceptions of human intellectual powers, preferring "the collected wisdom of ages to the abilities of any two men living";[2] the recommendation that human beings, often unruly and frightening, should have their passions restrained; and, accordingly, a suspicion toward extravagant claims for unbridled liberty.

All of this bubbles in Burke's mind, erupts from his pages on the French Revolution, and stamps him as "plainly the first of English conservative thinkers in influence and importance."[3] But Burke is too independent a thinker, too unclassifiable, too expansive and indeed boundless in his views, too enigmatic, to

---

1 Russell Kirk, *The Conservative Mind* (Regnery, 2001), 13.
2 Edmund Burke, *Letters on a Regicide Peace* (3rd letter), in *The Works and Correspondence of the Right Honourable Edmund Burke*, 8 vols. (Francis & John Rivington, 1852), vol. V, 358. Hereafter, references to this work will be cited as *Works* with volume and page number.
3 Anthony Quinton, *The Politics of Imperfection* (Faber & Faber, 1978), 56.

be sequestered solely within one tradition. His positions led him, indeed, at the end of his life to be outside of any party, and painfully isolated. Not that this sense of isolation would have been altogether unfamiliar to him: "I believe, in any body of men in England, I should have been in the Minority; I have always been in the Minority," he once remarked to James Boswell (1740–95).[1] Even in the *Reflections* his position is not unambiguous: "*à la fois libérale et contre-révolutionnaire*" is how it has been described.[2] As a result of his enlarged, moderate, and liberal perspective, Burke's thought has been treasured by thinking people across the political spectrum. Harold Laski (1893–1950), from the socialist left, regarded him not only as "the apostle of philosophic conservatism" but as one able "to give deep comfort to men of liberal temper": "Burke," he wrote, "has endured as the permanent manual of political wisdom without which statesmen are as sailors on an uncharted sea."[3]

Burke was in the twilight of a distinguished parliamentary career when he wrote the *Reflections*. His was a life peppered with achievements, both political and literary, and with no small share of mystery. The year of his birth, though most commonly listed as 1729, is a subject of dispute,[4] and while Dublin is generally regarded as his birthplace, this too has been contested.[5] A question mark even hangs over the location of Burke's place of burial: it is contended by some—though by no means all—that Burke, fearful that the French revolutionaries would desecrate his body, arranged for the true place of his interment to be kept secret.[6] The mists surrounding expanses of Burke's life seem in

---

1 James Boswell, *Life of Johnson* (1791; Oxford UP, 1990), 904.

2 Philippe Raynaud, preface to French edition of *Réflections sur la Révolution de France* (Hachette, 1989), lvi, qtd. in Conor Cruise O'Brien, *The Great Melody: A Thematic Biography of Edmund Burke* (U of Chicago P, 1992), lxxiv.

3 Harold Laski, *Political Thought in England from Locke to Bentham* (Thornton Butterworth, 1930), 172.

4 See F.P. Lock, *Edmund Burke: Volume I: 1730–1784* (Clarendon Press, 1999), 16–17.

5 Conor Cruise O'Brien (*Great Melody* 14) entertains the possibility that Burke was born in Shanballymore, in rural (and what would be regarded as suspiciously Catholic) County Cork.

6 The secret grave conspiracy, reported in *Notes and Queries*, vol. CXLIX, August 1925, p. 80, is accepted by Isaac Kramnick (*The Rage of Edmund Burke* [Basic Books, 1977], 189) and more recently

part born of his habitual circumspection with regard to personal matters. As early as 1746, we find him recommending caution and reserve to his friend Richard Shackleton (1729–92): "we live in a world where every one is on the Catch, and the only way to be Safe is to be Silent, Silent in any affair of Consequence, and I think it would not be a bad rule for every man to keep within what he thinks of others, of himself, and of his own Affairs."[1] That air of mystery also surrounds Burke's first years in London, where he relocated from Ireland in 1750 (ostensibly to study law at the Middle Temple), but he begins to emerge into the light in the later years of the decade with the publication (both initially anonymous) of two books of lasting significance. *A Vindication of Natural Society* (1756) was a parody of the philosophy of Lord Bolingbroke (Henry St. John, 1678–1751); anticipating the arguments of the *Reflections on the Revolution in France* over 30 years later, it ridiculed both the mischievous tendencies of rationalistic political theories and the calls for "perfect Liberty." Burke's extraordinary second book, *A Philosophical Enquiry into the Origin of Our Ideas of the Sublime and Beautiful* (1757; see Appendix A3), proved to be an influential contribution to the field of aesthetics, in which he distinguished and sharply demarcated the characteristics of the sublime (vast, rugged, obscure, terrifying, and enormous in its power) from those of the beautiful (small, smooth, clear, gentle, and delicate). As will be seen, the claims of that book also find an echo in Burke's later thoughts on the evils of revolution.

The political career that was to define the rest of Burke's life began in 1759, when he became private secretary to MP William Gerard Hamilton (1729–96). This was a trying and ultimately acrimonious relationship, but it opened the door to a more fulfilling and determinative connection, that with Charles Watson-Wentworth, 2nd Marquess of Rockingham (1730–82), the leader of the Whig Party and prime minister in two short-lived administrations. As Rockingham's secretary, Burke acted, with enormous energy and commitment, as spokesman and pamphleteer for the Rockingham Whigs. In this capacity he

---

by Greg Weiner (*Old Whigs: Burke, Lincoln and the Politics of Prudence* [Encounter Books, 2019], 1).

1 Letter to Richard Shackleton, 15 February 1746, *The Correspondence of Edmund Burke*, edited by Thomas W. Copeland et al., 10 vols. (U of Chicago P, 1958–78), vol. I, p. 62. Hereafter, references to this work will be cited as *Corr.* with volume and page number.

produced an eloquent defence of the concept of party politics[1] and, as a member of Parliament from 1765 until his retirement in 1794, was a colossus in the House of Commons, delivering widely admired speeches on the vital issues of the day. Until 1789 at least, Burke's political position was clearly identifiable with the cause of liberty and reform, and he became known for his exertions against what he would later call "the persecutions of oppressive power":[2] the plight of the Catholics of Ireland under the Protestant Ascendancy; that of the people of India suffering under the rapacious rule of Warren Hastings (1732–1818) and the East India Company; and the struggle of the American colonists against overbearing British rule.[3] Without being "one of those who think that the people are never in the wrong," Burke had nonetheless made it a point of principle "that in all disputes between them and their rulers, the presumption is at least upon a par in favour of the people."[4]

Given his disapprobation of authoritarianism and his sympathetic attitude toward rebellions,[5] it was not unreasonable for Burke's contemporaries to expect from him a positive response to the revolution that occurred in France in 1789. It was in such a spirit that Charles-Jean-François Depont (1767–96)—the "very young gentleman at Paris" to whom *Reflections on the Revolution in France* is addressed—wrote to Burke on 4 November of that year seeking his assurance that the French people were worthy to be free and could distinguish liberty from licence and

---

1 *Thoughts on the Cause of the Present Discontents* (J. Dodsley, 1770), originally published anonymously.
2 Edmund Burke, *Reflections on the Revolution in France*, 7th ed. (J. Dodsley, 1790), 217. Parts of the *Reflections* not contained in the present abridged edition will be cited from this edition as *Reflections* with page number.
3 For Burke's response to the American Revolution, see Appendix B.
4 Edmund Burke, *Thoughts on the Cause of the Present Discontents*, *Works* III, 114.
5 "At least five separate rebellions against authority can be cited as meeting with Burke's specific approval—the Glorious Revolution of 1688, the American War of Independence, the struggle of the Corsicans for freedom, the attempt of the Poles to preserve their national independence, and the various revolts against the minions of Warren Hastings in India." Alfred Cobban, *Edmund Burke and the Revolt against the Eighteenth Century* (George Allen & Unwin, 1960), 100.

legitimate government from despotic power.[1] This letter produced from Burke a measured, cautious response (see Appendix C2), and some months later the far lengthier, far more polemical, and far more negative, *Reflections*.

There were three objects of contemplation in Burke's mind as he wrote: the revolutionary events in France; the reception and impact in England of those events; and—transcending those contemporary matters—the abiding and eternal principles of social and political life. The English dimension of the book can be seen in its original title, *Reflections on certain Proceedings of the Revolution Society of the 4th of November, 1789, concerning the Affairs of France*. On that date, by coincidence the same date on which Depont wrote to Burke, Richard Price (1723–91) delivered an address to the Revolution Society in which he celebrated the recent French upheaval and asserted three principles upon which he claimed England's own revolution (that of 1688) had rested and upon which the French were now also acting: "The right to chuse our own governors; to cashier them for misconduct; and to frame a government for ourselves" (Appendix A5, p. 179). The first sections of the book consist of Burke's criticisms of this radical (and, to him, radically mistaken) interpretation of the events of 1688; in undertaking this critical task, Burke presents an account of the actual principles of the English constitution and casts himself as the spokesman for the people of England, enunciating the balanced features of their settled and cherished mode of life as opposed to the turbulent, sophistical, and ruin-bound innovations of the French. Those enthusiastic supporters of the French Revolution on Burke's side of the Channel are thus cast as being out of line with true English sentiments. Such enthusiasts are nonetheless dangerous, since they are vocal and noisy though small in number, since they sow discord concerning perceived faults in the English constitution, and since that unnecessarily sown discord may lead England on the road to French-style destruction. Hence the *Reflections* can be seen to possess at times a prophylactic character. That the revolutionary events are happening in a different country should not be a cause for complacency: "Whenever our neighbour's house is on fire, it cannot be amiss for the engines to play a little on our own" (p. 49).

---

1 "Si vous Daignez l'assurer que les françois sont Dignes d'être libres, qu'il Scauront Distinguer la liberté de la licence et un Gouvernement legitime d'un pouvoir Despotique." Letter from Depont to Burke, 4 November 1789, *Corr.* VI, 32.

The second object of Burke's contemplation was, of course, France itself. The French had thrown away a perfectly tolerable state of affairs which could, wherever required, have been happily reformed. The actions of the revolutionaries and the projects of the new National Assembly were unnecessary, and they served as monuments to the folly of thinking that any society can be torn down and then raised anew to match the plan of some abstract philosophical model. Destruction is natural to the psychology of the revolutionary ("Something they must destroy, or they seem to themselves to exist for no purpose," p. 79), and it is *easy* (a frenzied mob can do it); but the creation and maintenance of a constitution is another thing altogether, and it requires more skill and experience than a single person or generation can ever possess. This insight was confirmed, Burke held, by the new system in France, which he had already declared to be "a most bungling, and unworkmanlike performance."[1] The varieties and extent of this bungling, across the entire spectrum of French socio-economic life, are exposed and held up to excoriating ridicule in the *Reflections*. One particular act especially engages his attention, namely the disestablishment of the French Church and the confiscation of Church property as a means of resolving France's financial crisis. Burke rejects the economic thinking underlying the policy of expropriation, but he sees in that policy something still more insidious: the consciously pursued erosion of the religious basis of society. This erosion assisted the revolutionaries in the pursuit of their ends, since one of the vital functions of religion, Burke held, was the maintenance of the established order. The loss of religion would be felt elsewhere too. Its unique set of consolations was irreplaceable, and it functioned both as a source of moral instruction and as part of the "decent drapery of life" (p. 97) shielding us from naked reality. Once that drapery was torn off, the human person would be seen as nothing more than an animal, with murderous consequences following predictably from that downgraded status.

The worst excesses of the Revolution—the September Massacres, the guillotine, the executions of Louis XVI and Marie Antoinette, the Terror—lay still in the future when Burke wrote the *Reflections*. It is a mark of his understanding of the tendencies of human nature that Burke could sense where things were headed, even when many were greeting a new birthday of the world, and even when many could hold (as some of

---

1 Letter to unknown recipient, January 1790, *Corr.* VI, 80.

Figure 1: *Frontispiece to Reflections on the French Revolution*, attributed to Frederick George Byron, 1790. Library of Congress, Prints and Photographs Division, Cartoon Prints, British.

Burke's immediate critics did) that whatever violence had been unleashed was minimal and had passed. The seeds of what was to come were to be found not only in the "old Parisian ferocity" (Appendix C1, p. 195) and the punishment of the lamp-post, but also in the shameful mistreatment of Marie Antoinette at Versailles on 6 October 1789, the subject of a memorable and commonly mocked passage of the *Reflections* (see Figure 1). This revealed to Burke the change in manners that had come over France, and this was for him more than a merely superficial thing. "Manners," he wrote, "are of more importance than laws. Upon them, in a great measure, the laws depend" (Appendix D3a, p. 220). The new manners of revolutionary France were to be "coarse, rude, savage, and ferocious" (p. 220) and would also destabilize the French nation still further once the accompanying insubordination extended, as Burke felt it inevitably would, to the army. Here Burke almost preternaturally foresees the rise of Napoleon ("some popular general" who has the power to conciliate a mutinous soldiery and who becomes "master of your whole republic," p. 153); and thus the heady dreams of the Revolution and the Rights of Men, having passed through chaotic and bloody transmigrations, are augured to terminate in the nightmare of authoritarian military rule.

It would be a mistake to see the *Reflections* as simply an argument about the political situations of England and France in the eighteenth century. Though provoked by the events in France, Burke's arguments transcend any particular historical event and assume a more generalizable quality. One early reviewer, indeed, commented that the book should have been titled *An Essay on Government*, so as more accurately to describe its focus.[1] At the heart of these more generalizable positions concerning social and political problems—the third object of Burke's contemplation—lies the concept of *prescription*. In Burke's hands this idea signifies, not that any institution can be justified on the mere grounds that it has existed beyond memory or record (though he does often incline to that view),[2] but the more subtle and persuasive conception of a nation as a living organism of great intricacy and historical continuity. The consequences of this conception are numerous and profound. Social alterations should be

---

1 Review in the *St. James's Chronicle*, 2 November 1790.

2 See Burke's remarkable discussion of prescription and presumption in his speech on the Representation of the Commons in Parliament (*Works* VI, 128–36, and in Appendix E5).

regarded as something like surgical procedures performed on a living body, undertaken only when necessary, with reticence and solicitude, and with great awareness for how the procedure will affect the organism as a whole. The very complexity of the national organism requires a knowledge more extensive than that attainable by any single individual or generation, and hence an appeal, rooted in epistemological humility, is to be made to the wisdom of the ages: "We are afraid to put men to live and trade each on his own private stock of reason; because we suspect that this stock in each man is small, and that the individuals would be better to avail themselves of the general bank and capital of nations, and of ages" (p. 105). In contrast, then, to the radical's belief that each new generation has the ability and the obligation to investigate, assess, and refashion the existing order ("to begin the world over again"),[1] Burke laments the modish idea that "every thing is to be discussed" (p. 109) and stresses instead the importance in social life of accepted prejudice, habit, and custom.[2]

The stress on historical continuity, without which human beings "would become little better than the flies of a summer" (p. 112), asserts itself in Burke's distinctive gloss on the theory of the social contract. John Locke's (1632–1704) statement of this theory had become Whig orthodoxy, but there were elements in Locke's theory that Burke feared were dangerously open to radical readings. Rather than characterizing the social contract as akin to a mundane agreement or business partnership that might be dissolved according to the fancy of the involved parties, Burke widened its temporal scope, thereby restricting the right of any one generation to make sweeping and unprecedented changes to society, or to dissolve it altogether on a whim. "Society is indeed

---

1 Thomas Paine, *Common Sense* (1776; H.D. Symonds, 1792), 32.
2 Burke's use of "prejudice" is likely to vex the modern reader. It is therefore important to note the sense in which he uses it, which, as laid down in Samuel Johnson's 1755 *Dictionary of the English Language*, indicates a "judgment formed beforehand without examination." It should be understood as an opinion held on the basis of tradition. Johnson indeed advises against the "accidental" use of "prejudice" to indicate anything mischievous or harmful. The emphasis on the centrality of prejudice is part of Burke's anti-rationalistic understanding of politics and society: social relations are a function of habit and custom rather than of intellectualizing and theory.

a contract," he writes in one of the most famous passages in the *Reflections*, though not a contract of "a temporary and perishable nature":

It is a partnership in all science; a partnership in all art; a partnership in every virtue, and in all perfection. As the ends of such a partnership cannot be obtained in many generations, it becomes a partnership not only between those who are living, but between those who are living, those who are dead, and those who are to be born. (pp. 113–14)

Responsible and prudent political activity must be grounded in an understanding of history and of human nature and it must approach any reforming business with "pious awe and trembling sollicitude" (p. 113). The actions of the revolutionary French were undertaken in a markedly different manner, neglecting history in favour of metaphysics, and human nature in favour of an abstract concept of "man." The consequences of this neglect, of trusting in the "imbecility" of one generation when the collective wisdom of the past was available, and of seeing the order of society as a merely temporary arrangement, were now to be seen, disastrously, in the catastrophe unfolding in France.

It is clear that Depont was disappointed by Burke's response: "I would not have hazarded my question had I been aware what effect it would produce, and ... if your opinions had been then known to me, far from engaging you to disclose them, I should have intreated you to withhold them from the public."[1] Depont was not the only one to be surprised by Burke's condemnation of French events. A bemused reaction was common. How could the man who had most conspicuously supported the Americans in their struggle for liberty condemn those in France who were now pursuing that same goal? Appalled, both Thomas Paine (1737–1809) and Joseph Priestley (1733–1804) lamented that a great friend of liberty and humankind had been lost; Fanny Burney (1752–1840) wondered how anyone could "be so little resembling to himself at different periods as this man"; and Thomas Jefferson (1743–1826) declared himself to be less astonished by the Revolution of France than by "the Revolution of Mr. Burke."[2] Thomas

---

1 M. Depont, *Answer to the Reflections of the Right Hon. Edmund Burke* (P. Byrne et al., 1791), 3.

2 See Appendices G3, G7, G8, and G10 for these responses.

Moore (1779–1852), in his biography of Burke's Whig colleague-cum-foe Richard Brinsley Sheridan (1751–1816), wrote in dramatically seismic terms of Burke's "division of himself": "His mind, indeed, lies parted asunder in his works, like some vast continent severed by a convulsion of nature,—each portion peopled by its own giant race of opinions, differing altogether in features and language, and committed in eternal hostility with each other."[1] This view of the inconsistent and divided Burke—the liberal friend of humanity versus the reactionary defender of tyrannical monarchs—was (and continues to be) a source of puzzlement, generating a wide range of attempts to account for the apparent reversal of principle in Burke's views.

A first explanation, not infrequently invoked, is that Burke had altered his stance on rebellions, not on principle, but from venality. He had, in other words, sold out to the Court, abandoning his former positions in order to become the King's hired pen. Mary Wollstonecraft (1759–97) insinuated such a thing in her *Vindication of the Rights of Men*, claiming (without foundation) that "in a skulking, unmanly way, he has secured himself a pension,"[2] and the allegation that it was nothing other than secret remuneration that changed Burke—to be sure, always in need of money—from reformer of abuses to preserver of the status quo became something of a staple ingredient in attacks on the *Reflections*. We find the charge in Thomas Paine's *Rights of Man* (see Appendix G8), for example, and in a number of contemporary satirical cartoons. Pre-eminent among these, perhaps, is James Gillray's caricature *A Uniform Whig* (Figure 2), in which Burke is displayed as a comically divided figure: tattered clothes and shoes adorn his left side, while on the right he is opulently dressed, cash pouring from his pockets; the pedestal on which his arm rests supports a bust of George III, by implication the new patron for whom Burke writes. Gillray's cartoon gives us, in capsule form, the suspicious view of Burke: his inconsistency, his self-righteousness, his venality, and his monarchical obsequiousness are all uppermost. Paine, indeed, claimed that Burke wrote "in the fawning character of that creature known in all countries, and a friend to none,

---

1 Thomas Moore, *Memoirs of the Life of the Rt. Hon. Richard Brinsley Sheridan* (J.S. Redfield, 1858), vol. II, 101.
2 Mary Wollstonecraft, *A Vindication of the Rights of Men* (J. Johnson, 1790), 19–20. The charge is without foundation, since Burke did not receive a pension until 1794.

A Uniform Whig.

"I preserve consistency by varying my means, to secure the unity of my end." Burkes Reflections V. 216.

Figure 2: *A Uniform Whig*, James Gillray, 1791. Yale Center for British Art, Paul Mellon Collection.

a COURTIER" (Appendix G8, p. 275), and the conception of Burke as venal sycophant found its way, many decades later, into Marx's *Das Kapital*.[1]

A variant of this theme of the unprincipled agent holds that Burke's inconsistency was the result of his desire, not for monetary reward, but for renewed influence within the Whig Party. On this view, recently championed by L.G. Mitchell, Burke had lost his place as the intellectual leader of the Whig party, felt adrift and aggrieved (feeling only "perpetual failure" and fearing the arrival of an end "without Success and without reputation"[2]), and he launched his distinctive attack on the French Revolution in order to re-assert his claim to authority: "The momentous events in France demanded an intellectual response from Burke or the permanent resignation of his claim to a voice in the determination of English Whiggery."[3] This explanation— that Burke, hating his fallen position, sought (with desperation and a sense of wounded vanity) to recover his prominence—had also been levelled at him by Wollstonecraft:

> You were the Cicero of one side of the house for years; and then to sink into oblivion, to see your blooming honours fade before you, was enough to rouse all that was human in you—and make you produce the impassioned *Reflections* which have been a glorious revivification of your fame.— Richard is himself again![4]

On this view, Burke's stance is unprincipled and even narcissistic, born of a desire for status and continued recognition. He needed simply to be *noticed*. Hence Paine:

> Even his genius is without a constitution. It is a genius at random, and not a genius constituted. But he must say something.—He has therefore mounted in the air like a

---

1 See Karl Marx, *Capital* (1867; Oxford UP, 1999), 197.
2 Burke, letter to the Earl of Charlemont, 10 July 1789, *Corr*. VI, 1.
3 L.G. Mitchell, "Introduction," *The Writings and Speeches of Edmund Burke* (Oxford UP, 1981–2015), vol. VIII, p. 30.
4 Wollstonecraft, *Vindication* 101–02. The words "Richard is himself again!" are drawn from Colley Cibber's theatrical adaptation of Shakespeare's *Richard III* (1700). In Wollstonecraft's time the phrase was used to indicate that a person has returned to normal after an illness.

balloon, to draw the eyes of the multitude from the ground they stand upon.[1]

The failure of Burke's plan (ultimately there was, for him, "only the bitterness of the dishonoured prophet")[2] may be seen to account for the increased rage and petulance of his subsequent writings.

The surprising nature of Burke's apparent volte-face was in other quarters attributed to a dramatic change in personality rather than to a calculated and cynical shift of allegiance. That Burke had lost his reason was a view represented in many contemporary cartoons, which showed him insane, raging, or held in restraints. Henry Thomas Buckle, in his *History of Civilization in England*, advanced this interpretation clearly and with much lamentation. Before 1789, Buckle claims, Burke had been the most able and the most admirable of British politicians, a principled opponent of George III (r. 1760–1820) and of his policies toward America, of the slave trade, and of a great many cruel laws justified merely by ancient usage. When the tumultuous events in France began, and subsequently intensified, this overthrew the equipoise of Burke's great mind, and he "fell into a state of complete hallucination": "the balance tottered; the proportions of that gigantic intellect were disturbed."[3] Burke's mental deterioration worsened with the death of his beloved son in 1794, and in his writings from 1790 onwards "we may note the consecutive steps of an increasing, and at length an uncontrollable violence."[4] Thus it is that Burke's denunciations of the French, listed by Buckle in a memorable passage, become progressively unhinged: "As to France itself, it is 'Cannibal Castle;' it is 'the republic of assassins;' it is 'a hell;' its government is composed of 'the dirtiest, lowest, most fraudulent, most knavish, of chicaners;' its National Assembly are 'miscreants;' its people are 'an allied army of Amazonian and male cannibal Parisians;' they are 'a nation of murderers;' they are 'the basest of mankind;' they are 'murderous atheists;' they are 'a gang of robbers;' they are 'the prostitute outcasts of mankind;' they are 'a desperate gang of plunderers, murderers, tyrants, and

---

1 Paine, *Rights of Man* 63.
2 Mitchell, "Introduction" 51.
3 Henry Thomas Buckle, *The History of Civilization in England* (John W. Parker & Son, 1857), vol. I, p. 467.
4 Buckle, *History* 469.

atheists.'"[1] Can these be the words of a man in control of his reason, his passions? For those reluctant to draw the conclusion of insanity, there was an alternative: like a great many others before and after him, with age Burke had simply become more conservative, the great changes afoot around him a source not of hope for a better world, but of fear for the loss of things to which he had become attached. To be sure, the motif of the cautious elder statesman giving prudent advice to the "very young man at Paris" is part of the rhetorical architecture of the Reflections, but it was not age-produced wisdom but rather dotage and mental enfeeblement that some of Burke's critics wished to imply.

It is to be noted, however, that the premise on which all these interpretations rest—the premise, that is, of Burke's inconsistency—can be challenged. James Mackintosh (1765–1832), perhaps the most astute and compelling of Burke's earliest critics, wrote that careful observers of Burke's political life should not have been surprised by his judgment on the French Revolution: "An abhorrence for abstract politics, a predilection for aristocracy, and a dread of innovation, have ever been among the most sacred articles of his public creed."[2] Mackintosh is correct. From the *Vindication of Natural Society* onwards, Burke had consistently warned of the dangers of abstract and unrooted political theorizing, which he held to be in conflict with custom and prescription. Even in those campaigns of his most admired by

---

1 Buckle, *History* 472.
2 See Appendix G11, p. 277. In what follows, the focus will be on Burke's censure of innovation and abstract politics, but his lifelong "predilection for aristocracy" is not to be ignored and can be seen in a letter of 15 November 1772 to the Duke of Richmond: "You people of great families and hereditary Trusts and fortunes are not like such as I am, who whatever we may be by the Rapidity of our growth and of the fruit we bear, flatter ourselves that while we creep on the Ground we belly into melons that are exquisite for size and flavour, yet still we are but annual plants that perish with our Season and leave no sort of Traces behind us. You if you are what you ought to be are the great Oaks that shade a Country and perpetuate your benefits from Generation to Generation" (*Corr.* II, 377). One must see beyond the apparent obsequiousness of this letter: Burke is both engaging in something of an admonition of the aristocracy (they are maybe not what they "ought" to be) and also highlighting the functional importance of the aristocratic landowning class for maintaining the stability and continuity of a nation.

radicals—against the abuse of power in America and India—Burke's dislike of theory is conspicuous. The American crisis was not to be eased by determining the abstract issue of whether Britain had a right to tax the colonists; no, the proper guides to policy in the American business should be expediency and circumstance. There also, Burke distrusted the strangely novel approach of Britain's government, which had so unsettled the Americans, and declared himself an enemy of "tampering": instead of trying out speculative new projects, "I put my foot in the tracks of our forefathers; where I can neither wander nor stumble."[1] He here went so far as to declare, in words that could have come straight from the *Reflections*, "that Government is of divine *institution* and *sacred* authority, and no *arbitrary device of men*, to be modified at their *pleasure* or conducted by their *fancies*, or *feelings*."[2] Nor was this sentiment expressed lightly: it was, he said, something that "I ... believe from my soul."[3] Even when engaged in significant reforms, statesmen should be guided by ancient practice and by reverence for the wisdom of the ages, and not by the theoretical innovations of bold experimenters. As he declared in his speech on Charles James Fox's East India Bill, "I feel an insuperable reluctance in giving my hand to destroy any established institution of government, upon a theory, however plausible it may be."[4]

It is this same spirit that animates the writings on France. True, Burke's words are in this later case more dramatic, more extreme, but the intensification of his onslaught suited the subject matter, since the world had theretofore witnessed nothing so dramatic nor so extreme as the French Revolution. In his first substantial response to Depont's approach, Burke urged his young correspondent to be wary of the abstract politics engulfing France and to heed instead what he called "the late ripe fruit of mere experience" (Appendix C2, p. 199).[5] The French, he wrote, have "theories enough concerning the Rights of Men" but no understanding of what is essential, namely "Man in the

---

1 Edmund Burke, *Speech on Conciliation with America, Works* III, 276.
2 Edmund Burke, "Second Speech on Conciliation, 16 November 1775," *The Writings and Speeches of Edmund Burke*, vol. III, p. 208.
3 Burke, "Second Speech" 208.
4 Edmund Burke, *Speech on Mr. Fox's East-India Bill, Works* III, 454–55.
5 An emphasis on "the solid test of long experience" is found throughout the *Reflections*.

concrete" (p. 198). The *Reflections* documents the follies of the National Assembly (the best members of which were merely, Burke bewails, "men of theory")[1] in pursuing a whole series of rationalistic and theory-driven innovations in the system of finance, in electoral representation, and in the constitution of the executive power and of the judicature, indeed across the entirety of French society. He lambasts these political experiments as being against experience, against custom, and against nature. "I believe it will be found," he concludes, "that a more salutary lesson of caution against the daring spirit of innovators ... never was at any time furnished to mankind."[2] Burke's anti-theoretical guidance in the American crisis—"whether you will choose to abide by a profitable experience, or a mischievous theory"[3]—was here repeated in the case of the French Revolution, his readers urged to defer to the wisdom of the past, rather than "to follow in their desperate flights the aëronauts of France" (p. 157). Projects of reform and alteration are not precluded by these pieces of guidance, but renovation rather than innovation is to be the preferred method: "even when I changed, it should be to preserve ... In what I did, I should follow the example of our ancestors. I would make the reparation as nearly as possible in the style of the building" (p. 157). In all of this, Burke is consistent with what, two decades earlier, he had declared himself to be: "by opinion, principle, Constitution, an hater of *violence* and *innovation*" (Appendix E1, p. 225).

Burke himself was deeply concerned with the question of his own consistency, and he defended it energetically. "I believe," he wrote of himself, "if he could venture to value himself upon any thing, it is on the virtue of consistency that he would value himself the most. Strip him of this, and you leave him naked indeed."[4] So uppermost in Burke's mind is the threat of being labelled inconsistent that he concludes the *Reflections* with a vital and telling statement of the political constancy of his life—a life, he says, devoted to exertions against tyranny and for the liberty of others. That final sentence, of great length and building intensity, ends with the robust declaration that he is a man "who wishes to preserve consistency; but who would preserve

---

1 *Reflections* 59.
2 *Reflections* 343n.
3 Burke, *Speech on Conciliation, Works* III, 280.
4 Edmund Burke, *An Appeal from the New to the Old Whigs, Works* IV, 414.

consistency by varying his means to secure the unity of his end; and, when the equipoise of the vessel in which he sails, may be endangered by overloading it upon one side, is desirous of carrying the small weight of his reasons to that which may preserve its equipoise" (p. 158). One can note here how these words echo, in both form and substance, the defence of political "trimming," articulated a century earlier by the Marquis of Halifax (1633–95): "if Men are together in a Boat, and one part of the Company would weigh it down on one side, another would make it lean as much to the contrary; it happens there is a third Opinion of those, who conceive it would do as well, if the Boat went even, without endangering the Passengers."[1]

In significant and manifold ways, Burke's political stance mirrors Halifax's moderate and conservative disposition, with its desire to maintain balance and equipoise and to steer a prudent course between false and destabilizing extremes. The foundation of the *Reflections*, Burke maintained, was "laid in an opposition to extremes," and the doctrines he advanced there "do of themselves gravitate to a middle point, or to some point near a middle."[2] This attitude is clearly present when Burke rejects as alternatives both the total abolition and the unreformed maintenance of any problematic institution:

But in this, as in most questions of state, there is a middle. There is something else than the mere alternative of absolute destruction, or unreformed existence. *Spartam nactus es; hanc exorna.* This is, in my opinion, a rule of profound sense, and ought never to depart from the mind of an honest reformer. I cannot conceive how any man can have brought himself to that pitch of presumption, to consider his country

---

1 Sir George Savile, Marquis of Halifax, *The Character of a Trimmer* (1688), *Miscellanies by the Late Lord Marquis of Halifax* (W. Rogers, 1704), 88–89. Halifax (see Appendix A1) was one of the principal statesmen during the period of the English revolution, tendering the crown to William and Mary on 13 February 1689. In G.M. Trevelyan's view, the Glorious Revolution of 1688 was "a victory of moderation, a victory not of Whig or Tory passions, but of the spirit and mentality of Halifax the Trimmer" (G.M. Trevelyan, *The English Revolution 1688–1689* [Oxford UP, 1938], 241), a spirit and mentality that held fast to "the element of prudent compromise, preferring fact to theory" (153–54).

2 Burke, *Appeal, Works* IV, 485–86.

but *carte blanche*, upon which he may scribble whatever he pleases. A man full of warm speculative benevolence may wish his society otherwise constituted than he finds it; but a good patriot, and a true politician, always considers how he shall make the most of the existing materials of his country. A disposition to preserve, and an ability to improve, taken together, would be my standard of a statesman. (p. 138)

The "rule of profound sense" taken from Cicero ("Your lot is cast in Sparta; adorn it")[1] conveys the mean between preserving a situation, as if in aspic, and starting completely from scratch, making the world anew; "to make the most of my *actual situation*"[2] is thus the alternative both to reactionary politics and to revolutionary idealism.[3] It is the creed of the reformer, decrying those who would leave "nothing, no, nothing at all *unchanged*" (Appendix E8, p. 240), but willing to make improvements, where needed, with all due prudence and caution, gradually, and without endangering the entire structure. Burke's conservatism is therefore of a specific type. He is a *procedural* conservative, valuing an existing situation and, as a result of that, undertaking necessary and piecemeal reforms so as to preserve and maintain its integrity. This position contrasts with that of a substantive conservative who battles against any changes to an existing order, a project that Burke finds counterproductive: "A state without the means of some change is without the means of its conservation" (p. 58).[4]

---

1 Cicero, *Letters to Atticus*, Book IV, 6, itself a quotation from the *Telephus* of Euripides.

2 "It is a settled rule with me, to make the most of my *actual situation*; and not to refuse to do a proper thing, because there is something else more proper, which I am not able to do" (Edmund Burke, "Two Letters to Gentlemen in Bristol," *Works* III, 336).

3 "Halifax perhaps came nearer than any man in the seventeenth century to making this frame of mind [i.e., making the best of things] a working political hypothesis" (George H. Sabine, *A History of Political Theory* [Henry Holt & Company, 1937], 518).

4 The useful distinction between procedural and substantive conservatism is made by Iain Hampsher-Monk in his introduction to Burke's *Revolutionary Writings* (Cambridge UP, 2014), xxvii–xxviii. See also the characterization of Burke as a "pragmatic conservative" in Robert J. Lacey, *Pragmatic Conservatism: Edmund Burke and His American Heirs* (Palgrave Macmillan, 2016), and in Seth Vannatta, *Conservatism and Pragmatism* (Palgrave Macmillan, 2014), 22–37.

A vital element in this procedural stance is attention to *circumstances*, which again for Burke must undercut all the claims of mere theory.[1] "Circumstances (which with some gentlemen pass for nothing) give in reality to every political principle its distinguishing colour, and discriminating effect" (p. 47). This belief in the centrality of circumstances is perhaps most apparent in Burke's treatment of the American problem, in which the question of a timeless right (to tax, for example) is dismissed in favour of the appeal to an array of circumstances concerning the character and increasing number of the colonists, geographical distance, and other exigencies. The aim of that expedient appeal to circumstances is explicitly stated: "I am not determining a point of law; I am restoring tranquillity; and the general character and situation of a people must determine what sort of government is fitted for them."[2] One should here underscore two striking and typically Burkean elements of that declamation: first, there is no dogmatism about the type of government suitable for all people, independent of circumstances ("I reprobate no form of government merely upon abstract principles," p. 123); and second, the aim of policy should be the establishment of tranquility or, to return to the closing words of the *Reflections*, the preservation of equipoise. Burke's remaining energies, and the full "weight of his reasons," were to be utilized to restore that equipoise now disturbed by French events. For the languid and bucolic contentments of English life—with its settled and balanced constitution, its quiet inns and resting-places, and the freedom of "going about just as one pleases"[3]—might now be upended by the stormy revolutionary sentiment spawned from France and making its noise across Europe. England's government, Burke feared, "will be buffeted and beat forward and backward by the conflict of those billows; until at length, tumbling from the Gallic coast, the victorious tenth wave shall ride, like the bore, over all the rest, and poop the shattered, weather-beaten, leaky, water-logged vessel, and sink her to the bottom of the abyss."[4]

---

1 Compare again with Halifax: "Circumstances must come in, and are to be made a part of the matter of which we are to judge; positive *decisions* are always dangerous, more especially in *politics*" (*A Rough Draft of a New Model at Sea*, in *Miscellanies* 316; by "positive" is meant "theoretic").

2 Burke, *Speech on Conciliation*, *Works* III, 266.

3 Burke, "Letter to William Elliot," *Works* V, 141.

4 Burke, *Letters on a Regicide Peace* (4th Letter), *Works* V, 488.

Burke's depictions of the frightening power of revolutionary France, portrayed as an enormous and overwhelming wave or as "a vast, tremendous, unformed spectre" risen out of the tomb of the murdered French monarchy,[1] bear comparison with his youthful thoughts on the nature of the sublime. It was indeed the language of the sublime—language to do with astonishment, terror, vastness, destructive power, roughness, obscurity, things that were tremulous and jarring—that Burke here frequently evoked, mining the works of the greatest poets—Virgil, Spenser, Milton—in his search for an adequate depiction of the new French horror. The Revolution was "astonishing" (p. 49) and of almost supernatural power, a "hideous phantom" (Appendix D3a, p. 216), "a shapeless monster, born of hell and chaos" (Appendix H1, p. 295).[2] If revolutionary France exhibited characteristics of the sublime, then England, and its own Glorious Revolution of 1688, is at times depicted by Burke in terms of the contrasting features of the beautiful. Along with smallness and delicacy, the beautiful is characterized in the *Philosophical Enquiry* by two features by which Burke often depicts an ideal of English social and political life: smoothness and gradual variation. Beautiful objects inspire love and they produce in us a delightful feeling of bodily relaxation. In the presence of beauty, Burke writes, "the head reclines something on one side; the eyelids are more closed than usual, and the eyes roll gently with the inclination to the object; the mouth is a little opened, and the breath drawn slowly, with now and then a low sigh; the whole

---

1 Burke, *Letters on a Regicide Peace* (1st Letter), *Works* V, 256 (Appendix D3a, p. 216).

2 One should note that in order for something terrible to become properly sublime, the element of *distance* must be a factor. The sublime evokes "a sort of delightful horror, a sort of tranquillity tinged with terror" (what M.R. James called, in relation to the ghost story, "a pleasing terror" ["Some Remarks on Ghost Stories," *The Bookman*, Dec. 1929, p. 169]); but, "When danger or pain press too nearly, they are incapable of giving any delight, and are simply terrible; but at certain distances, and with certain modifications, they may be, and they are delightful, as we every day experience" (*A Philosophical Enquiry into the Origin of Our Ideas of the Sublime and Beautiful*, *Works* II, 653 and 585). The events in France were not distant enough from Burke to produce any sense of delight. Stripped of distance, they simply evoked *terror*, a passion similar to that evoked by the sublime.

body is composed, and the hands fall idly to the sides. All this is accompanied with an inward sense of melting and languor."[1] This contrasts with the markedly different physiological reaction which occurs when presented with something evocative of the sublime (something of great size or height, for example, or something threatening and powerful), for there a certain kind of bodily *tension* is produced.

One of the characteristics of the beautiful responsible for producing a state of relaxation is what Burke refers to as "the insensible deviation of line":

> Another principal property of beautiful objects is, that the line of their parts is continually varying its direction; but it varies it by a very insensible deviation; it never varies it so quickly as to surprise, or by the sharpness of its angle to cause any twitching or convulsion of the optic nerve. Nothing long continued in the same manner, nothing very suddenly varied, can be beautiful; because both are opposite to that agreeable relaxation which is the characteristic effect of beauty. (Appendix A3, p. 170)

Applied in the political realm, this can contribute to the Burkean defence of careful and incremental reform. Like the line of beauty, reforming changes should be almost imperceptibly gradual ("silent, as the extension of evening shadows," as Johnson put it[2]), and no alteration should shock the system with a disorienting and jolting disruption.[3] Burke's appreciative reading of the events and settlement of 1688 displays this conservative and beautifying ideal: in that moment when England "found itself without a king," the statesmen of 1688, utilizing "the two principles of conservation and correction," did everything they could to minimize disruption; though there was "a small and temporary deviation" from the order of hereditary succession,

---

1 Burke, *Philosophical Enquiry, Works* II, 663.
2 Samuel Johnson, "Adventurer, No. 137," *The Works of Samuel Johnson* (George Cowie & Co., 1825), vol. III, p. 137. See also the *Letter to Sir Hercules Langrishe* (*Works* IV, 507–40; Appendix E7) for Burke's clearest description and defence of gradualism.
3 It is a mark of Burke's respect for circumstances that even a convulsion may in some extreme case be required: "An irregular, convulsive movement may be necessary to throw off an irregular, convulsive disease" (p. 58).

the fabric of the nation was not dissolved, and "a politic, well-wrought veil" was thrown over any appearance of dramatic change.[1] The Revolution of 1688 thus differed markedly from the new and more sweeping one of 1789, which sought to change everything and threatened with its terrible power to overwhelm all things gentle and settled: "All the little quiet rivulets, that watered a humble, a contracted, but not an unfruitful field, are to be lost in the waste expanse, and boundless, barren ocean of the homicide philanthropy of France."[2]

These insights from Burke's thinking on beauty serve to highlight the conception of reform as a midway position between the twin perils of reactionary ossification (something "long continued in the same manner") and the sudden and convulsive changes of the revolutionary (*"tout détruire; oui, tout détruire; puisque tout est à recréer"*[3]). The first stages of Burke's political activity had largely been undertaken in opposition to that first peril, namely the reactionary tendencies and influence of George III. With the eruption of revolutionary events in France, however, Burke redirected his guns, "varying his means to secure the unity of his end," that end being equipoise, with timely reforms preserving a nation held together by smooth and lasting bonds of affection. It was indeed an emphasis on "love, veneration, admiration, or attachment" (p. 97) that lay close to the heart of Burke's political thought: "To be attached to the subdivision, to love the little platoon we belong to in society, is the first principle (the germ as it were) of public affections. It is the first link in the series by which we proceed towards a love to our country and to mankind" (p. 72). "To make us love our country," he then declares, "our country ought to be lovely" (p. 97). Rejecting fanciful political experiments and their predictably horrific consequences, Burke would have agreed with the familiar pragmatic conception of politics as the art of the possible, but his views also leave us with what is perhaps a more poetic conception, of politics as action directed toward tranquility, equipoise, and the maintenance of the beautiful.

---

1 See *Reflections* 23–30, pp. 55–58 in this edition.
2 Burke, *Letters on a Regicide Peace* (3rd Letter), *Works* V, 352.
3 M. Rabaud de St. Etienne (1743–93), quoted by Burke, p. 142, note 1 ("destroy everything; yes, destroy everything; since everything is to be recreated").

Edmund Burke: A Brief Chronology

1729/30 (?) Born in Dublin on 12 January, the son of a Protestant father and a Catholic mother
1744   Enters Trinity College, Dublin; graduates in 1748
1750   Settles in London as a law student in the Middle Temple
1756   Publishes *A Vindication of Natural Society*
1757   Publishes *A Philosophical Enquiry into the Origin of Our Ideas of the Sublime and Beautiful*
             Marries Jane Nugent
1758   Appointed editor of the *Annual Register*
             Birth of sons Richard and Christopher (Christopher dies in infancy)
1759–64   Private secretary to MP William Gerard Hamilton
1765   Becomes private secretary to Lord Rockingham
1765–74   MP for Wendover
1770   Publishes *Thoughts on the Cause of the Present Discontents*
1773   Visits France
1774–80   MP for Bristol
1774   19 April: Delivers *Speech on American Taxation*
1775   22 March: Delivers *Speech on Conciliation with America*
1776   4 July: American Declaration of Independence
1777   Publishes *A Letter to the Sheriffs of Bristol*
1780–94   MP for Malton
1782   Second Rockingham administration; Burke becomes Paymaster General. Rockingham dies on 1 July; Burke resigns as Paymaster General on 10 July
1783   Burke becomes Paymaster General again in the short-lived Fox-North coalition government (2 April–19 December)
1788–94   Takes leading role in the trial of Warren Hastings
1789   The French Revolution begins
             Richard Price delivers his sermon "A Discourse on the Love of Our Country" to the Revolution Society at the Old Jewry meeting house

1790	9 February: Burke's first public attack on the French Revolution in his Commons "Speech on the Army Estimates"
	1 November: Publishes *Reflections on the Revolution in France*
1791	6 May: Burke and Fox split over their differences with regard to France, publicly during the Commons debate on the Quebec Bill
	Publishes *A Letter to a Member of the National Assembly*, *An Appeal from the New to the Old Whigs*, and *Thoughts on French Affairs*
1792	Writes *Heads for Consideration on the Present State of Affairs*
1793	Executions of Louis XVI (21 January) and Marie Antoinette (16 October)
	Publishes *Observations on the Conduct of the Minority* and *Remarks on the Policy of the Allies*
1794	21 June: Retires from Parliament
	28 July: Execution of Robespierre
	2 August: Death of Burke's son Richard
1795	Receives pension from the Crown
	2 November: French Directory established
1796	Publishes *A Letter to a Noble Lord* and *Letters on a Regicide Peace*
1797	9 July: Dies in Beaconsfield

A Note on the Text

The publication history of *Reflections on the Revolution in France* has been thoroughly expounded by William B. Todd in the Editor's Note to his edition of the text (Holt, Rinehart and Winston, 1959). I follow Todd's recommendation in using here, as the basis of my abridgement, the "Seventh Edition" (or the tenth and final impression) of 1790, published by J. Dodsley in Pall-Mall, London. J.C.D. Clark, emphasizing the scholarly value of recovering an author's first thoughts, has made a good case for using the first edition, published on 1 November 1790, but I have opted to use as the basis of the following abridgement the text last corrected by Burke himself.

Unless where otherwise stated, the Burke selections presented in the appendices are drawn from the eight-volume *Works and Correspondence of the Right Honourable Edmund Burke* (Francis & John Rivington, 1852); the abbreviation *Works*, followed by the volume number, refers to this edition. Letters from and to Burke are drawn, with one exception, from *The Correspondence of Edmund Burke*, ed. Thomas W. Copeland et al., 10 vols. (Chicago: U of Chicago P, 1958–78). This is cited in the text by the abbreviation *Corr.*, followed by the volume number.

Some justification must always be required for the abridgement of a great text. The twin needs motivating this abridged edition of Edmund Burke's classic *Reflections on the Revolution in France* are those of pedagogy and accessibility. While the original text is not overly long, it does contain a number of sections which students and general readers alike will tend to find cumbersome. Discouraged, such readers may not make it to the soaring final passages of the *Reflections*, and that would be more than a shame. The potentially onerous sections, which may for many people impede an appreciation of Burke's book, concern such matters as the French National Assembly's novel systems of finance, legislature, and judicature. The details arrayed in Burke's presentation of these matters are famously problematic and not devoid of factual shortcomings (see L.G. Mitchell's introduction to Volume VIII of the Oxford edition of *The Writings and Speeches of Edmund Burke*). Since the abiding message of Burke's book can be preserved without the inclusion of those sections, it is these that form the core of the passages expurgated from this edition. While no abridgement can ever be a substitute for the complete text intended by the author (editions of which are suggested in the Select Bibliography at the end of this book), a digestible version, such as that offered in the following pages, has great beneficial value, familiarizing new readers with the major work of an enormously influential political thinker. The task of understanding is aided here by the inclusion of other vital writings by Burke and selections from the critical voices that responded to the *Reflections*.

Edits to the abridged text are indicated by an ellipsis (...). Since Burke used no ellipses in the original *Reflections*, the presence of an ellipsis invariably indicates here an editorial cut. There are two places in the text (pp. 72 and 136) where summaries are provided of lengthy passages that have been cut; these summaries are supplied so as to aid understanding of what follows in Burke's argument; they are identifiable by italic script within square brackets [*like this*]. No other changes to the text have been made, and Burke's punctuation and spellings (often inconsistent and irregular) have been retained. Burke's own footnotes are identified by the words "[Burke's note:]" at the beginning of each; all other footnotes are provided by the editor.

The "supporting texts" of this book's title are arranged in the form of a number of appendices. Appendix A consists of background materials that throw light on aspects of Burke's thinking on revolution. Appendix B is an overview of Burke's pronouncements on the American Revolution, containing selections from his writings and speeches on that matter. Appendices C and D focus on the French Revolution, illustrating both Burke's initial reactions to the events in France and his later calls for war against the "armed doctrine" of revolutionary France. Writings documenting Burke's consistently drawn contrast between innovative change and gradual reform are the subject of Appendix E, while Appendix F focuses on Burke's censure of the moral influence of Jean-Jacques Rousseau, which, though muted in the *Reflections*, is unleashed with fury in the later *Letter to a Member of the National Assembly*. *Reflections on the Revolution in France* was an instant sensation upon publication, and Appendix G provides a sampling from the numerous contemporary critical responses. Finally, Appendix H shows Burke in action, in the House of Commons debate on the Quebec Bill in May 1791; these selections provide further instances of Burke's horrified response to the French Revolution and show also the personal cost of his opposition to that event: political isolation and loss of friendship.

REFLECTIONS

ON THE

REVOLUTION IN FRANCE,

AND ON THE

PROCEEDINGS IN CERTAIN SOCIETIES
IN LONDON

RELATIVE TO THAT EVENT.

IN A

L E T T E R

INTENDED TO HAVE BEEN SENT TO A GENTLEMAN
IN PARIS.

BY THE RIGHT HONOURABLE

EDMUND BURKE.

THE SEVENTH EDITION.

LONDON:

PRINTED FOR J. DODSLEY, IN PALL-MALL.

M.DCC.XC.

REFLECTIONS

ON THE

REVOLUTION IN FRANCE
(ABRIDGED)

It may not be unnecessary to inform the Reader, that the following Reflections had their origin in a correspondence between the Author and a very young gentleman at Paris,[1] who did him the honour of desiring his opinion upon the important transactions, which then, and ever since, have so much occupied the attention of all men. An answer was written some time in the month of October 1789; but it was kept back upon prudential considerations. That letter is alluded to in the beginning of the following sheets. It has been since forwarded to the person to whom it was addressed. The reasons for the delay in sending it were assigned in a short letter to the same gentleman. This produced on his part a new and pressing application for the Author's sentiments.

The Author began a second and more full discussion on the subject. This he had some thoughts of publishing early in the last spring; but the matter gaining upon him, he found that what he had undertaken not only far exceeded the measure of a letter, but that its importance required rather a more detailed consideration than at that time he had any leisure to bestow upon it. However, having thrown down his first thoughts in the form of a letter, and indeed when he sat down to write, having intended it for a private letter, he found it difficult to change the form of address, when his sentiments had grown into a greater extent, and had received another direction. A different plan, he is sensible, might be more favourable to a commodious division and distribution of his matter.

---

1 Charles-Jean-François Depont (1767–96). Depont had met Burke in 1785 while on a visit to England. A moderate supporter of the revolution, he died by suicide in 1796.

DEAR SIR,

You are pleased to call again, and with some earnestness, for my thoughts on the late proceedings in France. I will not give you reason to imagine, that I think my sentiments of such value as to wish myself to be solicited about them. They are of too little consequence to be very anxiously either communicated or withheld. It was from attention to you, and to you only, that I hesitated at the time, when you first desired to receive them. In the first letter I had the honour to write to you, and which at length I send, I wrote neither for nor from any description of men; nor shall I in this. My errors, if any, are my own. My reputation alone is to answer for them.

You see, Sir, by the long letter I have transmitted to you, that, though I do most heartily wish that France may be animated by a spirit of rational liberty, and that I think you bound, in all honest policy, to provide a permanent body, in which that spirit may reside, and an effectual organ, by which it may act, it is my misfortune to entertain great doubts concerning several material points in your late transactions.

You imagined, when you wrote last, that I might possibly be reckoned among the approvers of certain proceedings in France, from the solemn public seal of sanction they have received from two clubs of gentlemen in London, called the Constitutional Society, and the Revolution Society.

I certainly have the honour to belong to more clubs than one, in which the constitution of this kingdom and the principles of the glorious Revolution, are held in high reverence: and I reckon myself among the most forward in my zeal for maintaining that constitution and those principles in their utmost purity and vigour. It is because I do so, that I think it necessary for me, that there should be no mistake. Those who cultivate the memory of our revolution, and those who are attached to the constitution of this kingdom, will take good care how they are involved with persons who, under the pretext of zeal towards the Revolution and Constitution, too frequently wander from their true principles; and are ready on every occasion to depart from the firm but cautious and deliberate spirit which produced the one, and which presides in the other. Before I proceed to answer the more material particulars in your letter, I shall beg leave to give you such information as I have been able to obtain of the two clubs which have thought proper, as bodies, to interfere in the concerns of France; first assuring you, that I am not, and that I have never been, a member of either of those societies.

The first, calling itself the Constitutional Society, or Society for Constitutional Information, or by some such title, is, I believe, of seven or eight years standing. The institution of this society appears to be of a charitable, and so far of a laudable, nature: it was intended for the circulation, at the expence of the members, of many books, which few others would be at the expence of buying; and which might lie on the hands of the booksellers, to the great loss of an useful body of men. Whether the books so charitably circulated, were ever as charitably read, is more than I know. Possibly several of them have been exported to France; and, like goods not in request here, may with you have found a market. I have heard much talk of the lights to be drawn from books that are sent from hence. What improvements they have had in their passage (as it is said some liquors are meliorated by crossing the sea) I cannot tell: But I never heard a man of common judgment, or the least degree of information, speak a word in praise of the greater part of the publications circulated by that society; nor have their proceedings been accounted, except by some of themselves, as of any serious consequence.

Your National Assembly[1] seems to entertain much the same opinion that I do of this poor charitable club. As a nation, you reserved the whole stock of your eloquent acknowledgments for the Revolution Society; when their fellows in the Constitutional were, in equity, entitled to some share. Since you have selected the Revolution Society as the great object of your national thanks and praises, you will think me excusable in making its late conduct the subject of my observations. The National Assembly of France has given importance to these gentlemen by adopting them; and they return the favour, by acting as a committee in England for extending the principles of the National Assembly. Henceforward we must consider them as a kind of privileged persons; as no inconsiderable members in the diplomatic body. This is one among the revolutions which have given splendour to obscurity, and distinction to undiscerned merit. Until very lately I do not recollect to have heard of this club. I am quite sure that it never occupied a moment of my thoughts; nor, I believe, those of any person out of

1 The National Assembly was the first revolutionary government in France, formed in June 1789 out of the previously convened Estates-General and comprised mostly of members of the Commons (or "Third Estate"), as distinct from the Nobility and the Clergy.

their own set. I find, upon enquiry, that on the anniversary of the Revolution in 1688, a club of dissenters, but of what denomination I know not, have long had the custom of hearing a sermon in one of their churches; and that afterwards they spent the day cheerfully, as other clubs do, at the tavern. But I never heard that any public measure, or political system, much less that the merits of the constitution of any foreign nation, had been the subject of a formal proceeding at their festivals; until, to my inexpressible surprize, I found them in a sort of public capacity, by a congratulatory address, giving an authoritative sanction to the proceedings of the National Assembly in France....

I flatter myself that I love a manly, moral, regulated liberty as well as any gentleman of that society, be he who he will; and perhaps I have given as good proofs of my attachment to that cause, in the whole course of my public conduct. I think I envy liberty as little as they do, to any other nation. But I cannot stand forward, and give praise or blame to any thing which relates to human actions, and human concerns, on a simple view of the object, as it stands stripped of every relation, in all the nakedness and solitude of metaphysical abstraction. Circumstances (which with some gentlemen pass for nothing) give in reality to every political principle its distinguishing colour, and discriminating effect. The circumstances are what render every civil and political scheme beneficial or noxious to mankind. Abstractedly speaking, government, as well as liberty, is good; yet could I, in common sense, ten years ago, have felicitated France on her enjoyment of a government (for she then had a government) without enquiry what the nature of that government was, or how it was administered? Can I now congratulate the same nation upon its freedom? Is it because liberty in the abstract may be classed amongst the blessings of mankind, that I am seriously to felicitate a madman, who has escaped from the protecting restraint and wholesome darkness of his cell, on his restoration to the enjoyment of light and liberty? Am I to congratulate an highwayman and murderer, who has broke prison, upon the recovery of his natural rights? This would be to act over again the scene of the criminals condemned to the gallies, and their heroic deliverer, the metaphysic Knight of the Sorrowful Countenance.[1]

---

1 The reference is to an episode in Cervantes' *Don Quixote* (Part
   I, Ch. XXII) (1605), in which Don Quixote (the Knight of the
   Sorrowful Countenance) releases some condemned criminals who
   proceed to beat and rob him.

When I see the spirit of liberty in action, I see a strong principle at work; and this, for a while, is all I can possibly know of it. The wild *gas*, the fixed air is plainly broke loose: but we ought to suspend our judgment until the first effervescence is a little subsided, till the liquor is cleared, and until we see something deeper than the agitation of a troubled and frothy surface. I must be tolerably sure, before I venture publicly to congratulate men upon a blessing, that they have really received one. Flattery corrupts both the receiver and the giver; and adulation is not of more service to the people than to kings. I should therefore suspend my congratulations on the new liberty of France, until I was informed how it had been combined with government; with public force; with the discipline and obedience of armies; with the collection of an effective and well-distributed revenue; with morality and religion; with the solidity of property; with peace and order; with civil and social manners. All these (in their way) are good things too; and, without them, liberty is not a benefit whilst it lasts, and is not likely to continue long. The effect of liberty to individuals is, that they may do what they please: We ought to see what it will please them to do, before we risque congratulations, which may be soon turned into complaints. Prudence would dictate this in the case of separate insulated private men; but liberty, when men act in bodies, is *power*. Considerate people, before they declare themselves, will observe the use which is made of *power*; and particularly of so trying a thing as *new* power in *new* persons, of whose principles, tempers, and dispositions, they have little or no experience, and in situations where those who appear the most stirring in the scene may possibly not be the real movers.

All these considerations however were below the transcendental dignity of the Revolution Society. Whilst I continued in the country, from whence I had the honour of writing to you, I had but an imperfect idea of their transactions. On my coming to town, I sent for an account of their proceedings, which had been published by their authority, containing a sermon of Dr. Price, with the Duke de Rochefoucault's and the Archbishop of Aix's letter, and several other documents annexed.[1] The whole of that

---

1 Richard Price (1723–91), dissenting minister and philosopher; Louis-Alexandre, duc de La Rochefoucauld d'Enville (1743–92), aristocratic member of the Third Estate, conveyed the Revolution Society's address to the National Assembly; Jean de Dieu-Raymond de Cucé Boisgelin, Archbishop of Aix (1732–1804), President of the National Assembly in November 1789.

publication, with the manifest design of connecting the affairs of France with those of England, by drawing us into an imitation of the conduct of the National Assembly, gave me a considerable degree of uneasiness. The effect of that conduct upon the power, credit, prosperity, and tranquility of France, became every day more evident. The form of constitution to be settled, for its future polity, became more clear. We are now in a condition to discern, with tolerable exactness, the true nature of the object held up to our imitation. If the prudence of reserve and decorum dictates silence in some circumstances, in others prudence of an higher order may justify us in speaking our thoughts. The beginnings of confusion with us in England are at present feeble enough; but with you, we have seen an infancy still more feeble, growing by moments into a strength to heap mountains upon mountains, and to wage war with Heaven itself. Whenever our neighbour's house is on fire, it cannot be amiss for the engines to play a little on our own. Better to be despised for too anxious apprehensions, than ruined by too confident a security.

Sollicitous chiefly for the peace of my own country, but by no means unconcerned for your's, I wish to communicate more largely, what was at first intended only for your private satisfaction. I shall still keep your affairs in my eye, and continue to address myself to you. Indulging myself in the freedom of epistolary intercourse, I beg leave to throw out my thoughts, and express my feelings, just as they arise in my mind, with very little attention to formal method. I set out with the proceedings of the Revolution Society; but I shall not confine myself to them. Is it possible I should? It looks to me as if I were in a great crisis, not of the affairs of France alone, but of all Europe, perhaps of more than Europe. All circumstances taken together, the French revolution is the most astonishing that has hitherto happened in the world. The most wonderful things are brought about in many instances by means the most absurd and ridiculous; in the most ridiculous modes; and apparently, by the most contemptible instruments. Every thing seems out of nature in this strange chaos of levity and ferocity, and of all sorts of crimes jumbled together with all sorts of follies. In viewing this monstrous tragi-comic scene, the most opposite passions necessarily succeed, and sometimes mix with each other in the mind; alternate contempt and indignation; alternate laughter and tears; alternate scorn and horror.

It cannot however be denied, that to some this strange scene appeared in quite another point of view. Into them it inspired no other sentiments than those of exultation and rapture. They saw nothing in what has been done in France, but a firm and temperate exertion of freedom; so consistent, on the whole, with morals and with piety, as to make it deserving not only of the secular applause of dashing Machiavelian politicians, but to render it a fit theme for all the devout effusions of sacred eloquence.

On the forenoon of the 4th of November last, Doctor Richard Price, a non-conforming minister of eminence, preached at the dissenting meeting-house of the Old Jewry,[1] to his club or society, a very extraordinary miscellaneous sermon, in which there are some good moral and religious sentiments, and not ill expressed, mixed up in a sort of porridge of various political opinions and reflections: but the revolution in France is the grand ingredient in the cauldron. I consider the address transmitted by the Revolution Society to the National Assembly, through Earl Stanhope,[2] as originating in the principles of the sermon, and as a corollary from them. It was moved by the preacher of that discourse. It was passed by those who came reeking from the effect of the sermon, without any censure or qualification, expressed or implied. If, however, any of the gentlemen concerned shall wish to separate the sermon from the resolution, they know how to acknowledge the one, and to disavow the other. They may do it: I cannot.

For my part, I looked on that sermon as the public declaration of a man much connected with literary caballers, and intriguing philosophers; with political theologians, and theological politicians, both at home and abroad. I know they set him up as a sort of oracle; because, with the best intentions in the world, he naturally *philippizes*,[3] and chaunts his prophetic song in exact unison with their designs.

---

1 The Old Jewry Meeting-house was a Dissenting chapel in the Old Jewry, a street between Gresham Street and Poultry in the City of London. Opened in 1701, it was demolished in 1846.

2 Charles, 3rd Earl Stanhope (1753–1816), chairman of the Revolution Society, and author of one of the earliest critical responses to Burke, *A Letter from Earl Stanhope to the Right Honourable Edmund Burke: Containing a Short Answer to His Late Speech on the French Revolution* (George Stafford, 1790). For the text of the Congratulatory Address, see Appendix A6.

3 "To favour or take the side of Philip of Macedon; (hence more generally) to speak or write as one who has been wrongly or corruptly inspired or influenced" (*OED*).

That sermon is in a strain which I believe has not been heard in this kingdom, in any of the pulpits which are tolerated or encouraged in it, since the year 1648, when a predecessor of Dr. Price, the Reverend Hugh Peters,[1] made the vault of the king's own chapel at St. James's ring with the honour and privilege of the Saints, who, with the "high praises of God in their mouths, and a *two*-edged sword in their hands, were to execute judgment on the heathen, and punishments upon the *people*; to bind their *kings* with chains, and their *nobles* with fetters of iron."[2] Few harangues from the pulpit, except in the days of your league in France, or in the days of our solemn league and covenant in England,[3] have ever breathed less of the spirit of moderation than this lecture in the Old Jewry. Supposing, however, that something like moderation were visible in this political sermon; yet politics and the pulpit are terms that have little agreement. No sound ought to be heard in the church but the healing voice of Christian charity. The cause of civil liberty and civil government gains as little as that of religion by this confusion of duties. Those who quit their proper character, to assume what does not belong to them, are, for the greater part, ignorant both of the character they leave, and of the character they assume. Wholly unacquainted with the world in which they are so fond of meddling, and inexperienced in all its affairs, on which they pronounce with so much confidence, they have nothing of politics but the passions they excite. Surely the church is a place where one day's truce ought to be allowed to the dissensions and animosities of mankind.

This pulpit style, revived after so long a discontinuance, had to me the air of novelty, and of a novelty not wholly without danger....

... His doctrines affect our constitution in its vital parts. He tells the Revolution Society, in this political sermon, that his majesty "is almost the *only* lawful king in the world, because the *only* one who owes his crown to the *choice of his people*." As to the kings of *the world*, all of whom (except one) this arch-pontiff of

---

1 Hugh Peters (1598–1660) was a radical minister who preached at the execution of Charles I in 1649 and was himself executed after the Restoration of the Monarchy in 1660.

2 [Burke's note:] Psalm cxlix.

3 The Leagues mentioned here were militant religious organizations, both of which acted in opposition to the monarchy of their respective countries.

the *rights of men*, with all the plenitude, and with more than the boldness of the papal deposing power in its meridian fervour of the twelfth century, puts into one sweeping clause of ban and anathema, and proclaims usurpers by circles of longitude and latitude, over the whole globe, it behoves them to consider how they admit into their territories these apostolic missionaries, who are to tell their subjects they are not lawful kings. That is their concern. It is ours, as a domestic interest of some moment, seriously to consider the solidity of the *only* principle upon which these gentlemen acknowledge a king of Great Britain to be entitled to their allegiance.

This doctrine, as applied to the prince now on the British throne, either is nonsense, and therefore neither true nor false, or it affirms a most unfounded, dangerous, illegal, and unconstitutional position. According to this spiritual doctor of politics, if his majesty does not owe his crown to the choice of his people, he is no *lawful* king. Now nothing can be more untrue than that the crown of this kingdom is so held by his majesty. Therefore if you follow their rule, the king of Great Britain, who most certainly does not owe his high office to any form of popular election, is in no respect better than the rest of the gang of usurpers, who reign, or rather rob, all over the face of this our miserable world, without any sort of right or title to the allegiance of their people. The policy of this general doctrine, so qualified, is evident enough. The propagators of this political gospel are in hopes their abstract principle (their principle that a popular choice is necessary to the legal existence of the sovereign magistracy) would be overlooked whilst the king of Great Britain was not affected by it. In the mean time the ears of their congregations would be gradually habituated to it, as if it were a first principle admitted without dispute. For the present it would only operate as a theory, pickled in the preserving juices of pulpit eloquence, and laid by for future use. *Condo et compono quæ mox depromere possim.*[1] By this policy, whilst our government is soothed with a reservation in its favour, to which it has no claim, the security, which it has in common with all governments, so far as opinion is security, is taken away.

Thus these politicians proceed, whilst little notice is taken of their doctrines; but when they come to be examined upon the plain meaning of their words and the direct tendency of their doctrines, then equivocations and slippery constructions come

---

1 "I am putting by and setting in order the stores on which I may some day draw." Horace (65–8 BCE), *Epistles*, Book I, i, 12.

into play. When they say the king owes his crown to the choice of his people, and is therefore the only lawful sovereign in the world, they will perhaps tell us they mean to say no more than that some of the king's predecessors have been called to the throne by some sort of choice; and therefore he owes his crown to the choice of his people. Thus, by a miserable subterfuge, they hope to render their proposition safe, by rendering it nugatory....

Whatever may be the success of evasion in explaining away the gross error of *fact*, which supposes that his majesty (though he holds it in concurrence with the wishes) owes his crown to the choice of his people, yet nothing can evade their full explicit declaration, concerning the principle of a right in the people to choose, which right is directly maintained, and tenaciously adhered to. All the oblique insinuations concerning election bottom in this proposition, and are referable to it. Lest the foundation of the king's exclusive legal title should pass for a mere rant of adulatory freedom, the political Divine proceeds dogmatically to assert,[1] that by the principles of the Revolution the people of England have acquired three fundamental rights, all which, with him, compose one system, and lie together in one short sentence; namely, that we have acquired a right

1. "To choose our own governors."
2. "To cashier them for misconduct."
3. "To frame a government for ourselves."

This new, and hitherto unheard-of bill of rights, though made in the name of the whole people, belongs to those gentlemen and their faction only. The body of the people of England have no share in it. They utterly disclaim it. They will resist the practical assertion of it with their lives and fortunes. They are bound to do so by the laws of their country, made at the time of that very Revolution, which is appealed to in favour of the fictitious rights claimed by the society which abuses its name.

These gentlemen of the Old Jewry, in all their reasonings on the Revolution of 1688, have a revolution which happened in England about forty years before,[2] and the late French revolu-

---

1 [Burke's note:] P. 34, *Discourse on the Love of our Country*, by Dr. Price.
2 Burke is referring here to the events and aftermath of the English Civil War (1642–51), sometimes called The Great Rebellion, which resulted in the execution of King Charles I (*continued*)

tion, so much before their eyes, and in their hearts, that they are constantly confounding all the three together. It is necessary that we should separate what they confound. We must recall their erring fancies to the *acts* of the Revolution which we revere, for the discovery of its true *principles*. If the *principles* of the Revolution of 1688 are anywhere to be found, it is in the statute called the *Declaration of Right*.[1] In that most wise, sober, and considerate declaration, drawn up by great lawyers and great statesmen, and not by warm and inexperienced enthusiasts, not one word is said, nor one suggestion made, of a general right "to choose our own *governors*; to cashier them for misconduct; and to *form* a government for *ourselves*."

This Declaration of Right (the act of the 1st of William and Mary, sess. 2. ch. 2.) is the cornerstone of our constitution, as reinforced, explained, improved, and in its fundamental principles for ever settled. It is called "An act for declaring the rights and liberties of the subject, and for *settling* the *succession* of the crown." You will observe that these rights and this succession are declared in one body, and bound indissolubly together.

A few years after this period, a second opportunity offered for asserting a right of election to the crown. On the prospect of a total failure of issue from King William, and from the Princess, afterwards Queen Anne, the consideration of the settlement of the crown, and of a further security for the liberties of the people, again came before the legislature. Did they this second time make any provision for legalizing the crown on the spurious Revolution principles of the Old Jewry? No. They followed the principles which prevailed in the Declaration of Right; indicating with more precision the persons who were to inherit in the Protestant line. This act also incorporated, by the same policy, our liberties, and an hereditary succession in the same act. Instead of a right to choose our own governors, they declared that the *succession* in that line (the protestant line drawn from James the First) was absolutely necessary "for the peace, quiet, and security of the realm," and that it was equally urgent on them "to maintain a *certainty in the succession* thereof, to which the subjects may safely have recourse for their protection."[2] Both

---

(on 30 January 1649) and in the establishment of a republican government from 1649 until the Restoration of the Monarchy in 1660.

1 Generally known as the Bill of Rights (reproduced in Appendix A2).

2 Act of Settlement, clause I.

these acts, in which are heard the unerring, unambiguous oracles of Revolution policy, instead of countenancing the delusive, gypsey predictions of a "right to choose our governors," prove to a demonstration how totally adverse the wisdom of the nation was from turning a case of necessity into a rule of law.

Unquestionably there was at the Revolution, in the person of King William, a small and a temporary deviation from the strict order of a regular hereditary succession; but it is against all genuine principles of jurisprudence to draw a principle from a law made in a special case, and regarding an individual person. *Privilegium non transit in exemplum.*[1] If ever there was a time favourable for establishing the principle, that a king of popular choice was the only legal king, without all doubt it was at the Revolution. Its not being done at that time is a proof that the nation was of opinion it ought not to be done at any time. There is no person so completely ignorant of our history, as not to know, that the majority in parliament of both parties were so little disposed to any thing resembling that principle, that at first they were determined to place the vacant crown, not on the head of the prince of Orange, but on that of his wife Mary, daughter of King James, the eldest born of the issue of that king, which they acknowledged as undoubtedly his. It would be to repeat a very trite story, to recall to your memory all those circumstances which demonstrated that their accepting King William was not properly a *choice*; but, to all those who did not wish, in effect to recall King James, or to deluge their country in blood, and again to bring their religion, laws, and liberties into the peril they had just escaped, it was an act of *necessity*, in the strictest moral sense in which necessity can be taken.

In the very act, in which for a time, and in a single case, parliament departed from the strict order of inheritance, in favour of a prince, who, though not next, was however very near in the line of succession, it is curious to observe how Lord Somers,[2] who drew the bill called the Declaration of Right, has comported himself on that delicate occasion. It is curious to observe with what address this temporary solution of continuity is kept from the eye; whilst all that could be found in this act of necessity to countenance the idea of an hereditary succession is brought

---

1 A special case must not be made a general rule (a maxim of Roman law).

2 John Somers, 1st Baron Somers (1651–1716), Whig jurist and statesman, solicitor general in 1689.

forward, and fostered, and made the most of, by this great man, and by the legislature who followed him. Quitting the dry, imperative style of an act of parliament, he makes the lords and commons fall to a pious, legislative ejaculation, and declare, that they consider it "as a marvellous providence, and merciful goodness of God to this nation, to preserve their said majesties *royal* persons, most happily to reign over us *on the throne of their ancestors*, for which, from the bottom of their hearts, they return their humblest thanks and praises."—The legislature plainly had in view the act of recognition of the first of Queen Elizabeth, Chap. 3d, and that of James the First, Chap. 1st, both acts strongly declaratory of the inheritable nature of the crown; and in many parts they follow, with a nearly literal precision, the words and even the form of thanksgiving, which is found in these old declaratory statutes.

The two houses, in the act of king William, did not thank God that they had found a fair opportunity to assert a right to choose their own governors, much less to make an election the *only lawful* title to the crown. Their having been in a condition to avoid the very appearance of it, as much as possible, was by them considered as a providential escape. They threw a politic, well-wrought veil over every circumstance tending to weaken the rights, which in the meliorated order of succession they meant to perpetuate; or which might furnish a precedent for any future departure from what they had then settled for ever. Accordingly, that they might not relax the nerves of their monarchy, and that they might preserve a close conformity to the practice of their ancestors, as it appeared in the declaratory statutes of queen Mary[1] and queen Elizabeth, in the next clause they vest, by recognition, in their majesties, *all* the legal prerogatives of the crown, declaring, "that in them they are most *fully*, rightfully, and *intirely* invested, incorporated, united, and annexed." In the clause which follows, for preventing questions, by reason of any pretended titles to the crown, they declare (observing also in this the traditionary language, along with the traditionary policy of the nation, and repeating as from a rubric the language of the preceding acts of Elizabeth and James) that on the preserving "a *certainty* in the SUCCESSION thereof, the unity, peace, and tranquillity of this nation doth, under God, wholly depend."

They knew that a doubtful title of succession would but too much resemble an election; and that an election would be utterly

---

1 [Burke's note:] 1st Mary, Sess. 3. ch. I.

destructive of the "unity, peace, and tranquillity of this nation," which they thought to be considerations of some moment. To provide for these objects, and therefore to exclude for ever the Old Jewry doctrine of "a right to choose our own governors," they follow with a clause, containing a most solemn pledge, taken from the preceding act of Queen Elizabeth, as solemn a pledge as ever was or can be given in favour of an hereditary succession, and as solemn a renunciation as could be made of the principles by this society imputed to them. "The lords spiritual and temporal, and commons, do, in the name of all the people aforesaid, most humbly and faithfully submit *themselves, their heirs and posterities for ever*; and do faithfully promise, that they will stand to, maintain, and defend their said majesties, and also the *limitation of the crown*, herein specified and contained, to the utmost of their powers," &c. &c.

So far is it from being true, that we acquired a right by the Revolution to elect our kings, that if we had possessed it before, the English nation did at that time most solemnly renounce and abdicate it, for themselves and for all their posterity for ever....

It is true that, aided with the powers derived from force and opportunity, the nation was at that time, in some sense, free to take what course it pleased for filling the throne; but only free to do so upon the same grounds on which they might have wholly abolished their monarchy, and every other part of their constitution. However they did not think such bold changes within their commission. It is indeed difficult, perhaps impossible, to give limits to the mere *abstract* competence of the supreme power, such as was exercised by parliament at that time; but the limits of a *moral* competence, subjecting, even in powers more indisputably sovereign, occasional will to permanent reason, and to the steady maxims of faith, justice, and fixed fundamental policy, are perfectly intelligible, and perfectly binding upon those who exercise any authority, under any name, or under any title, in the state....

It is far from impossible to reconcile, if we do not suffer ourselves to be entangled in the mazes of metaphysic sophistry, the use both of a fixed rule and an occasional deviation; the sacredness of an hereditary principle of succession in our government, with a power of change in its application in cases of extreme emergency. Even in that extremity (if we take the measure of our rights by our exercise of them at the Revolution) the change is to be confined to the peccant part only; to the part which produced the necessary deviation; and even then it is to be effected out a decomposition of the whole civil and political mass, the purpose of originating a new civil order out of the first elements of society.

A state without the means of some change is without the means of its conservation. Without such means it might even risque the loss of that part of the constitution which it wished the most religiously to preserve. The two principles of conservation and correction operated strongly at the two critical periods of the Restoration and Revolution, when England found itself without a king. At both those periods the nation had lost the bond of union in their antient edifice; they did not, however, dissolve the whole fabric. On the contrary, in both cases they regenerated the deficient part of the old constitution through the parts which were not impaired. They kept these old parts exactly as they were, that the part recovered might be suited to them. They acted by the ancient organized states in the shape of their old organization, and not by the organic *moleculæ* of a disbanded people. At no time, perhaps, did the sovereign legislature manifest a more tender regard to that fundamental principle of British constitutional policy, than at the time of the Revolution, when it deviated from the direct line of hereditary succession. The crown was carried somewhat out of the line in which it had before moved; but the new line was derived from the same stock. It was still a line of hereditary descent; still an hereditary descent in the same blood, though an hereditary descent qualified with protestantism. When the legislature altered the direction, but kept the principle, they shewed that they held it inviolable....

The gentlemen of the Society for Revolutions see nothing in that of 1688 but the deviation from the constitution; and they take the deviation from the principle for the principle....

... An irregular, convulsive movement may be necessary to throw off an irregular, convulsive disease. But the course of succession is the healthy habit of the British constitution. Was it that the legislature wanted, at the act for the limitation of the crown in the Hanoverian line, drawn through the female descendants of James the First, a due sense of the inconveniences of having two or three, or possibly more, foreigners in succession to the British throne? No!—they had a due sense of the evils which might happen from such foreign rule, and more than a due sense of them. But a more decisive proof cannot be given of the full conviction of the British nation, that the principles of the Revolution did not authorize them to elect kings at their pleasure, and without any attention to the antient fundamental principles of our government, than their continuing to adopt a plan of hereditary Protestant succession in the old line, with all the dangers and all the inconveniences of its being a foreign line full before their eyes, and operating with the utmost force upon their minds.

A few years ago I should be ashamed to overload a matter, so capable of supporting itself, by the then unnecessary support of any argument; but this seditious, unconstitutional doctrine is now publicly taught, avowed, and printed. The dislike I feel to revolutions, the signals for which have so often been given from pulpits; the spirit of change that is gone abroad; the total contempt which prevails with you, and may come to prevail with us, of all antient institutions, when set in opposition to a present sense of convenience, or to the bent of a present inclination: all these considerations make it not unadviseable, in my opinion, to call back our attention to the true principles of our own domestic laws; that you, my French friend, should begin to know, and that we should continue to cherish them. We ought not, on either side of the water, to suffer ourselves to be imposed upon by the counterfeit wares which some persons, by a double fraud, export to you in illicit bottoms, as raw commodities of British growth though wholly alien to our soil, in order afterwards to smuggle them back again into this country, manufactured after the newest Paris fashion of an improved liberty.

The people of England will not ape the fashions they have never tried; nor go back to those which they have found mischievous on trial. They look upon the legal hereditary succession of their crown as among their rights, not as among their wrongs; as a benefit, not as a grievance; as a security for their liberty, not as a badge of servitude. They look on the frame of their commonwealth, *such as it stands*, to be of inestimable value; and they conceive the undisturbed succession of the crown to be a pledge of the stability and perpetuity of all the other members of our constitution.

I shall beg leave, before I go any further, to take notice of some paltry artifices, which the abettors of election as the only lawful title to the crown, are ready to employ, in order to render the support of the just principles of our constitution a task somewhat invidious. These sophisters substitute a fictitious cause, and feigned personages, in whose favour they suppose you engaged, whenever you defend the inheritable nature of the crown. It is common with them to dispute as if they were in a conflict with some of those exploded fanatics of slavery, who formerly maintained, what I believe no creature now maintains, "that the crown is held by divine, hereditary, and indefeasible right."—These old fanatics of single arbitrary power dogmatized as if hereditary royalty was the only lawful government in the world, just as our new fanatics of popular arbitrary power, maintain that a popular election is the sole lawful source of authority. The old prerogative enthusiasts, it is true, did speculate foolishly, and perhaps impiously too, as if monarchy had more of a divine sanction than any other mode of government; and as if a right to govern by inheritance were in strictness *indefeasible* in every person, who should be found in the succession to a throne, and under every circumstance, which no civil or political right can be. But an absurd opinion concerning the king's hereditary right to the crown does not prejudice one that is rational, and bottomed upon solid principles of law and policy. If all the absurd theories of lawyers and divines were to vitiate the objects in which they are conversant, we should have no law, and no religion, left in the world. But an absurd theory on one side of a question forms no justification for alledging a false fact, or promulgating mischievous maxims on the other.

The second claim of the Revolution Society is "a right of cashiering their governors for *misconduct*." Perhaps the apprehensions our ancestors entertained of forming such a precedent as that "of cashiering for misconduct," was the cause that the declaration of the act which implied the abdication of king James, was, if it had any fault, rather too guarded, and too circumstantial.[1] But all this guard, and all this accumulation of circumstances, serves to shew the spirit of caution which predominated in the national councils, in a situation in which men irritated by oppression, and elevated by a triumph over it, are apt to abandon themselves to violent and extreme courses: it shews the anxiety of the great men who influenced the conduct of affairs at that great event, to make the Revolution a parent of settlement, and not a nursery of future revolutions.

No government could stand a moment, if it could be blown down with any thing so loose and indefinite as an opinion of

---

1 [Burke's note:] "That King James the second, having endeavoured to *subvert the constitution* of the kingdom, by breaking the *original contract* between king and people, and by the advice of jesuits, and other wicked persons, having violated the *fundamental* laws, and *having withdrawn himself out of the kingdom*, hath *abdicated* the government, and the throne is thereby *vacant*."

"*misconduct*." They who led at the Revolution, grounded their virtual abdication of King James upon no such light and uncertain principle. They charged him with nothing less than a design, confirmed by a multitude of illegal overt acts, to *subvert the Protestant church and state*, and their *fundamental*, unquestionable laws and liberties: they charged him with having broken the *original contract* between king and people. This was more than *misconduct*. A grave and overruling necessity obliged them to take the step they took, and took with infinite reluctance, as under that most rigorous of all laws. Their trust for the future preservation of the constitution was not in future revolutions. The grand policy of all their regulations was to render it almost impracticable for any future sovereign to compel the states of the kingdom to have again recourse to those violent remedies. They left the crown what, in the eye and estimation of law, it had ever been, perfectly irresponsible....

Dr. Price, in this sermon,[1] condemns very properly the practice of gross, adulatory addresses to kings. Instead of this fulsome style, he proposes that his majesty should be told, on occasions of congratulation, that "he is to consider himself as more properly the servant than the sovereign of his people." For a compliment, this new form of address does not seem to be very soothing. Those who are servants, in name, as well as in effect, do not like to be told of their situation, their duty, and their obligations....

I should have considered all this as no more than a sort of flippant vain discourse, in which, as in an unsavoury fume, several persons suffer the spirit of liberty to evaporate, if it were not plainly in support of the idea, and a part of the scheme of "cashiering kings for misconduct." In that light it is worth some observation.

Kings, in one sense, are undoubtedly the servants of the people, because their power has no other rational end than that of the general advantage; but it is not true that they are, in the ordinary sense (by our constitution, at least) any thing like servants; the essence of whose situation is to obey the commands of some other, and to be removeable at pleasure. But the king of Great Britain obeys no other person; all other persons are individually, and collectively too, under him, and owe to him a legal obedience. The law, which knows neither to flatter nor to insult, calls this high magistrate, not our servant, as this humble Divine

1 [Burke's note:] P. 22, 23, 24.

calls him, but *our sovereign Lord the King;*" and we, on our parts, have learned to speak only the primitive language of the law, and not the confused jargon of their Babylonian pulpits.

As he is not to obey us, but as we are to obey the law in him, our constitution has made no sort of provision towards render-.ing him, as a servant, in any degree responsible. Our constitution knows nothing of a magistrate like the *Justicia* of Arragon;[1] nor of any court legally appointed, nor of any process legally settled for submitting the king to the responsibility belonging to all servants. In this he is not distinguished from the commons and the lords; who, in their several public capacities, can never be called to an account for their conduct; although the Revolution Society chooses to assert, in direct opposition to one of the wisest and most beautiful parts of our constitution, that "a king is no more than the first servant of the public, created by it, *and responsible to it.*"

Ill would our ancestors at the Revolution have deserved their fame for wisdom, if they had found no security for their freedom, but in rendering their government feeble in its operations, and precarious in its tenure; if they had been able to contrive no better remedy against arbitrary power than civil confusion. Let these gentlemen state who that *representative* public is to whom they will affirm the king, as a servant, to be responsible. It will be then time enough for me to produce to them the positive statute law which affirms that he is not.

The ceremony of cashiering kings, of which these gentlemen talk so much at their ease, can rarely, if ever, be performed without force. It then becomes a case of war, and not of constitution. Laws are commanded to hold their tongues amongst arms; and tribunals fall to the ground with the peace they are no longer able to uphold. The Revolution of 1688 was obtained by a just war, in the only case in which any war, and much more a civil war, can be just. "Justa bella quibus *necessaria.*"[2] The question of dethroning, or, if these gentlemen like the phrase better, "cashiering kings," will always be, as it has always been, an extraordinary question of state, and wholly out of the law; a question (like all other questions of state) of dispositions, and of means, and of probable consequences, rather than of positive

---

1 Disputes between kings and nobility in medieval Aragon were submitted to the arbitration of a Justicia (or Chief Justice).

2 "That war is just which is necessary." Livy (64/59 BCE–12/17 CE), *History of Rome*, Book IX, i, 10.

rights. As it was not made for common abuses, so it is not to be agitated by common minds. The speculative line of demarcation, where obedience ought to end, and resistance must begin, is faint, obscure, and not easily definable. It is not a single act, or a single event, which determines it. Governments must be abused and deranged indeed, before it can be thought of; and the prospect of the future must be as bad as the experience of the past. When things are in that lamentable condition, the nature of the disease is to indicate the remedy to those whom nature has qualified to administer in extremities this critical, ambiguous, bitter portion to a distempered state. Times and occasions, and provocations, will teach their own lessons. The wise will determine from the gravity of the case; the irritable from sensibility to oppression; the high-minded from disdain and indignation at abusive power in unworthy hands; the brave and bold from the love of honourable danger in a generous cause: but, with or without right, a revolution will be the very last resource of the thinking and the good.

The third head of right, asserted by the pulpit of the Old Jewry, namely, the "right to form a government for ourselves," has, at least, as little countenance from any thing done at the Revolution, either in precedent or principle, as the two first of their claims. The Revolution was made to preserve our *antient* indisputable laws and liberties, and that *antient* constitution of government which is our only security for law and liberty. If you are desirous of knowing the spirit of our constitution, and the policy which predominated in that great period which has secured it to this hour, pray look for both in our histories, in our records, in our acts of parliament, and journals of parliament, and not in the sermons of the Old Jewry, and the after-dinner toasts of the Revolution Society.—In the former you will find other ideas and another language. Such a claim is as ill-suited by our temper and wishes as it is unsupported by any appearance of authority. The very idea of the fabrication of a new government, is enough to fill us with disgust and horror. We wished at the period of the Revolution, and do now wish, to derive all we possess as *an inheritance from our forefathers*. Upon that body and stock of inheritance we have taken care not to inoculate any cyon[1] alien to the nature of the original plant. All the reformations we have hitherto made, have proceeded upon the principle

---

1 Obsolete spelling of *scion*, namely a young shoot of a plant used for grafting or planting.

of reference to antiquity; and I hope, nay I am persuaded, that all those which possibly may be made hereafter, will be carefully formed upon analogical precedent, authority, and example.

Our oldest reformation is that of Magna Charta.[1] You will see that Sir Edward Coke, that great oracle of our law, and indeed all the great men who follow him, to Blackstone, are industrious to prove the pedigree of our liberties.[2] They endeavour to prove, that the antient charter, the Magna Charta of King John, was connected with another positive charter from Henry I. and that both the one and the other were nothing more than a re-affirmance of the still more antient standing law of the kingdom. In the matter of fact, for the greater part, these authors appear to be in the right; perhaps not always: but if the lawyers mistake in some particulars, it proves my position still the more strongly; because it demonstrates the powerful prepossession towards antiquity, with which the minds of all our lawyers and legislators, and of all the people whom they wish to influence, have been always filled; and the stationary policy of this kingdom in considering their most sacred rights and franchises as an *inheritance.*

In the famous law of the 3d of Charles I. called the *Petition of Right,* the parliament says to the king, "Your subjects have *inherited* this freedom," claiming their franchises not on abstract principles "as the rights of men," but as the rights of Englishmen, and as a patrimony derived from their forefathers. Selden,[3] and the other profoundly learned men, who drew this petition of right, were as well acquainted, at least, with all the general theories concerning the "rights of men," as any of the discoursers in our pulpits, or on your tribune; full as well as Dr. Price, or as the Abbé Seyes.[4] But, for reasons worthy of that practical

---

1 The Magna Carta ("Great Charter") of 1215, the foundational document of English liberty, guaranteed a number of rights, including inheritance, security of property, and a fair trial.

2 Sir Edward Coke (1552–1634) and Sir William Blackstone (1723–80) were the leading authorities on English law in the seventeenth and eighteenth centuries.

3 John Selden (1584–1654), jurist and Member of Parliament, one of the authors of the 1628 Petition of Right.

4 Abbé Emmanuel-Joseph Sieyès (1748–1836) was a radical priest and influential writer during the French Revolution, most famously the author of *What Is the Third Estate?*, published in January 1789, and an occasional focus of Burke's ire and ridicule: "Abbé

wisdom which superseded their theoretic science, they preferred this positive, recorded, *hereditary* title to all which can be dear to the man and the citizen, to that vague speculative right, which exposed their sure inheritance to be scrambled for and torn to pieces by every wild litigious spirit.

The same policy pervades all the laws which have since been made for the preservation of our liberties. In the 1st of William and Mary, in the famous statute, called the Declaration of Right, the two houses utter not a syllable of "a right to frame a government for themselves." You will see, that their whole care was to secure the religion, laws, and liberties, that had been long possessed, and had been lately endangered. "Taking[1] into their most serious consideration the *best* means for making such an establishment, that their religion, laws, and liberties, might not be in danger of being again subverted," they auspicate all their proceedings, by stating as some of those *best* means, "in the *first place*" to do "as their *ancestors in like cases have usually* done for vindicating their *antient* rights and liberties, to *declare*;"—and then they pray the king and queen, "that it may be *declared* and enacted, that *all and singular* the rights and liberties *asserted and declared* are the true *antient* and indubitable rights and liberties of the people of this kingdom."

You will observe, that from Magna Charta to the Declaration of Right, it has been the uniform policy of our constitution to

---

Sieyès has whole nests of pigeon-holes full of constitutions ready made, ticketed, sorted, and numbered; suited to every season and every fancy; some with the top of the pattern at the bottom, and some with the bottom at the top; some plain, some flowered; some distinguished for their simplicity, others for their complexity; some of blood colour; some of *boue de Paris*; some with directories, others without a direction; some with councils of elders, and councils of youngsters; some without any council at all. Some, where the electors choose the representatives; others, where the representatives choose the electors. Some in long coats, and some in short cloaks; some with pantaloons; some without breeches. Some with five-shilling qualifications; some totally unqualified. So that no constitution-fancier may go unsuited from his shop, provided he loves a pattern of pillage, oppression, arbitrary imprisonment, confiscation, exile, revolutionary judgment, and legalized premeditated murder, in any shapes into which they can be put" (*A Letter to a Noble Lord*, *Works* V, 242–43).

1 [Burke's note:] I W. and M.

claim and assert our liberties, as an *entailed inheritance* derived to us from our forefathers, and to be transmitted to our posterity; as an estate specially belonging to the people of this kingdom without any reference whatever to any other more general or prior right. By this means our constitution preserves an unity in so great a diversity of its parts. We have an inheritable crown; an inheritable peerage; and an house of commons and a people inheriting privileges, franchises, and liberties, from a long line of ancestors.

This policy appears to me to be the result of profound reflection; or rather the happy effect of following nature, which is wisdom without reflection, and above it. A spirit of innovation is generally the result of a selfish temper and confined views. People will not look forward to posterity, who never look backward to their ancestors. Besides, the people of England well know, that the idea of inheritance furnishes a sure principle of conservation, and a sure principle of transmission; without at all excluding a principle of improvement. It leaves acquisition free; but it secures what it acquires. Whatever advantages are obtained by a state proceeding on these maxims, are locked fast as in a sort of family settlement; grasped as in a kind of mortmain[1] for ever. By a constitutional policy, working after the pattern of nature, we receive, we hold, we transmit our government and our privileges, in the same manner in which we enjoy and transmit our property and our lives. The institutions of policy, the goods of fortune, the gifts of Providence, are handed down, to us and from us, in the same course and order. Our political system is placed in a just correspondence and symmetry with the order of the world, and with the mode of existence decreed to a permanent body composed of transitory parts; wherein, by the disposition of a stupendous wisdom, moulding together the great mysterious incorporation of the human race, the whole, at one time, is never old, or middle-aged, or young, but in a condition of unchangeable constancy, moves on through the varied tenour of perpetual decay, fall, renovation, and progression. Thus, by preserving the method of nature in the conduct of the state, in what we improve we are never wholly new; in what we retain we are never wholly obsolete. By adhering in this manner and on those principles to our forefathers, we are guided not by the superstition of antiquarians, but by the spirit of philosophic

---

1 An inalienable possession of lands by an ecclesiastical or other corporation.

analogy. In this choice of inheritance we have given to our frame of polity the image of a relation in blood; binding up the constitution of our country with our dearest domestic ties; adopting our fundamental laws into the bosom of our family affections; keeping inseparable, and cherishing with the warmth of all their combined and mutually reflected charities, our state, our hearths, our sepulchres, and our altars.

Through the same plan of a conformity to nature in our artificial institutions, and by calling in the aid of her unerring and powerful instincts, to fortify the fallible and feeble contrivances of our reason, we have derived several other, and those no small benefits, from considering our liberties in the light of an inheritance. Always acting as if in the presence of canonized forefathers, the spirit of freedom, leading in itself to misrule and excess, is tempered with an awful gravity. This idea of a liberal descent inspires us with a sense of habitual native dignity, which prevents that upstart insolence almost inevitably adhering to and disgracing those who are the first acquirers of any distinction. By this means our liberty becomes a noble freedom. It carries an imposing and majestic aspect. It has a pedigree and illustrating ancestors. It has its bearings and its ensigns armorial.[1] It has its gallery of portraits; its monumental inscriptions; its records, evidences, and titles. We procure reverence to our civil institutions on the principle upon which nature teaches us to revere individual men; on account of their age; and on account of those from whom they are descended. All your sophisters cannot produce any thing better adapted to preserve a rational and manly freedom than the course that we have pursued, who have chosen our nature rather than our speculations, our breasts rather than our inventions, for the great conservatories and magazines of our rights and privileges.

You might, if you pleased, have profited of our example, and have given to your recovered freedom a correspondent dignity. Your privileges, though discontinued, were not lost to memory. Your constitution, it is true, whilst you were out of possession, suffered waste and dilapidation; but you possessed in some parts the walls, and in all the foundations of a noble and venerable castle. You might have repaired those walls; you might have built on those old foundations. Your constitution was suspended before it was perfected; but you had the elements of a constitution very nearly as good as could be wished. In your old states

---

1 Heraldic symbols on flags or shields.

you possessed that variety of parts corresponding with the various descriptions of which your community was happily composed; you had all that combination, and all that opposition of interests, you had that action and counteraction which, in the natural and in the political world, from the reciprocal struggle of discordant powers, draws out the harmony of the universe. These opposed and conflicting interests, which you considered as so great a blemish in your old and in our present constitution, interpose a salutary check to all precipitate resolutions; They render deliberation a matter not of choice, but of necessity; they make all change a subject of *compromise*, which naturally begets moderation; they produce *temperaments*, preventing the sore evil of harsh, crude, unqualified reformations; and rendering all the headlong exertions of arbitrary power, in the few or in the many, for ever impracticable. Through that diversity of members and interests, general liberty had as many securities as there were separate views in the several orders; whilst by pressing down the whole by the weight of a real monarchy, the separate parts would have been prevented from warping and starting from their allotted places.

You had all these advantages in your antient states; but you chose to act as if you had never been moulded into civil society, and had every thing to begin anew. You began ill, because you began by despising every thing that belonged to you. You set up your trade without a capital. If the last generations of your country appeared without much lustre in your eyes, you might have passed them by, and derived your claims from a more early race of ancestors. Under a pious predilection for those ancestors, your imaginations would have realized in them a standard of virtue and wisdom, beyond the vulgar practice of the hour: and you would have risen with the example to whose imitation you aspired. Respecting your forefathers, you would have been taught to respect yourselves. You would not have chosen to consider the French as a people of yesterday, as a nation of low-born servile wretches until the emancipating year of 1789. In order to furnish, at the expence of your honour, an excuse to your apologists here for several enormities of yours, you would not have been content to be represented as a gang of Maroon slaves, suddenly broke loose from the house of bondage, and therefore to be pardoned for your abuse of the liberty to which you were not accustomed and ill fitted. Would it not, my worthy friend, have been wiser to have you thought, what I, for one, always thought you, a generous and gallant nation, long misled to your disadvantage by your high and romantic sentiments of fidelity, honour, and loyalty; that events had been unfavourable to you, but that you were not enslaved through any illiberal or servile disposition; that in your most devoted submission, you were actuated by a principle of public spirit, and that it was your country you worshipped, in the person of your king? Had you made it to be understood, that in the delusion of this amiable error you had gone further than your wise ancestors; that you were resolved to resume your ancient privileges, whilst you preserved the spirit of your ancient and your recent loyalty and honour; or, if diffident of yourselves, and not clearly discerning the almost obliterated constitution of your ancestors, you had looked to your neighbours in this land, who had kept alive the ancient principles and models of the old common law of Europe meliorated and adapted to its present state—by following wise examples you would have given new examples of wisdom to the world. You would have rendered the cause of liberty venerable in the eyes of every worthy mind in every nation. You would have shamed despotism from the earth, by shewing that freedom was not only reconcileable, but as, when well disciplined it is, auxiliary to law. You would have had an unoppressive but a productive revenue. You would have had a flourishing commerce to feed it. You would have had a free constitution; a potent monarchy; a disciplined army; a reformed and venerated clergy; a mitigated but spirited nobility, to lead your virtue, not to overlay it; you would have had a liberal order of commons, to emulate and to recruit that nobility; you would have had a protected, satisfied, laborious, and obedient people, taught to seek and to recognize the happiness that is to be found by virtue in all conditions; in which consists the true moral equality of mankind, and not in that monstrous fiction, which, by inspiring false ideas and vain expectations into men destined to travel in the obscure walk of laborious life, serves only to aggravate and imbitter that real inequality, which it never can remove; and which the order of civil life establishes as much for the benefit of those whom it must leave in an humble state, as those whom it is able to exalt to a condition more splendid, but not more happy. You had a smooth and easy career of felicity and glory laid open to you, beyond any thing recorded in the history of the world; but you have shewn that difficulty is good for man.

Compute your gains: see what is got by those extravagant and presumptuous speculations which have taught your leaders to despise all their predecessors, and all their contemporaries, and even to despise themselves, until the moment in which they become truly despicable. By following those false lights, France has bought undisguised calamities at a higher price than any nation has purchased the most unequivocal blessings! France has bought poverty by crime! France has not sacrificed her virtue to her interest; but she has abandoned her interest, that she might prostitute her virtue. All other nations have begun the fabric of a new government, or the reformation of an old, by establishing originally, or by enforcing with greater exactness some rites or other of religion. All other people have laid the foundations of civil freedom in severer manners, and a system of a more austere and masculine morality. France, when she let loose the reins of regal authority, doubled the licence, of a ferocious dissoluteness in manners, and of an insolent irreligion in opinions and practices; and has extended through all ranks of life, as if she were communicating some privilege, or laying open some secluded benefit, all the unhappy corruptions that usually were the disease of wealth and power. This is one of the new principles of equality in France.

France, by the perfidy of her leaders, has utterly disgraced the tone of lenient council in the cabinets of princes, and disarmed it of its most potent topics. She has sanctified the dark suspicious maxims of tyrannous distrust; and taught kings to tremble at (what will hereafter be called) the delusive plausibilities, of moral politicians. Sovereigns will consider those who advise them to place an unlimited confidence in their people, as subverters of their thrones; as traitors who aim at their destruction, by leading their easy good-nature, under specious pretences, to admit combinations of bold and faithless men into a participation of their power. This alone (if there were nothing else) is an irreparable calamity to you and to mankind. Remember that your parliament of Paris told your king, that in calling the states together, he had nothing to fear but the prodigal excess of their zeal in providing for the support of the throne. It is right that these men should hide their heads. It is right that they should bear their part in the ruin which their counsel has brought on their sovereign and their country. Such sanguine declarations tend to lull authority asleep; to encourage it rashly to engage in perilous adventures of untried policy; to neglect those provisions, preparations, and precautions, which distinguish benevolence from imbecillity; and without which no man can answer for the salutary effect of any abstract plan of government or of freedom. For want of these, they have seen the medicine of the state corrupted into its poison. They have seen the French rebel against a mild and lawful monarch, with more fury, outrage, and insult, than ever any people has been known to rise against the most illegal usurper, or the most sanguinary tyrant. Their resistance was made to concession; their revolt was from protection; their blow was aimed at an hand holding out graces, favours, and immunities.

This was unnatural. The rest is in order. They have found their punishment in their success. Laws overturned; tribunals subverted; industry without vigour; commerce expiring; the revenue unpaid, yet the people impoverished; a church pillaged, and a state not relieved; civil and military anarchy made the constitution of the kingdom; every thing human and divine sacrificed to the idol of public credit, and national bankruptcy the consequence; and to crown all, the paper securities of new, precarious, tottering power, the discredited paper securities of impoverished fraud, and beggared rapine, held out as a currency for the support of an empire, in lieu of the two great recognized species that represent the lasting conventional credit of mankind, which disappeared and hid themselves in the earth from whence they came, when the principle of property, whose creatures and representatives they are, was systematically subverted.

Were all these dreadful things necessary? were they the inevitable results of the desperate struggle of determined patriots, compelled to wade through blood and tumult, to the quiet shore of a tranquil and prosperous liberty? No! nothing like it. The fresh ruins of France, which shock our feelings wherever we can turn our eyes, are not the devastation of civil war; they are the sad but instructive monuments of rash and ignorant counsel in time of profound peace. They are the display of inconsiderate and presumptuous, because unresisted and irresistible authority. The persons who have thus squandered away the precious treasure of their crimes, the persons who have made this prodigal and wild waste of public evils (the last stake reserved for the ultimate ransom of the state) have met in their progress with little, or rather with no opposition at all. Their whole march was more like a triumphal procession than the progress of a war. Their pioneers have gone before them, and demolished and laid every thing level at their feet. Not one drop of *their* blood have they shed in the cause of the country they have ruined. They have made no sacrifices to their projects of greater consequence than their shoe-buckles, whilst they were imprisoning their king, murdering their fellow citizens, and bathing in tears, and plunging in poverty and distress, thousands of worthy men and worthy families. Their cruelty has not even been the base result of fear. It has been the effect of their sense of perfect safety, in authorizing treasons, robberies, rapes, assassinations, slaughters, and burnings throughout their harassed land. But the cause of all was plain from the beginning.

[*Burke next surveys the composition of the National Assembly, bewailing both the members' lack of practical experience (the best of them being "only men of theory") and the numerical balance in favour of the Third Estate (the Commons, in contradistinction to the First Estate [the Clergy] and the Second Estate [the Nobility]). He notes that the majority of the members of the Assembly were obscure and low-ranking practitioners in the law, and he declares that he saw distinctly and immediately all that was to follow. Such men—"habitually meddling, daring, subtle, active, of litigious dispositions and unquiet minds"—would be intoxicated with their new power and would pursue their private interests, at any expense to the state. "It was not an event depending on chance or contingency. It was inevitable; it was necessary; it was planted in the nature of things."*]

To observing men it must have appeared from the beginning, that the majority of the Third Estate, in conjunction with such a deputation from the clergy as I have described, whilst it pursued the destruction of the nobility, would inevitably become subservient to the worst designs of individuals in that class. In the spoil and humiliation of their own order these individuals would possess a sure fund for the pay of their new followers. To squander away the objects which made the happiness of their fellows, would be to them no sacrifice at all. Turbulent, discontented men of quality, in proportion as they are puffed up with personal pride and arrogance, generally despise their own order. One of the first symptoms they discover of a selfish and mischievous ambition, is a profligate disregard of a dignity which they partake with others. To be attached to the subdivision, to love the little platoon we belong to in society, is the first principle (the germ as it were) of public affections. It is the first link in the series by which we proceed towards a love to our country and to mankind. The interests of that portion of social arrangement is a trust in the hands of all those who compose it; and as none but bad men would justify it in abuse, none but traitors would barter it away for their own personal advantage....

... Believe me, Sir, those who attempt to level, never equalize. In all societies, consisting of various descriptions of citizens, some description must be uppermost. The levellers therefore only change and pervert the natural order of things; they load the edifice of society, by setting up in the air what the solidity of the structure requires to be on the ground. The associations of taylors and carpenters, of which the republic (of Paris, for instance) is composed, cannot be equal to the situation, into which, by the worst of usurpations, an usurpation on the prerogatives of nature, you attempt to force them.

The chancellor of France at the opening of the states, said, in a tone of oratorical flourish, that all occupations were honourable. If he meant only, that no honest employment was disgraceful, he would not have gone beyond the truth. But in asserting, that any thing is honourable, we imply some distinction in its favour. The occupation of an hair-dresser, or of a working tallow-chandler, cannot be a matter of honour to any person—to say nothing of a number of other more servile employments. Such descriptions of men ought not to suffer oppression from the state; but the state suffers oppression, if such as they, either individually or collectively, are permitted to rule. In this you think you are combatting prejudice, but you are at war with nature.[1]

I do not, my dear Sir, conceive you to be of that sophistical captious spirit, or of that uncandid dulness, as to require, for every general observation or sentiment, an explicit detail of the correctives and exceptions, which reason will presume to be included in all the general propositions which come from reasonable men.

---

1 [Burke's note:] Ecclesiasticus, chap. xxxviii. verse 24, 25. "The wisdom of a learned man cometh by opportunity of leisure: and he that hath little business shall become wise."—"How can he get wisdom that holdeth the plough, and that glorieth in the goad; that driveth oxen; and is occupied in their labours; and whose talk is of bullocks."

Ver. 27. "So every carpenter and work-master that laboureth night and day." &c.

Ver. 33. "They shall not be sought for in public counsel, nor sit high in the congregation: They shall not sit on the judges seat, nor understand the sentence of judgment: they cannot declare justice and judgment, and they shall not be found where parables are spoken."

Ver. 34. "But they will maintain the state of the world."

I do not determine whether this book be canonical, as the Gallican church (till lately) has considered it, or apocryphal, as here it is taken. I am sure it contains a great deal of sense, and truth.

I do not imagine, that I wish to confine power, authority, and distinction to blood, and names, and titles. No, Sir. There is no qualification for government, but virtue and wisdom, actual or presumptive. Wherever they are actually found, they have, in whatever state, condition, profession or trade, the passport of Heaven to human place and honour. Woe to the country which would madly and impiously reject the service of the talents and virtues, civil, military, or religious, that are given to grace and to serve it; and would condemn to obscurity every thing formed to diffuse lustre and glory around a state. Woe to that country too, that passing into the opposite extreme, considers a low education, a mean contracted view of things, a sordid mercenary occupation, as a preferable title to command. Every thing ought to be open; but not indifferently to every man. No rotation; no appointment by lot; no mode of election operating in the spirit of sortition[1] or rotation, can be generally good in a government conversant in extensive objects. Because they have no tendency, direct or indirect, to select the man with a view to the duty, or to accommodate the one to the other. I do not hesitate to say, that the road to eminence and power, from obscure condition, ought not to be made too easy, nor a thing too much of course. If rare merit be the rarest of all rare things, it ought to pass through some sort of probation. The temple of honour ought to be seated on an eminence. If it be open through virtue, let it be remembered too, that virtue is never tried but by some difficulty, and some struggle.

Nothing is a due and adequate representation of a state, that does not represent its ability, as well as its property. But as ability is a vigorous and active principle, and as property is sluggish, inert, and timid, it never can be safe from the invasions of ability, unless it be, out of all proportion, predominant in the representation. It must be represented too in great masses of accumulation, or it is not rightly protected. The characteristic essence of property, formed out of the combined principles of its acquisition and conservation, is to be *unequal.* The great masses therefore which excite envy, and tempt rapacity, must be put out of the possibility of danger. Then they form a natural rampart about the lesser properties in all their gradations. The same quantity of property, which is by the natural course of things divided among many, has not the same operation. Its defensive power is weakened as it is diffused. In this diffusion each man's portion is less than what, in the eagerness of his desires, he may

Everything should be open and allowed for every man and nothing bitter to him

Communism?

He says land and property is not equal to man

---

1 The selection of political representatives by lottery.

He will do what he can

flatter himself to obtain by dissipating the accumulations of oth-) ers. The plunder of the few would indeed give but a share inconceivably small in the distribution to the many. But the many are not capable of making this calculation; and those who lead them to rapine, never intend this distribution.

The power of perpetuating our property in our families is one of the most valuable and interesting circumstances belonging to it, and that which tends the most to the perpetuation of society itself. It makes our weakness subservient to our virtue; it grafts benevolence even upon avarice. The possessors of family wealth, and of the distinction which attends hereditary possession (as most concerned in it) are the natural securities for this transmission. With us, the house of peers is formed upon this principle. It is wholly composed of hereditary property and hereditary distinction; and made therefore the third of the legislature; and in the last event, the sole judge of all property in all its subdivisions. The house of commons too, though not necessarily, yet in fact, is always so composed in the far greater part. Let those large proprietors be what they will, and they have their chance of being amongst the best, they are at the very worst, the ballast in the vessel of the commonwealth. For though hereditary wealth, and the rank which goes with it, are too much idolized by creeping sycophants, and the blind abject admirers of power, they are too rashly slighted in shallow speculations of the petulant, assuming, short-sighted coxcombs of philosophy. Some decent regulated pre-eminence, some preference (not exclusive appropriation) given to birth, is neither unnatural, nor unjust, nor impolitic.

Touching store of this point of view and what builds our virtue

It is said, that twenty-four millions ought to prevail over two hundred thousand. True; if the constitution of a kingdom be a problem of arithmetic. This sort of discourse does well enough with the lamp-post for its second: to men who *may* reason calmly, it is ridiculous. The will of the many, and their interest, must very often differ; and great will be the difference when they make an evil choice. A government of five hundred country attorneys and obscure curates is not good for twenty-four millions of men, though it were chosen by eight and forty millions; nor is it the better for being guided by a dozen of persons of quality, who have betrayed their trust in order to obtain that power. At present, you seem in every thing to have strayed out of the high road of nature....

think what he saying is that small gov't is not good for a large population

If this be your actual situation, compared to the situation to which you were called, as it were by the voice of God and man, I cannot find it in my heart to congratulate you on the choice you have made, or the success which has attended your endeavours. I can as little recommend to any other nation a conduct grounded on such principles, and productive of such effects. That I must leave to those who can see further into your affairs than I am able to do, and who best know how far your actions are favourable to their designs. The gentlemen of the Revolution Society, who were so early in their congratulations, appear to be strongly of opinion that there is some scheme of politics relative to this country, in which your proceedings may, in some way, be useful. For your Dr. Price, who seems to have speculated himself into no small degree of fervour upon this subject, addresses his auditory in the following very remarkable words: "I cannot conclude without recalling *particularly* to your recollection a consideration which I have *more than once alluded to*, and which probably your thoughts have *been all along anticipating*; a consideration with which my *mind is impressed more than I can express*. I mean the consideration of the *favourableness of the present times to all exertions in the cause of liberty*."

It is plain that the mind of this *political* Preacher was at the time big with some extraordinary design; and it is very probable, that the thoughts of his audience, who understood him better than I do, did all along run before him in his reflection, and in the whole train of consequences to which it led.

Before I read that sermon, I really thought I had lived in a free country; and it was an error I cherished, because it gave me a greater liking to the country I lived in. I was indeed aware, that a jealous, ever-waking vigilance, to guard the treasure of our liberty, not only from invasion, but from decay and corruption, was our best wisdom and our first duty. However, I considered that treasure rather as a possession to be secured than as a prize to be contended for. I did not discern how the present time came to be so very favourable to all *exertions* in the cause of freedom. The present time differs from any other only by the circumstance of what is doing in France. If the example of that nation is to have an influence on this, I can easily conceive why some of their proceedings which have an unpleasant aspect, and are not quite reconcileable to humanity, generosity, good faith, and justice, are palliated with so much milky good-nature towards the actors, and borne with so much heroic fortitude towards the sufferers. It is certainly not prudent to discredit the authority of an example we mean to follow. But allowing this, we are led to a very natural question;—What is that cause of liberty, and what are those

[margin notes:] Their Opinion is Strong with Politics in Society

[margin notes:] Characteristics of ones in Society

EDMUND BURKE

[handwritten:] what Characteristics brings that about?

exertions in its favour, to which the example of France is so singularly auspicious? Is our monarchy to be annihilated, with all the laws, all the tribunals, and all the antient corporations of the kingdom? . — Is it one Person or a democracy.

I see that your example is held out to shame us. I know that we are supposed a dull sluggish race, rendered passive by finding our situation tolerable; and prevented by a mediocrity of freedom from ever attaining to its full perfection.[1] Your leaders in France began by affecting to admire, almost to adore, the British constitution; but as they advanced they came to look upon it with a sovereign contempt. The friends of your National Assembly amongst us have full as mean an opinion of what was formerly thought the glory of their country. The Revolution Society has discovered that the English nation is not free. They are convinced that the inequality in our representation is a "defect in our constitution *so gross and palpable*, as to make it excellent chiefly in *form* and *theory*."[2] That a representation in the legislature of a kingdom is not only the basis of all constitutional liberty in it, but of "*all legitimate government*; that without it a *government* is nothing but an *usurpation*;"—that "when the representation is *partial*, the kingdom possesses liberty only *partially*; and if extremely partial it gives only a *semblance*; and if not only extremely partial, but corruptly chosen, it becomes a *nuisance.*" Dr. Price considers this inadequacy of representation as our *fundamental grievance;* and though, as to the corruption of this semblance of representation, he hopes it is not yet arrived to its full perfection of depravity; he fears that "nothing will be done towards gaining for us this *essential blessing*, until some

[marginalia: English nation is Corrupt and broke within Society]

[marginalia: He is Saying their all now and what causes Problems]

---

1 Compare this with the sentiment in Burke's "Letter to William Elliot": "I admit, indeed, that my praises of the British government, loaded with all its incumbrances; clogged with its peers and its beef; its parsons and its pudding; its commons and its beer; and its dull slavish liberty of going about just as one pleases, had something to provoke a jockey of Norfolk, who was inspired with the resolute ambition of becoming a citizen of France, to do something which might render him worthy of naturalization in that grand asylum of persecuted merit ..." (*Works* V, 141). The "jockey of Norfolk" is Thomas Paine (1737–1809), who hailed from Thetford, Norfolk; the relevant sense of "jockey" here is that of "A crafty or fraudulent bargainer; a cheat" (*OED*).

2 [Burke's note:] Discourse on the Love of our Country, 3d edit. p. 39.

great abuse of power again provokes our resentment, or some *great calamity* again alarms our fears, or perhaps till the acquisition of a *pure and equal representation by other countries*, whilst we are *mocked* with the *shadow*, kindles our shame." To this he subjoins a note in these words. "A representation, chosen chiefly by the Treasury, and a *few* thousands of the *dregs* of the people, who are generally paid for their votes."

You will smile here at the consistency of those democratists, who, when they are not on their guard, treat the humbler part of the community with the greatest contempt, whilst, at the same time, they pretend to make them the depositories of all power. It would require a long discourse to point out to you the many fallacies that lurk in the generality and equivocal nature of the terms "inadequate representation." I shall only say here, in justice to that old-fashioned constitution, under which we have long prospered, that our representation has been found perfectly adequate to all the purposes for which a representation of the people can be desired or devised. I defy the enemies of our constitution to shew the contrary. To detail the particulars in which it is found so well to promote its ends, would demand a treatise on our practical constitution. I state here the doctrine of the Revolutionists, only that you and others may see, what an opinion these gentlemen entertain of the constitution of their country, and why they seem to think that some great abuse of power, or some great calamity, as giving a chance for the blessing of a constitution according to their ideas, would be much palliated to their feelings; you see *why they* are so much enamoured of your fair and equal representation, which being once obtained, the same effects might follow. You see they consider our house of commons as only "a semblance," "a form," "a theory," "a shadow," "a mockery," perhaps "a nuisance."

These gentlemen value themselves on being systematic; and not without reason. They must therefore look on this gross and palpable defect of representation, this fundamental grievance (so they call it) as a thing not only vicious in itself, but as rendering our whole government absolutely *illegitimate*, and not at all better than a downright *usurpation*. Another revolution, to get rid of this illegitimate and usurped government, would of course be perfectly justifiable, if not absolutely necessary. Indeed their principle, if you observe it with any attention, goes much further than to an alteration in the election of the house of commons; for, if popular representation, or choice, is necessary to the *legitimacy* of all government, the house of lords is, at one stroke, bastardized and corrupted in blood. That house is no representative of the people at all, even in "semblance or in form." The case of the crown is altogether as bad. In vain the crown may endeavour to screen itself against these gentlemen by the authority of the establishment made on the Revolution.[1] The Revolution which is resorted to for a title, on their system, wants a title itself. The Revolution is built, according to their theory, upon a basis not more solid than our present formalities, as it was made by an house of lords not representing any one but themselves; and by an house of commons exactly such as the present, that is, as they term it, by a mere "shadow and mockery" of representation.

Something they must destroy, or they seem to themselves to exist for no purpose. One set is for destroying the civil power through the ecclesiastical; another for demolishing the ecclesiastick through the civil. They are aware that the worst consequences might happen to the public in accomplishing this double ruin of church and state; but they are so heated with their theories, that they give more than hints, that this ruin, with all the mischiefs that must lead to it and attend it, and which to themselves appear quite certain, would not be unacceptable to them, or very remote from their wishes. A man amongst them of great authority, and certainly of great talents, speaking of a supposed alliance between church and state, says, "perhaps *we must wait for the fall of the civil powers* before this most unnatural alliance be broken. Calamitous no doubt will that time be. But what convulsion in the political world ought to be a subject of lamentation, if it be attended with so desirable an effect?"[2] You see with what a steady eye these gentlemen are prepared to view the greatest calamities which can befall their country!

It is no wonder therefore, that with these ideas of every thing in their constitution and government at home, either in church or state, as illegitimate and usurped, or, at best as a vain mockery, they look abroad with an eager and passionate enthusiasm. Whilst they are possessed by these notions, it is vain to talk to them of the practice of their ancestors, the fundamental laws of their country, the fixed form of a constitution, whose merits are confirmed by the solid test of long experience, and an increasing public strength and national prosperity. They despise

---

1 I.e., the Revolution of 1688.
2 The quoted passage is from Joseph Priestley's *History of the Corruptions of Christianity* (1782), vol. II, p. 484.

experience as the wisdom of unlettered men; and as for the rest, they have wrought under-ground a mine that will blow up at one grand explosion all examples of antiquity, all precedents, charters, and acts of parliament. They have "the rights of men." Against these there can be no prescription; against these no agreement is binding: these admit no temperament, and no compromise: any thing withheld from their full demand is so much of fraud and injustice. Against these their rights of men let no government look for security in the length of its continuance, or in the justice and lenity of its administration. The objections of these speculatists, if its forms do not quadrate with their theories, are as valid against such an old and beneficent government as against the most violent tyranny, or the greenest usurpation. They are always at issue with governments, not on a question of abuse, but a question of competency, and a question of title. I have nothing to say to the clumsy subtilty of their political metaphysics. Let them be their amusement in the schools.—"Illa se jactet in aula—Æolus, et clauso ventorum carcere regnet."[1]—But let them not break prison to burst like a Levanter,[2] to sweep the earth with their hurricane, and to break up the fountains of the great deep to overwhelm us.

Far am I from denying in theory; full as far is my heart from withholding in practice (if I were of power to give or to withhold) the real rights of men. In denying their false claims of right, I do not mean to injure those which are real, and are such as their pretended rights would totally destroy. If civil society be made for the advantage of man, all the advantages for which it is made become his right. It is an institution of beneficence; and law itself is only beneficence acting by a rule. Men have a right to live by that rule; they have a right to justice; as between their fellows, whether their fellows are in politic function or in ordinary occupation. They have a right to the fruits of their industry; and to the means of making their industry fruitful. They have a right to the acquisitions of their parents; to the nourishment and improvement of their offspring; to instruction in life, and to consolation in death. Whatever each man can separately do, without trespassing upon others, he has a right to do for himself; and he has a right to a fair portion of all which society, with all its combinations of skill and force, can do in his favour.

---

1 "In that hall let Aeolus lord it and rule within the barred prison of the winds." Virgil (70–19 BCE), *Aeneid*, Book I, 140–41.
2 A strong easterly wind in the Mediterranean region.

In this partnership all men have equal rights; but not to equal things. He that has but five shillings in the partnership, has as good a right to it, as he that has five hundred pound has to his larger proportion. But he has not a right to an equal dividend in the product of the joint stock; and as to the share of power, authority, and direction which each individual ought to have in the management of the state, that I must deny to be amongst the direct original rights of man in civil society; for I have in my contemplation the civil social man, and no other. It is a thing to be settled by convention.

If civil society be the offspring of convention, that convention must be its law. That convention must limit and modify all the descriptions of constitution which are formed under it. Every sort of legislative, judicial, or executory power are its creatures. They can have no being in any other state of things; and how can any man claim, under the conventions of civil society, rights which do not so much as suppose its existence? Rights which are absolutely repugnant to it? One of the first motives to civil society, and which becomes one of its fundamental rules, is, *that no man should be judge in his own cause*. By this each person has at once divested himself of the first fundamental right of uncovenanted man, that is, to judge for himself, and to assert his own cause. He abdicates all right to be his own governor. He inclusively, in a great measure, abandons the right of self-defence, the first law of nature. Men cannot enjoy the rights of an uncivil and of a civil state together. That he may obtain justice he gives up his right of determining what it is in points the most essential to him. That he may secure some liberty, he makes a surrender in trust of the whole of it.

Government is not made in virtue of natural rights, which may and do exist in total independence of it; and exist in much greater clearness, and in a much greater degree of abstract perfection: but their abstract perfection is their practical defect. By having a right to every thing they want every thing. Government is a contrivance of human wisdom to provide for human *wants*. Men have a right that these wants should be provided for by this wisdom. Among these wants is to be reckoned the want, out of civil society, of a sufficient restraint upon their passions. Society requires not only that the passions of individuals should be subjected, but that even in the mass and body as well as in the individuals, the inclinations of men should frequently be thwarted, their will controlled, and their passions brought into subjection. This can only be done *by a power out of themselves*; and not, in the exercise of its function, subject to that will and to those passions which it is its office to bridle and subdue. In this sense the restraints on men, as well as their liberties, are to be reckoned among their rights. But as the liberties and the restrictions vary with times and circumstances, and admit of infinite modifications, they cannot be settled upon any abstract rule; and nothing is so foolish as to discuss them upon that principle.

The moment you abate any thing from the full rights of men, each to govern himself, and suffer any artificial positive limitation upon those rights, from that moment the whole organization of government becomes a consideration of convenience. This it is which makes the constitution of a state, and the due distribution of its powers, a matter of the most delicate and complicated skill. It requires a deep knowledge of human nature and human necessities, and of the things which facilitate or obstruct the various ends which are to be pursued by the mechanism of civil institutions. The state is to have recruits to its strength, and remedies to its distempers. What is the use of discussing a man's abstract right to food or to medicine? The question is upon the method of procuring and administering them. In that deliberation I shall always advise to call in the aid of the farmer and the physician, rather than the professor of metaphysics.

The science of constructing a commonwealth, or renovating it, or reforming it, is, like every other experimental science, not to be taught à priori. Nor is it a short experience that can instruct us in that practical science; because the real effects of moral causes are not always immediate; but that which in the first instance is prejudicial may be excellent in its remoter operation; and its excellence may arise even from the ill effects it produces in the beginning. The reverse also happens; and very plausible schemes, with very pleasing commencements, have often shameful and lamentable conclusions. In states there are often some obscure and almost latent causes, things which appear at first view of little moment, on which a very great part of its prosperity or adversity may most essentially depend. The science of government being therefore so practical in itself, and intended for such practical purposes, a matter which requires experience, and even more experience than any person can gain in his whole life, however sagacious and observing he may be, it is with infinite caution that any man ought to venture upon pulling down an edifice which has answered in any tolerable degree for ages the common purposes of society, or on building it up again, without having models and patterns of approved utility before his eyes.

These metaphysic rights entering into common life, like rays of light which pierce into a dense medium, are, by the laws of nature, refracted from their straight line. Indeed in the gross and complicated mass of human passions and concerns, the primitive rights of men undergo such a variety of refractions and reflections, that it becomes absurd to talk of them as if they continued in the simplicity of their original direction. The nature of man is intricate; the objects of society are of the greatest possible complexity; and therefore no simple disposition or direction of power can be suitable either to man's nature, or to the quality of his affairs. When I hear the simplicity of contrivance aimed at and boasted of in any new political constitutions, I am at no loss to decide that the artificers are grossly ignorant of their trade, or totally negligent of their duty. The simple governments are fundamentally defective, to say no worse of them. If you were to contemplate society in but one point of view, all these simple modes of polity are infinitely captivating. In effect each would answer its single end much more perfectly than the more complex is able to attain all its complex purposes. But it is better that the whole should be imperfectly and anomalously answered, than that, while some parts are provided for with great exactness, others might be totally neglected, or perhaps materially injured, by the over-care of a favourite member.

The pretended rights of these theorists are all extremes; and in proportion as they are metaphysically true, they are morally and politically false. The rights of men are in a sort of *middle*, incapable of definition, but not impossible to be discerned. The rights of men in governments are their advantages; and these are often in balances between differences of good; in compromises sometimes between good and evil, and sometimes, between evil and evil. Political reason is a computing principle; adding, subtracting, multiplying, and dividing, morally and not metaphysically or mathematically, true moral denominations.

By these theorists the right of the people is almost always sophistically confounded with their power. The body of the community, whenever it can come to act, can meet with no effectual resistance; but till power and right are the same, the whole body of them has no right inconsistent with virtue, and the first of all virtues, prudence. Men have no right to what is not reasonable, and to what is not for their benefit; for though a pleasant writer said, *Liceat perire poetis*, when one of them, in cold blood, is said to have leaped into the flames of a volcanic revolution, *Ardentem frigidus Ætnam insiluit*, I consider such a frolic rather as an unjustifiable poetic licence, than as one of the franchises of Parnassus; and whether he were poet or divine, or politician that chose to exercise this kind of right, I think that more wise, because more charitable thoughts would urge me rather to save the man, than to preserve his brazen slippers as the monuments of his folly.[1]

The kind of anniversary sermons, to which a great part of what I write refers, if men are not shamed out of their present course, in commemorating the fact, will cheat many out of the principles, and deprive them of the benefits of the Revolution they commemorate. I confess to you, Sir, I never liked this continual talk of resistance and revolution, or the practice of making the extreme medicine of the constitution its daily bread. It renders the habit of society dangerously valetudinary: it is taking periodical doses of mercury sublimate, and swallowing down repeated provocatives of cantharides to our love of liberty.[2]

This distemper of remedy, grown habitual, relaxes and wears out, by a vulgar and prostituted use, the spring of that spirit which is to be exerted on great occasions. It was in the most patient period of Roman servitude that themes of tyrannicide made the ordinary exercise of boys at school—*cum perimit sævos classis numerosa tyrannos.*[3] In the ordinary state of things, it produces in a country like ours the worst effects, even on the cause of that liberty which it abuses with the dissoluteness of an extravagant speculation. Almost all the high-bred republicans of my time have, after a short space, become the most

---

1 The reference is to Horace's account, in *De Arte Poetica* (465–66), of Empedocles leaping into the erupting Mount Etna: "Let poets have the right and power to destroy themselves." The "franchises of Parnassus" are the liberties or privileges granted to poets, Parnassus being a mountain in Greece sacred to Apollo and the muses.

2 Mercury sublimate was, before the advent of penicillin, a common though ineffective treatment for syphilis, with toxic side-effects including irritability and mania. Cantharides (also called "Spanish Fly") was a drug made of powdered beetles and used as a diuretic and aphrodisiac. The overall intention of the passage, with its references to medicines and health-anxiety, is to leave the reader with the impression that revolutionaries suffer from a "distemper of remedy," recommending toxic remedies for a disease of their own making.

3 "While the crowded class is killing off the cruel tyrants." Juvenal (1st/2nd centuries CE), *Satires*, VII, 151.

decided, thorough-paced courtiers; they soon left the business of a tedious, moderate, but practical resistance to those of us whom, in the pride and intoxication of their theories, they have slighted, as not much better than tories. Hypocrisy, of course, delights in the most sublime speculations; for, never intending to go beyond speculation, it costs nothing to have it magnificent. But even in cases where rather levity than fraud was to be suspected in these ranting speculations, the issue has been much the same. These professors, finding their extreme principles not applicable to cases which call only for a qualified, or, as I may say, civil and legal resistance, in such cases employ no resistance at all. It is with them a war or a revolution, or it is nothing. Finding their schemes of politics not adapted to the state of the world in which they live, they often come to think lightly of all public principle; and are ready, on their part, to abandon for a very trivial interest what they find to be of very trivial value. Some indeed are of more steady and persevering natures; but these are eager politicians out of parliament, who have little to tempt them to abandon their favourite projects. They have some change in the church or state, or both, constantly in their view. When that is the case, they are always bad citizens, and perfectly unsure connexions. For, considering their speculative designs as of infinite value, and the actual arrangement of the state as of no estimation, they are at best indifferent about it. They see no merit in the good, and no fault in the vicious management of public affairs; they rather rejoice in the latter, as more propitious to revolution. They see no merit or demerit in any man, or any action, or any political principle, any further than as they may forward or retard their design of change: they therefore take up, one day, the most violent and stretched prerogative, and another time the wildest democratic ideas of freedom, and pass from the one to the other without any sort of regard to cause, to person, or to party.

In France you are now in the crisis of a revolution, and in the transit from one form of government to another—you cannot see that character of men exactly in the same situation in which we see it in this country. With us it is militant; with you it is triumphant; and you know how it can act when its power is commensurate to its will. I would not be supposed to confine those observations to any description of men, or to comprehend all men of any description within them—No! far from it. I am as incapable of that injustice, as I am of keeping terms with those who profess principles of extremes; and who under the name of religion teach little else than wild and dangerous politics. The worst of these politics of revolution is this; they temper and harden the breast, in order to prepare it for the desperate strokes which are sometimes used in extreme occasions. But as these occasions may never arrive, the mind receives a gratuitous taint; and the moral sentiments suffer not a little, when no political purpose is served by the depravation. This sort of people are so taken up with their theories about the rights of man, that they have totally forgot his nature. Without opening one new avenue to the understanding, they have succeeded in stopping up those that lead to the heart. They have perverted in themselves, and in those that attend to them, all the well-placed sympathies of the human breast.

This famous sermon of the Old Jewry breathes nothing but this spirit through all the political part. Plots, massacres, assassinations, seem to some people a trivial price for obtaining a revolution. A cheap, bloodless reformation, a guiltless liberty, appear flat and vapid to their taste. There must be a great change of scene; there must be a magnificent stage effect; there must be a grand spectacle to rouze the imagination, grown torpid with the lazy enjoyment of sixty years security, and the still unanimating repose of public prosperity. The Preacher found them all in the French revolution. This inspires a juvenile warmth through his whole frame. His enthusiasm kindles as he advances; and when he arrives at his peroration, it is in a full blaze. Then viewing, from the Pisgah of his pulpit,[1] the free, moral, happy, flourishing, and glorious state of France, as in a bird-eye landscape of a promised land, he breaks out into the following rapture:

"What an eventful period is this! I am *thankful* that I have lived to it; I could almost say, *Lord, now lettest thou thy servant depart in peace, for mine eyes have seen thy salvation.*—I have lived to see a *diffusion* of knowledge, which has undermined superstition and error.—I have lived to see *the rights of men* better understood than ever; and nations panting for liberty which seemed to have lost the idea of it.—I have lived to see *Thirty Millions of People,* indignant and resolute, spurning at slavery, and demanding

---

1 God's words to Moses in Deuteronomy 3:27: "Get thee up into the top of Pisgah, and lift up thy eyes westward, and northward, and southward, and eastward, and behold it with thy eyes: for thou shalt not go over this Jordan." From this summit, Moses was afforded a first glimpse of the Promised Land.

liberty with an irresistible voice. *Their King led in triumph, and an arbitrary monarch surrendering himself to his subjects.*"[1]

Before I proceed further, I have to remark, that Dr. Price seems rather to over-value the great acquisitions of light which he has obtained and diffused in this age. The last century appears to me to have been quite as much enlightened. It had, though in a different place, a triumph as memorable as that of Dr. Price; and some of the great preachers of that period partook of it as eagerly as he has done in the triumph of France. On the trial of the Rev. Hugh Peters for high treason, it was deposed, that when King Charles was brought to London for his trial, the Apostle of Liberty in that day conducted the *triumph*. "I saw," says the witness, "his majesty in the coach with six horses, and Peters riding before the king *triumphing*." Dr. Price, when he talks as if he had made a discovery, only follows a precedent; for, after the commencement of the king's trial, this precursor, the same Dr. Peters, concluding a long prayer at the royal chapel at Whitehall, (he had very triumphantly chosen his place) said, "I have prayed and preached these twenty years; and now I may say with old Simeon, *Lord, now lettest thou thy servant depart in peace, for mine eyes have seen thy salvation.*"[2] Peters had not the fruits of his prayer; for he neither departed so soon as he wished, nor in peace. He became (what I heartily hope none of his followers may be in this country) himself a sacrifice to the triumph which he led as Pontiff. They dealt at the Restoration, perhaps, too hardly with this poor good man.[3] But we owe it to his memory and his sufferings, that he had as much illumination, and as much zeal, and had as effectually undermined all *the superstition and error* which might impede the great business he was engaged in, as any who follow and repeat after him, in this age, which would assume to itself an exclusive title to the knowledge of the rights of men, and all the glorious consequences of that knowledge.

---

1 [Burke's note:] Another of these reverend gentlemen, who was witness to some of the spectacles which Paris has lately exhibited— expresses himself thus, *"A king dragged in submissive triumph by his conquering subjects* is one of those appearances of grandeur which seldom rise in the prospect of human affairs, and which, during the remainder of my life, I shall think of with wonder and gratification." These gentlemen agree marvellously in their feelings. [For Price's response to this passage, see Appendix G4.]

2 [Burke's note:] State Trials, vol. ii. p. 360, 363.

3 Peters was hanged, drawn, and quartered on 16 October 1660.

After this sally of the preacher of the Old Jewry, which differs only in place and time, but agrees perfectly with the spirit and letter of the rapture of 1648, the Revolution Society, the fabricators of governments, the heroic band of *cashierers* of *monarchs*, electors of sovereigns, and leaders of kings in triumph, strutting with a proud consciousness of the diffusion of knowledge, of which every member had obtained so large a share in the donative, were in haste to make a generous diffusion of the knowledge they had thus gratuitously received. To make this bountiful communication, they adjourned from the church in the Old Jewry, to the London Tavern; where the same Dr. Price, in whom the fumes of his oracular tripod were not entirely evaporated, moved and carried the resolution, or address of congratulation, transmitted by Lord Stanhope to the National Assembly of France.[1]

I find a preacher of the gospel prophaning the beautiful and prophetic ejaculation, commonly called *"nunc dimittis,"*[2] made on the first presentation of our Saviour in the Temple, and applying it, with an inhuman and unnatural rapture, to the most horrid, atrocious, and afflicting spectacle, that perhaps ever was exhibited to the pity and indignation of mankind. This *"leading in triumph,"* a thing in its best form unmanly and irreligious, which fills our Preacher with such unhallowed transports, must shock, I believe, the moral taste of every well-born mind. Several English were the stupified and indignant spectators of that triumph. It was (unless we have been strangely deceived) a spectacle more resembling a procession of American savages, entering into Onondaga, after some of their murders called victories, and leading into hovels hung round with scalps, their captives, overpowered with the scoffs and buffets of women as ferocious as themselves, much more than it resembled the triumphal pomp of a civilized martial nation;—if a civilized nation, or any men who had a sense of generosity, were capable of a personal triumph over the fallen and afflicted.

This, my dear Sir, was not the triumph of France. I must believe, that, as a nation, it overwhelmed you with shame and horror. I must believe that the National Assembly find

---

1 See Appendix A6.
2 Meaning "now let depart," and also known as the Song of Simeon, the "nunc dimittis" is the hymn of praise sung by the aged Simeon (Luke 2:29–32), who had been promised by the Holy Spirit that he would not die until he had seen the Messiah.

themselves in a state of the greatest humiliation, in not being able to punish the authors of this triumph, or the actors in it; and that they are in a situation in which any enquiry they may make upon the subject, must be destitute even of the appearance of liberty or impartiality. The apology of that Assembly is found in their situation; but when we approve what they *must* bear, it is in us the degenerate choice of a vitiated mind.

With a compelled appearance of deliberation, they vote under the dominion of a stern necessity. They sit in the heart, as it were, of a foreign republic: they have their residence in a city whose constitution has emanated neither from the charter of their king, nor from their legislative power. There they are surrounded by an army not raised either by the authority of their crown, or by their command; and which, if they should order to dissolve itself, would instantly dissolve them. There they sit, after a gang of assassins had driven away some hundreds of the members; whilst those who held the same moderate principles, with more patience or better hope, continued every day exposed to outrageous insults and murderous threats. There a majority, sometimes real, sometimes pretended, captive itself, compels a captive king to issue as royal edicts, at third hand, the polluted nonsense of their most licentious and giddy coffee-houses. It is notorious, that all their measures are decided before they are debated. It is beyond doubt, that under the terror of the bayonet, and the lamp-post, and the torch to their houses, they are obliged to adopt all the crude and desperate measures suggested by clubs composed of a monstrous medley of all conditions, tongues, and nations. Among these are found persons, in comparison of whom Catiline would be thought scrupulous, and Cethegus a man of sobriety and moderation.[1] Nor is it in these clubs alone that the publick measures are deformed into monsters. They undergo a previous distortion in academies, intended as so many seminaries for these clubs, which are set up in all the places of publick resort. In these meetings of all sorts, every counsel, in proportion as it is daring, and violent, and perfidious, is taken for the mark of superior genius. Humanity and compassion are ridiculed as the fruits of superstition and ignorance. Tenderness to individuals is considered as treason to the public. Liberty is always to be estimated perfect as property

---

1 Lucius Sergius Catilina (c. 108–62 BCE), Roman aristocrat and demagogue; Publius Cornelius Cethegus (d. 63 BCE), notoriously dissolute Roman patrician, and associate of Catilina.

is rendered insecure. Amidst assassination, massacre, and confiscation, perpetrated or meditated, they are forming plans for the good order of future society. Embracing in their arms the carcases of base criminals, and promoting their relations on the title of their offences, they drive hundreds of virtuous persons to the same end, by forcing them to subsist by beggary or by crime.

The Assembly, their organ, acts before them the farce of deliberation with as little decency as liberty. They act like the comedians of a fair before a riotous audience; they act amidst the tumultuous cries of a mixed mob of ferocious men, and of women lost to shame, who, according to their insolent fancies, direct, control, applaud, explode them; and sometimes mix and take their seats amongst them; domineering over them with a strange mixture of servile petulance and proud presumptuous authority. As they have inverted order in all things, the gallery is in the place of the house. This Assembly, which overthrows kings and kingdoms, has not even the physiognomy and aspect of a grave legislative body—*nec color imperii, nec frons erat ulla senatus.*[1] They have a power given to them, like that of the evil principle, to subvert and destroy; but none to construct, except such machines as may be fitted for further subversion and further destruction.

Who is it that admires, and from the heart is attached to national representative assemblies, but must turn with horror and disgust from such a profane burlesque, and abominable perversion of that sacred institute? Lovers of monarchy, lovers of republicks, must alike abhor it. The members of your Assembly must themselves groan under the tyranny of which they have all the shame, none of the direction, and little of the profit. I am sure many of the members who compose even the majority of that body, must feel as I do, notwithstanding the applauses of the Revolution Society.—Miserable king! miserable Assembly! How must that assembly be silently scandalized with those of their members, who could call a day which seemed to blot the sun out of Heaven, "un beau jour!"[2] How must they be inwardly indignant at hearing others, who thought fit to declare to them, "that the vessel of the state would fly forward in her course

---

1   "Nor will there be the external form of government nor any appearance of a legislative authority." Lucan (39–65 CE), *Pharsalia*, Book IX, 207.

2   [Burke's note:] 6th of October, 1789.

towards regeneration with more speed than ever,"[1] from the stiff gale of treason and murder, which preceded our Preacher's triumph! What must they have felt, whilst with outward patience and inward indignation they heard of the slaughter of innocent gentlemen in their houses, that "the blood spilled was not the most pure?"[2] What must they have felt, when they were besieged by complaints of disorders which shook their country to its foundations, at being compelled coolly to tell the complainants, that they were under the protection of the law, and that they would address the king (the captive king) to cause the laws to be enforced for their protection; when the enslaved ministers of that captive king had formally notified to them, that there were neither law, nor authority, nor power left to protect? What must they have felt at being obliged, as a felicitation on the present new year, to request their captive king to forget the stormy period of the last, on account of the great good which *he* was likely to produce to his people; to the complete attainment of which good they adjourned the practical demonstrations of their loyalty, assuring him of their obedience, when he should no longer possess any authority to command?

This address was made with much good-nature and affection, to be sure. But among the revolutions in France, must be reckoned a considerable revolution in their ideas of politeness. In England we are said to learn manners at second-hand from your side of the water, and that we dress our behaviour in the frippery of France. If so, we are still in the old cut; and have not so far conformed to the new Parisian mode of good-breeding, as to think it quite in the most refined strain of delicate compliment (whether in condolence or congratulation) to say, to the most humiliated creature that crawls upon the earth, that great public benefits are derived from the murder of his servants, the attempted assassination of himself and of his wife, and the mortification, disgrace, and degradation that he has personally suffered. It is a topic of consolation which our ordinary of Newgate[3] would be too humane to use to a criminal at the foot of the gallows. I should have thought that the hangman of Paris, now that he is liberalized by the vote of the National Assembly, and is

---

1 Words reportedly spoken by Honoré Gabriel Riqueti, Comte de Mirabeau (1749–91) in the National Assembly.

2 The words used by Antoine Barnave (1761–93) on hearing of the murder of Foullon and Berthier, two Parisian officials, in July 1789.

3 The prison chaplain at London's Newgate Prison.

allowed his rank and arms in the Herald's College of the rights of men, would be too generous, too gallant a man, too full of the sense of his new dignity, to employ that cutting consolation to any of the persons whom the *leze nation*[1] might bring under the administration of his *executive powers*.

A man is fallen indeed, when he is thus flattered. The anodyne draught of oblivion, thus drugged, is well calculated to preserve a galling wakefulness, and to feed the living ulcer of a corroding memory. Thus to administer the opiate potion of amnesty, powdered with all the ingredients of scorn and contempt, is to hold to his lips, instead of "the balm of hurt minds,"[2] the cup of human misery full to the brim, and to force him to drink it to the dregs.

Yielding to reasons, at least as forcible as those which were so delicately urged in the compliment on the new year, the king of France will probably endeavour to forget these events, and that compliment. But history, who keeps a durable record of all our acts, and exercises her awful censure over the proceedings of all sorts of sovereigns, will not forget, either those events, or the æra of this liberal refinement in the intercourse of mankind. History will record, that on the morning of the 6th of October 1789, the king and queen of France, after a day of confusion, alarm, dismay, and slaughter, lay down, under the pledged security of public faith, to indulge nature in a few hours of respite, and troubled melancholy repose. From this sleep the queen was first startled by the voice of the centinel at her door, who cried out to her, to save herself by flight—that this was the last proof of fidelity he could give—that they were upon him, and he was dead. Instantly he was cut down. A band of cruel ruffians and assassins, reeking with his blood, rushed into the chamber of the queen, and pierced with an hundred strokes of bayonets and poniards the bed, from whence this persecuted woman had but just time to fly almost naked, and through ways unknown to the murderers had escaped to seek refuge at the feet of a king and husband, not secure of his own life for a moment.

This king, to say no more of him, and this queen, and their infant children (who once would have been the pride and hope of a great and generous people) were then forced to abandon the

---

1 In English law, lese-majesty was treason against the monarch; Burke invents the term "leze nation" to suggest the idea of treason against the nation.
2 Shakespeare, *Macbeth* 2.2.51.

sanctuary of the most splendid palace in the world, which they left swimming in blood, polluted by massacre, and strewed with scattered limbs and mutilated carcases. Thence they were conducted into the capital of their kingdom. Two had been selected from the unprovoked, unresisted, promiscuous slaughter, which was made of the gentlemen of birth and family who composed the king's body guard. These two gentlemen, with all the parade of an execution of justice, were cruelly and publickly dragged to the block, and beheaded in the great court of the palace. Their heads were stuck upon spears, and led the procession; whilst the royal captives who followed in the train were slowly moved along, amidst the horrid yells, and shrilling screams, and frantic dances, and infamous contumelies, and all the unutterable abominations of the furies of hell, in the abused shape of the vilest of women. After they had been made to taste, drop by drop, more than the bitterness of death, in the slow torture of a journey of twelve miles, protracted to six hours, they were, under a guard, composed of those very soldiers who had thus conducted them through this famous triumph, lodged in one of the old palaces of Paris, now converted into a Bastile for kings.

Is this a triumph to be consecrated at altars? to be commemorated with grateful thanksgiving? to be offered to the divine humanity with fervent prayer and enthusiastick ejaculation?—These Theban and Thracian Orgies, acted in France, and applauded only in the Old Jewry, I assure you, kindle prophetic enthusiasm in the minds but of very few people in this kingdom; although a saint and apostle, who may have revelations of his own, and who has so completely vanquished all the mean superstitions of the heart, may incline to think it pious and decorous to compare it with the entrance into the world of the Prince of Peace, proclaimed in a holy temple by a venerable sage, and not long before not worse announced by the voice of angels to the quiet innocence of shepherds.[1]

At first I was at a loss to account for this fit of unguarded transport. I knew, indeed, that the sufferings of monarchs make a delicious repast to some sort of palates. There were reflexions which might serve to keep this appetite within some bounds of temperance. But when I took one circumstance into my consideration, I was obliged to confess, that much allowance ought to be made for the Society, and that the temptation was too

---

1 Price vigorously rejected Burke's claim that he had celebrated the events of 6 October (see Appendix G4).

strong for common discretion; I mean, the circumstance of the Io Pæan[1] of the triumph, the animating cry which called "for all the BISHOPS to be hanged on the lamp-posts,"[2] might well have brought forth a burst of enthusiasm on the foreseen consequences of this happy day. I allow to so much enthusiasm some little deviation from prudence. I allow this prophet to break forth into hymns of joy and thanksgiving on an event which appears like the precursor of the Millennium, and the projected fifth monarchy,[3] in the destruction of all church establishments. There was, however (as in all human affairs there is) in the midst of this joy something to exercise the patience of these worthy gentlemen, and to try the long-suffering of their faith. The actual murder of the king and queen, and their child, was wanting to the other auspicious circumstances of this *"beautiful day."* The actual murder of the bishops, though called for by so many holy ejaculations, was also wanting. A groupe of regicide and sacrilegious slaughter, was indeed boldly sketched, but it was only sketched. It unhappily was left unfinished, in this great history-piece of the massacre of innocents. What hardy pencil of a great master, from the school of the rights of men, will finish it, is to be seen hereafter. The age has not yet the compleat benefit of that diffusion of knowledge that has undermined superstition and error; and the king of France wants another object or two, to consign to oblivion, in consideration of all the good which is to arise from his own sufferings, and the patriotic crimes of an enlightened age.[4]

Although this work of our new light and knowledge, did not

---

1 Greek hymn of praise to Apollo, signifying in English a song of triumph.

2 [Burke's note:] Tous les Eveques à la lanterne.

3 The Fifth Monarchy Men were an extreme Puritan sect in the seventeenth century, who believed that a fifth monarchy (that of Christ) would imminently succeed the Assyrian, Persian, Greek, and Roman monarchies.

4 Burke inserted here a lengthy footnote, written in French, by an eyewitness to the events of 6 October, M. de Lally Tollendal (1751–1830), who documents the bloody horrors he saw and the mocking, mirthful responses of Bailley, Mirabeau, and Barnave. It was these sights, Lally Tollendal says, that made him swear never again to set foot *"dans cette caverne d'Antropophages"* (in this "cave of cannibals," namely the National Assembly), and to go instead into voluntary exile.

go to the length, that in all probability it was intended it should be carried; yet I must think, that such treatment of any human creatures must be shocking to any but those who are made for accomplishing Revolutions. But I cannot stop here. Influenced by the inborn feelings of my nature, and not being illuminated by a single ray of this new-sprung modern light, I confess to you, Sir, that the exalted rank of the persons suffering, and particularly the sex, the beauty, and the amiable qualities of the descendant of so many kings and emperors, with the tender age of royal infants, insensible only through infancy and innocence of the cruel outrages to which their parents were exposed, instead of being a subject of exultation, adds not a little to my sensibility on that most melancholy occasion.

I hear that the august person, who was the principal object of our preacher's triumph, though he supported himself, felt much on that shameful occasion. As a man, it became him to feel for his wife and his children, and the faithful guards of his person, that were massacred in cold blood about him; as a prince, it became him to feel for the strange and frightful transformation of his civilized subjects, and to be more grieved for them, than solicitous for himself. It derogates little from his fortitude, while it adds infinitely to the honour of his humanity. I am very sorry to say it, very sorry indeed, that such personages are in a situation in which it is not unbecoming in us to praise the virtues of the great.

I hear, and I rejoice to hear, that the great lady, the other object of the triumph, has borne that day (one is interested that beings made for suffering should suffer well) and that she bears all the succeeding days, that she bears the imprisonment of her husband, and her own captivity, and the exile of her friends, and the insulting adulation of addresses, and the whole weight of her accumulated wrongs, with a serene patience, in a manner suited to her rank and race, and becoming the offspring of a sovereign distinguished for her piety and her courage; that like her she has lofty sentiments; that she feels with the dignity of a Roman matron; that in the last extremity she will save herself from the last disgrace, and that if she must fall, she will fall by no ignoble hand.

It is now sixteen or seventeen years since I saw the queen of France, then the dauphiness, at Versailles; and surely never lighted on this orb, which she hardly seemed to touch, a more delightful vision. I saw her just above the horizon, decorating and cheering the elevated sphere she just began to move in,— glittering like the morning-star, full of life, and splendor, and

The revolution is going insane

;.(Oh! what a revolution!) and what an heart must I have, to contemplate without emotion that elevation and that fall! Little did I dream when she added titles of veneration to those of enthusiastic, distant, respectful love, that she should ever be obliged to carry the sharp antidote against disgrace concealed in that bosom; little did I dream that I should have lived to see such disasters fallen upon her in a nation of gallant men, in a nation of men of honour and of cavaliers. I thought ten thousand swords must have leaped from their scabbards to avenge even a look that threatened her with insult.—But the age of chivalry is gone.—That of sophisters, œconomists, and calculators, has succeeded; and the glory of Europe is extinguished for ever. Never, never more, shall we behold that generous loyalty to rank and sex, that proud submission, that dignified obedience, that subordination of the heart, which kept alive, even in servitude itself, the spirit of an exalted freedom. The unbought grace of life, the cheap defence of nations, the nurse of manly sentiment and heroic enterprize is gone! It is gone, that sensibility of principle, that chastity of honour, which felt a stain like a wound, which inspired courage whilst it mitigated ferocity, which ennobled whatever it touched, and under which vice itself lost half its evil, by losing all its grossness.

(This mixed system of opinion and sentiment had its origin in the antient chivalry;) and the principle, though varied in its appearance by the varying state of human affairs, subsisted and influenced through a long succession of generations, even to the time we live in. If it should ever be totally extinguished, the loss I fear will be great. It is this which has given its character to modern Europe. It is this which has distinguished it under all its forms of government, and distinguished it to its advantage, from the states of Asia, and possibly from those states which flourished in the most brilliant periods of the antique world. It was this, which, without confounding ranks, had produced a noble equality, and handed it down through all the gradations of social life. It was this opinion which mitigated kings into companions, and raised private men to be fellows with kings. Without force, or opposition, it subdued the fierceness of pride and power; it obliged sovereigns to submit to the soft collar of social esteem, compelled stern authority to submit to elegance, and gave a domination vanquisher of laws, to be subdued by manners.

But now all is to be changed. All the pleasing illusions, which made power gentle, and obedience liberal, which harmonized the different shades of life, and which, by a bland assimilation,

Whole system of rights feels it must be completly changed

incorporated into politics the sentiments which beautify and soften private society, are to be dissolved by this new conquering empire of light and reason. All the decent drapery of life is to be rudely torn off. All the superadded ideas, furnished from the wardrobe of a moral imagination, which the heart owns, and the understanding ratifies, as necessary to cover the defects of our naked shivering nature, and to raise it to dignity in our own estimation, are to be exploded as a ridiculous, absurd, and antiquated fashion.

On this scheme of things, a king is but a man; a queen is but a woman; a woman is but an animal; and an animal not of the highest order. All homage paid to the sex in general as such, and without distinct views, is to be regarded as romance and folly. Regicide, and parricide, and sacrilege, are but fictions of superstition, corrupting jurisprudence by destroying its simplicity. The murder of a king, or a queen, or a bishop, or a father, are only common homicide; and if the people are by any chance, or in any way gainers by it, a sort of homicide much the most pardonable, and into which we ought not to make too severe a scrutiny.

On the scheme of this barbarous philosophy, which is the offspring of cold hearts and muddy understandings, and which is as void of solid wisdom, as it is destitute of all taste and elegance, laws are to be supported only by their own terrors, and by the concern, which each individual may find in them, from his own private speculations, or can spare to them from his own private interests. In the groves of *their* academy, at the end of every visto, you see nothing but the gallows. Nothing is left which engages the affections on the part of the commonwealth. On the principles of this mechanic philosophy, our institutions can never be embodied, if I may use the expression, in persons; so as to create in us love, veneration, admiration, or attachment. But that sort of reason which banishes the affections is incapable of filling their place. These public affections, combined with manners, are required sometimes as supplements, sometimes as correctives, always as aids to law. The precept given by a wise man, as well as a great critic, for the construction of poems, is equally true as to states. *Non satis est pulchra esse poemata, dulcia sunto.* There ought to be a system of manners in every nation which a well-formed mind would be disposed to relish. To make us love our country, our country ought to be lovely.

_____

1 "It is not enough for poems to be beautiful; they must also be sweet." Horace, *De Arte Poetica*, 99–100.

But power, of some kind or other, will survive the shock in which manners and opinions perish; and it will find other and worse means for its support. The usurpation which, in order to subvert antient institutions, has destroyed antient principles, will hold power by arts similar to those by which it has acquired it. When the old feudal and chivalrous spirit of *Fealty*, which, by freeing kings from fear, freed both kings and subjects from the precautions of tyranny, shall be extinct in the minds of men, plots and assassinations will be anticipated by preventive murder and preventive confiscation, and that long roll of grim and bloody maxims, which form the political code of all power not standing on its own honour, and the honour of those who are to obey it. Kings will be tyrants from policy when subjects are rebels from principle.

When antient opinions and rules of life are taken away, the loss cannot possibly be estimated. From that moment we have no compass to govern us; nor can we know distinctly to what port we steer. Europe undoubtedly, taken in a mass, was in a flourishing condition the day on which your Revolution was compleated. How much of that prosperous state was owing to the spirit of our old manners and opinions is not easy to say; but as such causes cannot be indifferent in their operation, we must presume, that, on the whole, their operation was beneficial.

We are but too apt to consider things in the state in which we find them, without sufficiently adverting to the causes by which they have been produced, and possibly may be upheld. Nothing is more certain, than that our manners, our civilization, and all the good things which are connected with manners, and with civilization, have, in this European world of ours, depended for ages upon two principles; and were indeed the result of both combined; I mean the spirit of a gentleman, and the spirit of religion. The nobility and the clergy, the one by profession, the other by patronage, kept learning in existence, even in the midst of arms and confusions, and whilst governments were rather in their causes than formed. Learning paid back what it received to nobility and to priesthood; and paid it with usury, by enlarging their ideas, and by furnishing their minds. Happy if they had all continued to know their indissoluble union, and their proper place! Happy if learning, not debauched by ambition, had been satisfied to continue the instructor, and not aspired to be the master! Along with its natural protectors and guardians, learning will be cast into the mire, and trodden down under the hoofs of a swinish multitude.

If, as I suspect, modern letters owe more than they are always willing to own to antient manners, so do other interests which we value full as much as they are worth. Even commerce, and trade, and manufacture, the gods of our œconomical politicians, are themselves perhaps but creatures; are themselves but effects, which, as first causes, we choose to worship. They certainly grew under the same shade in which learning flourished. They too may decay with their natural protecting principles. With you, for the present at least, they all threaten to disappear together. Where trade and manufactures are wanting to a people, and the spirit of nobility and religion remains, sentiment supplies, and not always ill supplies their place; but if commerce and the arts should be lost in an experiment to try how well a state may stand without these old fundamental principles, what sort of thing must be a nation of gross, stupid, ferocious, and at the same time, poor and sordid barbarians, destitute of religion, honour, or manly pride, possessing nothing at present, and hoping for nothing hereafter?

I wish you may not be going fast, and by the shortest cut, to that horrible and disgustful situation. Already there appears a poverty of conception, a coarseness and vulgarity in all the proceedings of the assembly and of all their instructors. Their liberty is not liberal. Their science is presumptuous ignorance. Their humanity is savage and brutal.

It is not clear, whether in England we learned those grand and decorous principles, and manners, of which considerable traces yet remain, from you, or whether you took them from us. But to you, I think, we trace them best. You seem to me to be—*gentis incunabula nostræ*.[1] France has always more or less influenced manners in England; and when your fountain is choaked up and polluted, the stream will not run long, or not run clear with us, or perhaps with any nation. This gives all Europe, in my opinion, but too close and connected a concern in what is done in France. Excuse me, therefore, if I have dwelt too long on the atrocious spectacle of the sixth of October 1789, or have given too much scope to the reflections which have arisen in my mind on occasion of the most important of all revolutions, which may be dated from that day, I mean a revolution in sentiments, manners, and moral opinions. As things now stand, with every thing respectable destroyed without us, and an attempt to destroy within us every principle of

---

1 "The cradle of our people." Virgil, *Aeneid*, Book III, 105.

respect, one is almost forced to apologize for harbouring the common feelings of men.

Why do I feel so differently from the Reverend Dr. Price, and those of his lay flock, who will choose to adopt the sentiments of his discourse?—For this plain reason—because it is *natural* I should; because we are so made as to be affected at such spectacles with melancholy sentiments upon the unstable condition of mortal prosperity, and the tremendous uncertainty of human greatness; because in those natural feelings we learn great lessons; because in events like these our passions instruct our reason; because when kings are hurl'd from their thrones by the Supreme Director of this great drama, and become the objects of insult to the base, and of pity to the good, we behold such disasters in the moral, as we should behold a miracle in the physical order of things. We are alarmed into reflexion; our minds (as it has long since been observed) are purified by terror and pity; our weak unthinking pride is humbled, under the dispensations of a mysterious wisdom.—Some tears might be drawn from me, if such a spectacle were exhibited on the stage. I should be truly ashamed of finding in myself that superficial, theatric sense of painted distress, whilst I could exult over it in real life. With such a perverted mind, I could never venture to shew my face at a tragedy. People would think the tears that Garrick formerly, or that Siddons not long since, have extorted from me, were the tears of hypocrisy; I should know them to be the tears of folly.[1]

Indeed the theatre is a better school of moral sentiments than churches, where the feelings of humanity are thus outraged. Poets, who have to deal with an audience not yet graduated in the school of the rights of men, and who must apply themselves to the moral constitution of the heart, would not dare to produce such a triumph as a matter of exultation. There, where men follow their natural impulses, they would not bear the odious maxims of a Machiavelian policy, whether applied to the attainment of monarchical or democratic tyranny. They would reject them on the modern, as they once did on the antient stage, where they could not bear even the hypothetical proposition of such wickedness in the mouth of a personated tyrant, though suitable to the character he sustained. No theatric audience in Athens would bear what has been borne, in the midst of the real tragedy of this triumphal day; a principal actor weighing, as it were in

---

1 David Garrick (1717–79) and Sarah Siddons (1755–1831) were the principal stage actors of Burke's time.

scales hung in a shop of horrors,—so much actual crime against so much contingent advantage,—and after putting in and out weights, declaring that the balance was on the side of the advantages. They would not bear to see the crimes of new democracy posted as in a ledger against the crimes of old despotism, and the book-keepers of politics finding democracy still in debt, but by no means unable or unwilling to pay the balance. In the theatre, the first intuitive glance, without any elaborate process of reasoning, would shew, that this method of political computation, would justify every extent of crime. They would see, that on these principles, even where the very worst acts were not perpetrated, it was owing rather to the fortune of the conspirators than to their parsimony in the expenditure of treachery and blood. They would soon see, that criminal means once tolerated are soon preferred. They present a shorter cut to the object than through the highway of the moral virtues. Justifying perfidy and murder for public benefit, public benefit would soon become the pretext, and perfidy and murder the end; until rapacity, malice, revenge, and fear more dreadful than revenge, could satiate their insatiable appetites. Such must be the consequences of losing in the splendour of these triumphs of the rights of men, all natural sense of wrong and right.

But the Reverend Pastor exults in this "leading in triumph," because truly Louis XVIth was "an arbitrary monarch;" that is, in other words, neither more nor less, than because he was Louis the XVIth, and because he had the misfortune to be born king of France, with the prerogatives of which, a long line of ancestors, and a long acquiescence of the people, without any act of his, had put him in possession. A misfortune it has indeed turned out to him, that he was born king of France. But misfortune is not crime, nor is indiscretion always the greatest guilt. I shall never think that a prince, the acts of whose whole reign were a series of concessions to his subjects, who was willing to relax his authority, to remit his prerogatives, to call his people to a share of freedom, not known, perhaps not desired by their ancestors; such a prince, though he should be subject to the common frailties attached to men and to princes, though he should have once thought it necessary to provide force against the desperate designs manifestly carrying on against his person, and the remnants of his authority; though all this should be taken into consideration, I shall be led with great difficulty to think he deserves the cruel and insulting triumph of Paris, and of Dr. Price. I tremble for the cause of liberty, from such an example to kings. I tremble for the cause of humanity, in the unpunished outrages of the most wicked of mankind. But there are some people of that low and degenerate fashion of mind, that they look up with a sort of complacent awe and admiration to kings, who know to keep firm in their seat, to hold a strict hand over their subjects, to assert their prerogative, and by the awakened vigilance of a severe despotism, to guard against the very first approaches of freedom. Against such as these they never elevate their voice. Deserters from principle, listed with fortune, they never see any good in suffering virtue, nor any crime in prosperous usurpation.

If it could have been made clear to me, that the king and queen of France (those I mean who were such before the triumph) were inexorable and cruel tyrants, that they had formed a deliberate scheme for massacring the National Assembly (I think I have seen something like the latter insinuated in certain publications) I should think their captivity just. If this be true, much more ought to have been done, but done, in my opinion, in another manner. The punishment of real tyrants is a noble and awful act of justice; and it has with truth been said to be consolatory to the human mind. But if I were to punish a wicked king, I should regard the dignity in avenging the crime. Justice is grave and decorous, and in its punishments rather seems to submit to a necessity, than to make a choice. Had Nero, or Agrippina, or Louis the Eleventh, or Charles the Ninth, been the subject; if Charles the Twelfth of Sweden, after the murder of Patkul, or his predecessor Christina, after the murder of Monaldeschi, had fallen into your hands, Sir, or into mine, I am sure our conduct would have been different.[1]

If the French King, or the King of the French, (or by whatever name he is known in the new vocabulary of your constitution) has in his own person, and that of his Queen, really deserved these unavowed but unavenged murderous attempts, and those frequent indignities more cruel than murder, such a person would ill deserve even that subordinate executory trust, which I understand is to be placed in him; nor is he fit to be called chief in a nation which he has outraged and oppressed. A worse choice for such an office in a new commonwealth, than that of a deposed tyrant, could not possibly be made. But to degrade and insult a man as the worst of criminals, and afterwards to trust

---

1 The names listed in this sentence are examples of rulers guilty of murder or unlawful execution.

him in your highest concerns, as a faithful, honest, and zealous servant, is not consistent in reasoning, nor prudent in policy, nor safe in practice. Those who could make such an appointment must be guilty of a more flagrant breach of trust than any they have yet committed against the people. As this is the only crime in which your leading politicians could have acted inconsistently, I conclude that there is no sort of ground for these horrid insinuations. I think no better of all the other calumnies....

To tell you the truth, my dear Sir, I think the honour of our nation to be somewhat concerned in the disclaimer of the proceedings of the society of the Old Jewry and the London Tavern. I have no man's proxy. I speak only from myself; when I disclaim, as I do with all possible earnestness, all communion with the actors in that triumph, or with the admirers of it. When I assert any thing else, as concerning the people of England, I speak from observation not from authority; but I speak from the experience I have had in a pretty extensive and mixed communication with the inhabitants of this kingdom, of all descriptions and ranks, and after a course of attentive observation, began early in life, and continued for near forty years. I have often been astonished, considering that we are divided from you but by a slender dyke of about twenty-four miles, and that the mutual intercourse between the two countries has lately been very great, to find how little you seem to know of us. I suspect that this is owing to your forming a judgment of this nation from certain publications, which do, very erroneously, if they do at all, represent the opinions and dispositions generally prevalent in England. The vanity, restlessness, petulance, and spirit of intrigue of several petty cabals, who attempt to hide their total want of consequence in bustle and noise, and puffing, and mutual quotation of each other, makes you imagine that our contemptuous neglect of their abilities is a mark of general acquiescence in their opinions. No such thing, I assure you. Because half a dozen grasshoppers[1] under a fern make the field ring with their importunate chink, whilst thousands of great cattle, reposed beneath the shadow of the British oak, chew the cud and are silent, pray do not imagine, that those who make the noise are the only inhabitants of the field; that of course, they are many in number; or that, after all, they are other than the little shrivelled, meagre, hopping, though loud and troublesome insects of the hour.

---

1 This is the only place in this abridgement in which Burke's spelling has been altered (from *grashoppers* in the original).

I almost venture to affirm, that not one in a hundred amongst us participates in the "triumph" of the Revolution Society. If the king and queen of France, and their children, were to fall into our hands by the chance of war, in the most acrimonious of hostilities (I deprecate such an event, I deprecate such hostility) they would be treated with another sort of triumphal entry into London. We formerly have had a king of France in that situation; you have read how he was treated by the victor in the field; and in what manner he was afterwards received in England.[1] Four hundred years have gone over us; but I believe we are not materially changed since that period. Thanks to our sullen resistance to innovation, thanks to the cold sluggishness of our national character, we still bear the stamp of our forefathers. We have not (as I conceive) lost the generosity and dignity of thinking of the fourteenth century; nor as yet have we subtilized ourselves into savages. We are not the converts of Rousseau; we are not the disciples of Voltaire; Helvetius has made no progress amongst us.[2] Atheists are not our preachers; madmen are not our lawgivers. We know that *we* have made no discoveries; and we think that no discoveries are to be made, in morality; nor many in the great principles of government, nor in the ideas of liberty, which were understood long before we were born, altogether as well as they will be after the grave has heaped its mould upon our presumption, and the silent tomb shall have imposed its law on our pert loquacity. In England we have not yet been completely embowelled of our natural entrails; we still feel within us, and we cherish and cultivate, those inbred sentiments which are the faithful guardians, the active monitors of our duty, the true supporters of all liberal and manly morals. We have not been drawn and trussed, in order that we may be filled, like stuffed birds in a museum, with chaff and rags, and paltry, blurred shreds of paper about the rights of man. We preserve the whole of our

---

1 John II (r. 1350–64), captured by the Black Prince at the battle of Poitiers and held captive in London from 1356–60.

2 Jean-Jacques Rousseau (1712–78); Voltaire (1694–1778); Claude Adrien Helvetius (1715–71): French philosophers beloved by the revolutionaries. Burke was horrified that these were the leading intellectual inspirations of revolutionary France: "Such masters, such scholars. Who ever dreamt of Voltaire and Rousseau as legislators?" (*Corr.* VI, 81); a lengthy attack on Rousseau and his influence is contained in Burke's *Letter to a Member of the National Assembly* (see Appendix F).

feelings still native and entire, unsophisticated by pedantry and infidelity. We have real hearts of flesh and blood beating in our bosoms. We fear God; we look up with awe to kings; with affection to parliaments; with duty to magistrates; with reverence to priests; and with respect to nobility. Why? Because when such ideas are brought before our minds, it is *natural* to be so affected; because all other feelings are false and spurious, and tend to corrupt our minds, to vitiate our primary morals, to render us unfit for rational liberty; and by teaching us a servile, licentious, and abandoned insolence, to be our low sport for a few holidays, to make us perfectly fit for, and justly deserving of slavery, through the whole course of our lives.

You see, Sir, that in this enlightened age I am bold enough to confess, that we are generally men of untaught feelings; that instead of casting away all our old prejudices, we cherish them to a very considerable degree, and, to take more shame to ourselves, we cherish them because they are prejudices; and the longer they have lasted, and the more generally they have prevailed, the more we cherish them. We are afraid to put men to live and trade each on his own private stock of reason; because we suspect that this stock in each man is small, and that the individuals would do better to avail themselves of the general bank and capital of nations, and of ages. Many of our men of speculation, instead of exploding general prejudices, employ their sagacity to discover the latent wisdom which prevails in them. If they find what they seek, and they seldom fail, they think it more wise to continue the prejudice, with the reason involved, than to cast away the coat of prejudice, and to leave nothing but the naked reason; because prejudice, with its reason, has a motive to give action to that reason, and an affection which will give it permanence. Prejudice is of ready application in the emergency; it previously engages the mind in a steady course of wisdom and virtue, and does not leave the man hesitating in the moment of decision, sceptical, puzzled, and unresolved. Prejudice renders a man's virtue his habit; and not a series of unconnected acts. Through just prejudice, his duty becomes part of his nature.

Your literary men, and your politicians, and so do the whole clan of the enlightened among us, essentially differ in these points. They have no respect for the wisdom of others; but they pay it off by a very full measure of confidence in their own. With them it is a sufficient motive to destroy an old scheme of things, because it is an old one. As to the new, they are in no sort of fear with regard to the duration of a building run up in haste;

because duration is no object to those who think little or nothing has been done before their time, and who place all their hopes in discovery. They conceive, very systematically, that all things which give perpetuity are mischievous, and therefore they are at inexpiable war with all establishments. They think that government may vary like modes of dress, and with as little ill effect. That there needs no principle of attachment, except a sense of present conveniency, to any constitution of the state. They always speak as if they were of opinion that there is a singular species of compact between them and their magistrates, which binds the magistrate, but which has nothing reciprocal in it, but that the majesty of the people has a right to dissolve it without any reason, but its will. Their attachment to their country itself, is only so far as it agrees with some of their fleeting projects; it begins and ends with that scheme of polity which falls in with their momentary opinion.

These doctrines, or rather sentiments, seem prevalent with your new statesmen. But they are wholly different from those on which we have always acted in this country.

I hear it is sometimes given out in France, that what is doing among you is after the example of England. I beg leave to affirm, that scarcely any thing done with you has originated from the practice or the prevalent opinions of this people, either in the act or in the spirit of the proceeding. Let me add, that we are as unwilling to learn these lessons from France, as we are sure that we never taught them to that nation. The cabals here who take a sort of share in your transactions as yet consist but of an handful of people. If unfortunately by their intrigues, their sermons, their publications, and by a confidence derived from an expected union with the counsels and forces of the French nation, they should draw considerable numbers into their faction, and in consequence should seriously attempt any thing here in imitation of what has been done with you, the event, I dare venture to prophesy, will be, that, with some trouble to their country, they will soon accomplish their own destruction. This people refused to change their law in remote ages, from respect to the infallibility of popes; and they will not now alter it from a pious implicit faith in the dogmatism of philosophers; though the former was armed with the anathema and crusade, and though the latter should act with the libel and the lamp-iron.

Formerly your affairs were your own concern only. We felt for them as men; but we kept aloof from them, because we were not citizens of France. But when we see the model held up to ourselves, we must feel as Englishmen, and feeling, we must provide as Englishmen. Your affairs, in spite of us, are made a part of our interest; so far at least as to keep at a distance your panacea, or your plague. If it be a panacea, we do not want it. We know the consequences of unnecessary physic. If it be a plague; it is such a plague, that the precautions of the most severe quarantine ought to be established against it.

I hear on all hands that a cabal, calling itself philosophic, receives the glory of many of the late proceedings; and that their opinions and systems are the true actuating spirit of the whole of them. I have heard of no party in England, literary or political, at any time, known by such a description. It is not with you composed of those men, is it? whom the vulgar, in their blunt, homely style, commonly call Atheists and Infidels? If it be, I admit that we too have had writers of that description, who made some noise in their day. At present they repose in lasting oblivion. Who, born within the last forty years, has read one word of Collins, and Toland, and Tindal, and Chubb, and Morgan, and that whole race who called themselves Freethinkers?[1] Who now reads Bolingbroke?[2] Who ever read him through? Ask the booksellers of London what is become of all these lights of the world. In as few years their few successors will go to the family vault of "all the Capulets."[3] But whatever they were, or are, with us, they were and are wholly unconnected individuals. With us they kept the common nature of their kind, and were not gregarious. They never acted in corps, not were known as a faction in the state, nor presumed to influence, in that name or character, or for the purposes of such a faction, on any of our public concerns. Whether they ought so to exist, and so be permitted to act, is another question. As such cabals have not existed in England, so neither has the spirit of them had any influence in establishing the original frame of our constitution, or in any one of the several reparations and improvements it has undergone. The whole

---

1 Anthony Collins (1676–1729), John Toland (1670–1722), Matthew Tindal (1657–1733), Thomas Chubb (1679–1747), and Thomas Morgan (1671/2–1743): prominent English deists.
2 The Tory statesman and freethinker Henry St. John, Viscount Bolingbroke (1678–1751), was especially disliked by Burke, and this is the first of two critical mentions he receives in the *Reflections*; Burke's first book, *A Vindication of Natural Society*, was a parody of Bolingbroke's philosophy.
3 Shakespeare, *Romeo and Juliet* 4.1.114.

has been done under the auspices, and is confirmed by the sanctions of religion and piety. The whole has emanated from the simplicity of our national character, and from a sort of native plainness and directness of understanding, which for a long time characterized those men who have successively obtained authority amongst us. This disposition still remains, at least in the great body of the people.

We know, and what is better we feel inwardly, that religion is the basis of civil society, and the source of all good and of all comfort. In England we are so convinced of this, that there is no rust of superstition, with which the accumulated absurdity of the human mind might have crusted it over in the course of ages, that ninety-nine in an hundred of the people of England would not prefer to impiety. We shall never be such fools as to call in an enemy to the substance of any system to remove its corruptions, to supply its defects, or to perfect its construction. If our religious tenets should ever want a further elucidation, we shall not call on atheism to explain them. We shall not light up our temple from that unhallowed fire. It will be illuminated with other lights. It will be perfumed with other incense, than the infectious stuff which is imported by the smugglers of adulterated metaphysics. If our ecclesiastical establishment should want a revision, it is not avarice or rapacity, public or private, that we shall employ for the audit, or receipt, or application of its consecrated revenue.—Violently condemning neither the Greek nor the Armenian, nor, since heats are subsided, the Roman system of religion, we prefer the Protestant; not because we think it has less of the Christian religion in it, but because, in our judgment, it has more. We are protestants, not from indifference, but from zeal.

We know, and it is our pride to know, that man is by his constitution a religious animal; that atheism is against, not only our reason but our instincts; and that it cannot prevail long. But if, in the moment of riot, and in a drunken delirium from the hot spirit drawn out of the alembick of hell, which in France is now so furiously boiling, we should uncover our nakedness by throwing off that Christian religion which has hitherto been our boast and comfort, and one great source of civilization amongst us, and among many other nations, we are apprehensive (being well aware that the mind will not endure a void) that some uncouth, pernicious, and degrading superstition, might take place of it.

For that reason, before we take from our establishment the natural human means of estimation, and give it up to contempt, as you have done, and in doing it have incurred the penalties you well deserve to suffer, we desire that some other may be presented to us in the place of it. We shall then form our judgment.

On these ideas, instead of quarrelling with establishments, as some do, who have made a philosophy and a religion of their hostility to such institutions, we cleave closely to them. We are resolved to keep an established church, an established monarchy, an established aristocracy, and an established democracy, each in the degree it exists, and in no greater. I shall shew you presently how much of each of these we possess.

It has been the misfortune (not as these gentlemen think it, the glory) of this age, that every thing is to be discussed, as if the constitution of our country were to be always a subject rather of altercation than enjoyment. For this reason, as well as for the satisfaction of those among you (if any such you have among you) who may wish to profit of examples, I venture to trouble you with a few thoughts upon each of these establishments. I do not think they were unwise in antient Rome, who, when they wished to new-model their laws, sent commissioners to examine the best constituted republics within their reach.

First, I beg leave to speak of our church establishment, which is the first of our prejudices, not a prejudice destitute of reason, but involving in it profound and extensive wisdom. I speak of it first. It is first, and last, and midst in our minds. For, taking ground on that religious system, of which we are now in possession, we continue to act on the early received, and uniformly continued sense of mankind. That sense not only, like a wise architect, hath built up the august fabric of states, but like a provident proprietor, to preserve the structure from prophanation and ruin, as a sacred temple, purged from all the impurities of fraud, and violence, and injustice, and tyranny, hath solemnly and for ever consecrated the commonwealth, and all that officiate in it. This consecration is made, that all who administer in the government of men, in which they stand in the person of God himself, should have high and worthy notions of their function and destination; that their hope should be full of immortality; that they should not look to the paltry pelf of the moment, nor to the temporary and transient praise of the vulgar, but to a solid, permanent existence, in the permanent part of their nature, and to a permanent fame and glory, in the example they leave as a rich inheritance to the world.

Such sublime principles ought to be infused into persons of exalted situations; and religious establishments provided, that may continually revive and enforce them. Every sort of moral, every sort of civil, every sort of politic institution, aiding the rational and natural ties that connect the human understanding and affections to the divine, are not more than necessary, in order to build up that wonderful structure, Man; whose prerogative it is, to be in a great degree a creature of his own making; and who when made as he ought to be made, is destined to hold no trivial place in the creation. But whenever man is put over men, as the better nature ought ever to preside, in that case more particularly, he should as nearly as possible be approximated to his perfection.

The consecration of the state, by a state religious establishment, is necessary also to operate with an wholesome awe upon free citizens; because, in order to secure their freedom, they must enjoy some determinate portion of power. To them therefore a religion connected with the state, and with their duty towards it, becomes even more necessary than in such societies, where the people by the terms of their subjection are confined to private sentiments, and the management of their own family concerns. All persons possessing any portion of power ought to be strongly and awefully impressed with an idea that they act in trust; and that they are to account for their conduct in that trust to the one great master, author and founder of society.

This principle ought even to be more strongly impressed upon the minds of those who compose the collective sovereignty than upon those of single princes. Without instruments, these princes can do nothing. Whoever uses instruments, in finding helps, finds also impediments. Their power is therefore by no means compleat; nor are they safe in extreme abuse. Such persons, however elevated by flattery, arrogance, and self-opinion, must be sensible that, whether covered or not by positive law, in some way or other they are accountable even here for the abuse of their trust. If they are not cut off by a rebellion of their people, they may be strangled by the very Janissaries[1] kept for their security against all other rebellion. Thus we have seen the king of France sold by his soldiers for an encrease of pay. But where popular authority is absolute and unrestrained, the people have an infinitely greater, because a far better founded confidence in their own power. They are themselves, in a great measure, their own instruments. They are nearer to their objects. Besides, they are less under responsibility to one of the greatest controlling

---

1 The Ottoman Sultan's elite military guard.

powers on earth, the sense of fame and estimation. The share of infamy that is likely to fall to the lot of each individual in public acts, is small indeed; the operation of opinion being in the inverse ratio to the number of those who abuse power. Their own approbation of their own acts has to them the appearance of a public judgment in their favour. A perfect democracy is therefore the most shameless thing in the world. As it is the most shameless, it is also the most fearless. No man apprehends in his person he can be made subject to punishment. Certainly the people at large never ought: for as all punishments are for example towards the conservation of the people at large, the people at large can never become the subject of punishment by any human hand.[1] It is therefore of infinite importance that they should not be suffered to imagine that their will, any more than that of kings, is the standard of right and wrong. They ought to be persuaded that they are full as little entitled, and far less qualified, with safety to themselves, to use any arbitrary power whatsoever; that therefore they are not, under a false shew of liberty, but, in truth, to exercise an unnatural inverted domination, tyrannically to exact, from those who officiate in the state, not an entire devotion to their interest, which is their right, but an abject submission to their occasional will; extinguishing thereby, in all those who serve them, all moral principle, all sense of dignity, all use of judgment, and all consistency of character, whilst by the very same process they give themselves up a proper, a suitable, but a most contemptible prey to the servile ambition of popular sycophants or courtly flatterers.

When the people have emptied themselves of all the lust of selfish will, which without religion it is utterly impossible they ever should, when they are conscious that they exercise, and exercise perhaps in an higher link of the order of delegation, the power, which to be legitimate must be according to that eternal immutable law, in which will and reason are the same, they will be more careful how they place power in base and incapable hands. In their nomination to office, they will not appoint to the exercise of authority, as to a pitiful job, but as to an holy function; not according to their sordid selfish interest, nor to their wanton caprice, nor to their arbitrary will; but they will confer that power (which any man may well tremble to give or to

---

1 [Burke's note:] Quicquid multis peccatur inultum. ["The sin of thousands always goes unpunished." Lucan, *Pharsalia*, Book V, 260.]

receive) on those only, in whom they may discern that predominant proportion of active virtue and wisdom, taken together and fitted to the charge, such, as in the great and inevitable mixed mass of human imperfections and infirmities, is to be found.

When they are habitually convinced that no evil can be acceptable, either in the act or the permission, to him whose essence is good, they will be better able to extirpate out of the minds of all magistrates, civil, ecclesiastical, or military, any thing that bears the least resemblance to a proud and lawless domination.

But one of the first and most leading principles on which the commonwealth and the laws are consecrated, is lest the temporary possessors and life-renters in it, unmindful of what they have received from their ancestors, or of what is due to their posterity, should act as if they were the entire masters; that they should not think it amongst their rights to cut off the entail, or commit waste on the inheritance, by destroying at their pleasure the whole original fabric of their society; hazarding to leave to those who come after them, a ruin instead of an habitation—and teaching these successors as little to respect their contrivances, as they had themselves respected the institutions of their forefathers. By this unprincipled facility of changing the state as often, and as much, and in as many ways as there are floating fancies or fashions, the whole chain and continuity of the commonwealth would be broken. No one generation could link with the other. Men would become little better than the flies of a summer.

And first of all the science of jurisprudence, the pride of the human intellect, which, with all its defects, redundancies, and errors, is the collected reason of ages, combining the principles of original justice with the infinite variety of human concerns, as a heap of old exploded errors, would be no longer studied. Personal self-sufficiency and arrogance (the certain attendants upon all those who have never experienced a wisdom greater than their own) would usurp the tribunal. Of course, no certain laws, establishing invariable grounds of hope and fear, would keep the actions of men in a certain course, or direct them to a certain end. Nothing stable in the modes of holding property, or exercising function, could form a solid ground on which any parent could speculate in the education of his offspring, or in a choice for their future establishment in the world. No principles would be early worked into the habits. As soon as the most able instructor had completed his laborious course of institution, instead of sending forth his pupil, accomplished in a virtuous discipline, fitted to procure him attention and respect, in his place in society, he would find every thing altered; and that he had turned out a poor creature to the contempt and derision of the world, ignorant of the true grounds of estimation. Who would insure a tender and delicate sense of honour to beat almost with the first pulses of the heart, when no man could know what would be the test of honour in a nation, continually varying the standard of its coin? No part of life would retain its acquisitions. Barbarism with regard to science and literature, unskilfulness with regard to arts and manufactures, would infallibly succeed to the want of a steady education and settled principle; and thus the commonwealth itself would, in a few generations, crumble away, be disconnected into the dust and powder of individuality, and at length dispersed to all the winds of heaven.

To avoid therefore the evils of inconstancy and versatility, ten thousand times worse than those of obstinacy and the blindest prejudice, we have consecrated the state, that no man should approach to look into its defects or corruptions but with due caution; that he should never dream of beginning its reformation by its subversion; that he should approach to the faults of the state as to the wounds of a father, with pious awe and trembling sollicitude. By this wise prejudice we are taught to look with horror on those children of their country who are prompt rashly to hack that aged parent in pieces, and put him into the kettle of magicians, in hopes that by their poisonous weeds, and wild incantations, they may regenerate the paternal constitution, and renovate their father's life.[1]

Society is indeed a contract. Subordinate contracts for objects of mere occasional interest may be dissolved at pleasure—but the state ought not to be considered as nothing better than a partnership agreement in a trade of pepper and coffee, callico or tobacco, or some other such low concern, to be taken up for a little temporary interest, and to be dissolved by the fancy of the parties. It is to be looked on with other reverence; because it is not a partnership in things subservient only to the gross animal existence of a temporary and perishable nature. It is a partnership in all science; a partnership in all art; a partnership

1 The content and dramatic imagery of this paragraph had been used by Burke some years previously, in his "Speech on a Motion Made in the House of Commons for a Committee to Inquire into the State of the Representation of the Commons in Parliament" (*Works* VI, 136). See Appendix E5.

in every virtue, and in all perfection. As the ends of such a partnership cannot be obtained in many generations, it becomes a partnership not only between those who are living, but between those who are living, those who are dead, and those who are to be born. Each contract of each particular state is but a clause in the great primæval contract of eternal society, linking the lower with the higher natures, connecting the visible and invisible world, according to a fixed compact sanctioned by the inviolable oath which holds all physical and all moral natures, each in their appointed place. This law is not subject to the will of those, who by an obligation above them, and infinitely superior, are bound to submit their will to that law. The municipal corporations of that universal kingdom are not morally at liberty at their pleasure, and on their speculations of a contingent improvement, wholly to separate and tear asunder the bands of their subordinate community, and to dissolve it into an unsocial, uncivil, unconnected chaos of elementary principles. It is the first and supreme necessity only, a necessity that is not chosen but chooses, a necessity paramount to deliberation, that admits no discussion, and demands no evidence, which alone can justify a resort to anarchy. This necessity is no exception to the rule; because this necessity itself is a part too of that moral and physical disposition of things to which man must be obedient by consent or force; but if that which is only submission to necessity should be made the object of choice, the law is broken, nature is disobeyed, and the rebellious are outlawed, cast forth, and exiled, from this world of reason, and order, and peace, and virtue, and fruitful penitence, into the antagonist world of madness, discord, vice, confusion, and unavailing sorrow.

These, my dear Sir, are, were, and I think long will be the sentiments of not the least learned and reflecting part of this kingdom. They who are included in this description, form their opinions on such grounds as such persons ought to form them. The less enquiring receive them from an authority which those whom Providence dooms to live on trust need not be ashamed to rely on. These two sorts of men move in the same direction, tho' in a different place. They both move with the order of the universe. They all know or feel this great antient truth: "Quod illi principi et præpotenti Deo qui omnem hunc mundum regit, nihil eorum quæ quidem fiant in terris acceptius quam concilia et cætus hominum jure sociati quæ civitates appellantur."[1] They

---

1 "To that supreme God who rules the universe, nothing on earth

take this tenet of the head and heart, not from the great name which it immediately bears, nor from the greater from whence it is derived;[1] but from that which alone can give true weight and sanction to any learned opinion, the common nature and common relation of men. Persuaded that all things ought to be done with reference, and referring all to the point of reference to which all should be directed, they think themselves bound, not only as individuals in the sanctuary of the heart, or as congregated in that personal capacity, to renew the memory of their high origin and cast; but also in their corporate character to perform their national homage to the institutor, and author and protector of civil society; without which civil society man could not by any possibility arrive at the perfection of which his nature is capable, nor even make a remote and faint approach to it. They conceive that He who gave our nature to be perfected by our virtue, willed also the necessary means of its perfection—He willed therefore the state—He willed its connexion with the source and original archetype of all perfection. They who are convinced of this his will, which is the law of laws and the sovereign of sovereigns, cannot think it reprehensible, that this our corporate fealty and homage, that this our recognition of a signiory paramount, I had almost said this oblation of the state itself, as a worthy offering on the high altar of universal praise, should be performed as all publick solemn acts are performed, in buildings, in musick, in decoration, in speech, in the dignity of persons, according to the customs of mankind, taught by their nature; that is, with modest splendour, with unassuming state, with mild majesty and sober pomp. For those purposes they think some part of the wealth of the country is as usefully employed as it can be, in fomenting the luxury of individuals. It is the publick ornament. It is the publick consolation. It nourishes the publick hope. The poorest man finds his own importance and dignity in it, whilst the wealth and pride of individuals at every moment makes the man of humble

---

is more welcome than those communities and associations of men that are called states." Cicero (106–43 BCE), *De Republica*, Book VI, xiii.

1 The line quoted from *De Republica* is from Cicero's imaginative telling of the dream of Scipio, a dream rich in content about governance, ambition, the relation of soul and body, immortality, and man's small place in the world. The Roman statesman Scipio (185–129 BCE) is "the great name which it immediately bears"; Cicero is "the greater from whence it is derived."

rank and fortune sensible of his inferiority, and degrades and vilifies his condition. It is for the man in humble life, and to raise his nature, and to put him in mind of a state in which the privileges of opulence will cease, when he will be equal by nature, and may be more than equal by virtue, that this portion of the general wealth of his country is employed and sanctified.

I assure you I do not aim at singularity. I give you opinions which have been accepted amongst us, from very early times to this moment, with a continued and general approbation, and which indeed are so worked into my mind, that I am unable to distinguish what I have learned from others from the results of my own meditation....

So tenacious are we are of the old ecclesiastical modes and fashions of institution, that very little alteration has been made in them since the fourteenth or fifteenth century; adhering in this particular, as in all things else, to our old settled maxim, never entirely nor at once to depart from antiquity. We found these old institutions, on the whole, favourable to morality and discipline; and we thought they were susceptible of amendment, without altering the ground. We thought that they were capable of receiving and meliorating, and above all of preserving the accessions of science and literature, as the order of Providence should successively produce them. And after all, with this Gothic and monkish education (for such it is in the groundwork) we may put in our claim to as ample and as early a share in all the improvements in science, in arts, and in literature, which have illuminated and adorned the modern world, as any other nation in Europe; we think one main cause of this improvement was our not despising the patrimony of knowledge which was left us by our forefathers.

It is from our attachment to a church establishment that the English nation did not think it wise to entrust that great fundamental interest of the whole to what they trust no part of their civil or military public service, that is to the unsteady and precarious contribution of individuals. They go further. They certainly never have suffered and never will suffer the fixed estate of the church to be converted into a pension, to depend on the treasury, and to be delayed, withheld, or perhaps to be extinguished by fiscal difficulties; which difficulties may sometimes be pretended for political purposes, and are in fact often brought on by the extravagance, negligence, and rapacity of politicians. The people of England think that they have constitutional motives, as well as religious, against any project of turning their independent clergy into ecclesiastical pensioners of state. They tremble for their liberty, from the influence of a clergy dependent on the crown; they tremble for the public tranquillity from the disorders of a factious clergy, if it were made to depend upon any other than the crown. They therefore made their church, like their king and their nobility, independent.

From the united considerations of religion and constitutional policy, from their opinion of a duty to make a sure provision for the consolation of the feeble and the instruction of the ignorant, they have incorporated and identified the estate of the church with the mass of *private property*, of which the state is not the proprietor, either for use or dominion, but the guardian only and the regulator. They have ordained that the provision of this establishment might be as stable as the earth on which it stands, and should not fluctuate with the Euripus[1] of funds and actions.

The men of England, the men, I mean, of light and leading in England, whose wisdom (if they have any) is open and direct, would be ashamed, as of a silly deceitful trick, to profess any religion in name, which by their proceedings they appear to contemn. If by their conduct (the only language that rarely lies) they seemed to regard the great ruling principle of the moral and the natural world, as a mere invention to keep the vulgar in obedience, they apprehend that by such a conduct they would defeat the politic purpose they have in view. They would find it difficult to make others to believe in a system to which they manifestly gave no credit themselves. The Christian statesmen of this land would indeed first provide for the *multitude*; because it is the *multitude*; and is therefore, as such, the first object in the ecclesiastical institution, and in all institutions. They have been taught, that the circumstance of the gospel's being preached to the poor, was one of the great tests of its true mission. They think, therefore, that those do not believe it, who do not take care it should be preached to the poor. But as they know that charity is not confined to any one description, but ought to apply itself to all men who have wants, they are not deprived of a due and anxious sensation of pity to the distresses of the miserable great. They are not repelled through a fastidious delicacy, at the stench of their arrogance and presumption, from a medicinal attention to their mental blotches and running sores. They are sensible, that religious instruction is of more consequence to them than to any others; from the greatness of the

---

1 A narrow strait of water with a violently flowing current, named after a channel in Greece separating Euboea from Boeotia.

temptation to which they are exposed; from the important consequences that attend their faults; from the contagion of their ill example; from the necessity of bowing down the stubborn neck of their pride and ambition to the yoke of moderation and virtue; from a consideration of the fat stupidity and gross ignorance concerning what imports men most to know, which prevails at courts, and at the head of armies, and in senates, as much as at the loom and in the field.

The English people are satisfied, that to the great the consolations of religion are as necessary as its instructions. They too are among the unhappy. They feel personal pain and domestic sorrow. In these they have no privilege, but are subject to pay their full contingent to the contributions levied on mortality. They want this sovereign balm under their gnawing cares and anxieties, which being less conversant about the limited wants of animal life, range without limit, and are diversified by infinite combinations in the wild and unbounded regions of imagination. Some charitable dole is wanting to these, our often very unhappy brethren, to fill the gloomy void that reigns in minds which have nothing on earth to hope or fear; something to relieve in the killing languor and over-laboured lassitude of those who have nothing to do; something to excite an appetite to existence in the palled satiety which attends on all pleasures which may be bought, where nature is not left to her own process, where even desire is anticipated, and therefore fruition defeated by meditated schemes and contrivances of delight; and no interval, no obstacle, is interposed between the wish and the accomplishment....

... For these reasons, whilst we provide first for the poor, and with a parental solicitude, we have not relegated religion (like something we were ashamed to shew) to obscure municipalities or rustic villages. No! We will have her to exalt her mitred front in courts and parliaments. We will have her mixed throughout the whole mass of life, and blended with all the classes of society....

With these ideas rooted in their minds, the commons of Great Britain, in the national emergencies, will never seek their resource from the confiscation of the estates of the church and poor. Sacrilege and proscription are not among the ways and means in our committee of supply. The Jews in Change Alley have not yet dared to hint their hopes of a mortgage on the revenues belonging to the see of Canterbury. I am not afraid that I shall be disavowed, when I assure you that there is not *one* public man in this kingdom, whom you wish to quote; no not one of any party or description, who does not reprobate the dishonest, perfidious, and cruel confiscation which the national assembly has been compelled to make of that property which it was their first duty to protect.

It is with the exultation of a little natural pride[1] I tell you, that those amongst us who have wished to pledge the societies of Paris in the cup of their abominations,[2] have been disappointed. The robbery of your church has proved a security to the possessions of ours. It has roused the people. They see with horror and alarm the enormous and shameless act of proscription. It has opened, and will more and more open their eyes upon the selfish enlargement of mind, and the narrow liberality of sentiment of insidious men, which commencing in close hypocrisy and fraud have ended in open violence and rapine. At home we behold similar beginnings. We are on our guard against similar conclusions.

I hope we shall never be so totally lost to all sense of the duties imposed upon us by the law of social union, as, upon any pretext of public service, to confiscate the goods of a single unoffending citizen. Who but a tyrant (a name expressive of every thing which can vitiate and degrade human nature) could think of seizing on the property of men, unaccused, unheard, untried, by whole descriptions, by hundreds and thousands together? who that had not lost every trace of humanity could think of casting down men of exalted rank and sacred function, some of them of an age to call at once for reverence and compassion, of casting them down from the highest situation in the commonwealth, wherein they were maintained by their own landed property, to a state of indigence, depression and contempt?

The confiscators truly have made some allowance to their victims from the scraps and fragments of their own tables from which they have been so harshly driven, and which have been so bountifully spread for a feast to the harpies of usury. But to drive men from independence to live on alms is itself great cruelty. That which might be a tolerable condition to men in one state

---

1 In some other editions of the text, this reads "a little national pride."

2 Revelation 17:4: "And the woman was arrayed in purple and scarlet colour, and decked with gold and precious stone and pearls, having a golden cup in her hand full of abominations and filthiness of her fornication."

of life, and not habituated to other things, may, when all these circumstances are altered, be a dreadful revolution; and one to which a virtuous mind would feel pain in condemning any guilt except that which would demand the life of the offender. But to many minds this punishment of *degradation* and *infamy* is worse than death. Undoubtedly it is an infinite aggravation of this cruel suffering, that the persons who were taught a double prejudice in favour of religion, by education and by the place they held in the administration of its functions, are to receive the remnants of their property as alms from the profane and impious hands of those who had plundered them of all the rest; to receive (if they are at all to receive) not from the charitable contributions of the faithful, but from the insolent tenderness of known and avowed Atheism, the maintenance of religion, measured out to them on the standard of the contempt in which it is held; and for the purpose of rendering those who receive the allowance vile and of no estimation in the eyes of mankind.

But this act of seizure of property, it seems, is a judgment in law, and not a confiscation. They have, it seems, found out in the academies of the *Palais Royale*, and the *Jacobins*,[1] that certain men had no right to the possessions which they held under law, usage, the decisions of courts, and the accumulated prescription of a thousand years. They say that ecclesiastics are fictitious persons, creatures of the state; whom at pleasure they may destroy, and of course limit and modify in every particular; that the goods they possess are not properly theirs, but belong to the state which created the fiction; and we are therefore not to trouble ourselves with what they may suffer in their natural feelings and natural persons, on account of what is done towards them in this their constructive character. Of what import is it, under what names you injure men, and deprive them of the just

---

1 The *Palais-Royal* was the residence of the duc d'Orléans (later the self-styled Philippe Égalité, guillotined in 1793); its courtyard was the meeting-place of incendiary orators who benefitted from the Duke's protection. The *Jacobins* was a political club, so named because it met in the monastery of the Dominicans ("Jacobins"). The name of Jacobins was initially given as a term of ridicule but was later adopted by the members of the club; they were to become the most radical of the French revolutionary groups and, with Robespierre at their head, they instituted the Terror of 1793–94. The Jacobins became the loathed focus of Burke's later writings on the Revolution, particularly in the *Letters on a Regicide Peace*.

emoluments of a profession, in which they were not only permitted but encouraged by the state to engage; and upon the supposed certainty of which emoluments they had formed the plan of their lives, contracted debts, and led multitudes to an entire dependence upon them? ...

Few barbarous conquerors have ever made so terrible a revolution in property. None of the heads of the Roman factions, when they established *"crudelem illam Hastam"*[1] in all their auctions of rapine, have ever set up to sale the goods of the conquered citizen to such an enormous amount. It must be allowed in favour of those tyrants of antiquity, that what was done by them could hardly be said to be done in cold blood. Their passions were inflamed, their tempers soured, their understandings confused, with the spirit of revenge, with the innumerable reciprocated and recent inflictions and retaliations of blood and rapine. They were driven beyond all bounds of moderation by the apprehension of the return of power with the return of property to the families of those they had injured beyond all hope of forgiveness.

These Roman confiscators, who were yet only in the elements of tyranny, and were not instructed in the rights of men to exercise all sorts of cruelties on each other without provocation, thought it necessary to spread a sort of colour over their injustice. They considered the vanquished party as composed of traitors who had borne arms, or otherwise had acted with hostility against the commonwealth. They regarded them as persons who had forfeited their property by their crimes. With you, in your improved state of the human mind, there was no such formality. You seized upon five millions sterling of annual rent, and turned forty or fifty thousand human creatures out of their houses, because "such was your pleasure." The tyrant, Harry the Eighth of England,[2] as he was not bet-

---

1 "That cruel spear." It was customary for Roman auctions to be conducted around a spear stuck in the ground, originally a sign of booty gained in war.

2 King Henry VIII (r. 1509–47) instituted in the early stages of the English Reformation a set of legal and administrative processes known as the Dissolution of the Monasteries, by means of which the lands and wealth of the monasteries of England and Wales were lucratively confiscated. Burke compares Henry with two Roman figures with reputations for greed and power-lust: Gaius Marius (157–86 BCE), and Lucius Cornelius Sulla (138–78 BCE).

ter enlightened than the Roman Marius's and Sylla's, and had not studied in your new schools, did not know what an effectual instrument of despotism was to be found in that grand magazine of offensive weapons, the rights of men. When he resolved to rob the abbies, as the club of the Jacobins have robbed all the ecclesiastics, he began by setting on foot a commission to examine into the crimes and abuses which prevailed in those communities. As it might be expected, his commission reported truths, exaggerations, and falshoods. But truly or falsely it reported abuses and offences. However, as abuses might be corrected, as every crime of persons does not infer a forfeiture with regard to communities, and as property, in that dark age, was not discovered to be a creature of prejudice, all those abuses (and there were enough of them) were hardly thought sufficient ground for such a confiscation as it was his purposes to make. He therefore procured the formal surrender of these estates. All these operose proceedings were adopted by one of the most decided tyrants in the rolls of history, as necessary preliminaries, before he could venture, by bribing the members of his two servile houses with a share of the spoil, and holding out to them an eternal immunity from taxation, to demand a confirmation of his iniquitous proceedings by an act of parliament. Had fate reserved him to our times, four technical terms would have done his business, and saved him all this trouble; he needed nothing more than one short form of incantation—"*Philosophy, Light, Liberality, the Rights of Men.*" ...

When all the frauds, impostures, violences, rapines, burnings, murders, confiscations, compulsory paper currencies, and every description of tyranny and cruelty employed to bring about and to uphold this revolution, have their natural effect, that is, to shock the moral sentiments of all virtuous and sober minds, the abettors of this philosophic system immediately strain their throats in a declamation against the old monarchical government of France. When they have rendered that deposed power sufficiently black, they then proceed in argument, as if all those who disapprove of their new abuses, must of course be partizans of the old; that those who reprobate their crude and violent schemes of liberty ought to be treated as advocates for servitude. I admit that their necessities do compel them to this base and contemptible fraud. Nothing can reconcile men to their proceedings and projects but the supposition that there is no third option between them, and some tyranny as odious as can be furnished by the records of history, or by the invention of poets. This prattling of theirs hardly deserves the name of sophistry. It is nothing but plain impudence. Have these gentlemen never heard, in the whole circle of the worlds of theory and practice, of any thing between the despotism of the monarch and the despotism of the multitude? Have they never heard of a monarchy directed by laws, controlled and balanced by the great hereditary wealth and hereditary dignity of a nation; and both again controlled by a judicious check from the reason and feeling of the people at large acting by a suitable and permanent organ? Is it then impossible that a man may be found who, without criminal ill intention, or pitiable absurdity, shall prefer such a mixed and tempered government to either of the extremes; and who may repute that nation to be destitute of all wisdom and of all virtue, which, having in its choice to obtain such a government with ease, *or rather to confirm it when actually possessed*, thought proper to commit a thousand crimes, and to subject their country to a thousand evils, in order to avoid it? Is it then a truth so universally acknowledged, that a pure democracy is the only tolerable form into which human society can be thrown, that a man is not permitted to hesitate about its merits, without the suspicion of being a friend to tyranny, that is, of being a foe to mankind?

I do not know under what description to class the present ruling authority in France. It affects to be a pure democracy, though I think it in a direct train of becoming shortly a mischievous and ignoble oligarchy. But for the present I admit it to be a contrivance of the nature and effect of what it pretends to. I reprobate no form of government merely upon abstract principles. There may be situations in which the purely democratic form will become necessary. There may be some (very few, and very particularly circumstanced) where it would be clearly desireable. This I do not take to be the case of France, or of any other great country. Until now, we have seen no examples of considerable democracies. The antients were better acquainted with them. Not being wholly unread in the authors, who had seen the most of those constitutions, and who best understood them, I cannot help concurring with their opinion, that an absolute democracy, no more than absolute monarchy, is to be reckoned among the legitimate forms of government. They think it rather the corruption and degeneracy, than the sound constitution of a republic. If I recollect rightly, Aristotle observes, that a democracy has many striking points of resemblance with a tyranny.[1] Of this I am certain, that in a democracy, the majority of the citizens is capable of exercising the most cruel oppressions upon the minority, whenever strong divisions prevail in that kind of polity, as they often must; and that oppression of the minority will extend to far greater numbers, and will be carried on with much greater fury, than can almost ever be apprehended from the dominion of a single sceptre. In such a popular persecution, individual sufferers are in a much more deplorable condition than in any other. Under a cruel prince they have the balmy compassion of mankind to assuage the smart of their wounds; they have the plaudits of the people to animate their generous constancy under their sufferings: but those who are subjected to wrong under multitudes, are deprived of all external consolation. They seem deserted by mankind; overpowered by a conspiracy of their whole species.

But admitting democracy not to have that inevitable tendency to party tyranny, which I suppose it to have, and admitting it to possess as much good in it when unmixed, as I am sure it possesses when compounded with other forms; does monarchy, on its part, contain nothing at all to recommend it? I do not often quote Bolingbroke, nor have his works in general, left any permanent impression on my mind. He is a presumptuous and a superficial writer. But he has one observation, which, in my opinion, is not without depth and solidity. He says, that he prefers a monarchy to other governments; because you can better ingraft any description of republic on a monarchy than any thing of monarchy upon the republican forms.[2] I think him perfectly in the right. The fact is so historically; and it agrees well with the speculation.

---

1 [Burke's note:] When I wrote this I quoted from memory, after many years had elapsed from my reading the passage. A learned friend has found it, and it is as follows: ... "The ethical character is the same; both exercise despotism over the better class of citizens; and decrees are in the one, what ordinances and arrêts are in the other: the demagogue too, and the court favourite, are not unfrequently the same identical men, and always bear a close analogy; and these have the principal power, each in their respective forms of government, favourites with the absolute monarch, and demagogues with a people such as I have described." Arist[otle]. Politic[s]. lib. iv. cap. 4.
2 See Henry St. John, Viscount Bolingbroke, *The Idea of a Patriot King* (Clarendon Press, [1738] 1926), 57–58.

I know how easy a topic it is to dwell on the faults of departed greatness. By a revolution in the state, the fawning sycophant of yesterday, is converted into the austere critic of the present hour. But steady independent minds, when they have an object of so serious a concern to mankind as government, under their contemplation, will disdain to assume the part of satirists and declaimers. They will judge of human institutions as they do of human characters. They will sort out the good from the evil, which is mixed in mortal institutions as it is in mortal men.

Your government in France, though usually, and I think justly, reputed the best of the unqualified or ill-qualified monarchies, was still full of abuses. These abuses accumulated in a length of time, as they must accumulate in every monarchy not under the constant inspection of a popular representative. I am no stranger to the faults and defects of the subverted government of France; and I think I am not inclined by nature or policy to make a panegyric upon any thing which is a just and natural object of censure. But the question is not now of the vices of that monarchy, but of its existence. Is it then true, that the French government was such as to be incapable or undeserving of reform; so that it was of absolute necessity the whole fabric should be at once pulled down, and the area cleared for the erection of a theoretic experimental edifice in its place? All France was of a different opinion in the beginning of the year 1789. The instructions to the representatives to the states-general, from every district in that kingdom, were filled with projects for the reformation of that government, without the remotest suggestion of a design to destroy it. Had such a design been then even insinuated, I believe there would have been but one voice, and that voice for rejecting it with scorn and horror. Men have been sometimes led by degrees, sometimes hurried into things, of which, if they could have seen the whole together, they never would have permitted the most remote approach. When those instructions were given, there was no question but that abuses existed, and that they demanded a reform; nor is there now. In the interval between the instructions and the revolution, things changed their shape; and in consequence of that change, the true question at present is, Whether those who would have reformed, or those who have destroyed, are in the right?

To hear some men speak of the late monarchy of France, you would imagine that they were talking of Persia bleeding under the ferocious sword of Tæhmas Kouli Khân;[1] or at least describing the barbarous anarchic despotism of Turkey, where the finest countries in the most genial climates in the world are wasted by peace more than any countries have been worried by war; where arts are unknown, where manufactures languish, where science is extinguished, where agriculture decays, where the human race itself melts away and perishes under the eye of the observer. Was this the case of France? I have no way of determining the question but by a reference to facts. Facts do not support the resemblance. Along with much evil, there is some good in monarchy itself; and some corrective to its evil, from religion, from laws, from manners, from opinions, the French monarchy must have received; which rendered it (though by no means a free, and therefore by no means a good constitution) a despotism rather in appearance than in reality.

Among the standards upon which the effects of government on any country are to be estimated, I must consider the state of its population as not the least certain. No country in which population flourishes, and is in progressive improvement, can be under a *very* mischievous government. About sixty years ago, the Intendants of the generalities of France made, with other matters, a report of the population of their several districts. I have not the books, which are very voluminous, by me, nor do I know where to procure them (I am obliged to speak by memory, and therefore the less positively) but I think the population of France was by them, even at that period, estimated at twenty-two millions of souls. At the end of the last century it had been generally calculated at eighteen. On either of these estimations France was not ill-peopled. Mr. Necker,[2] who is an authority for his own time at least equal to the Intendants for theirs, reckons, and upon apparently sure principles, the people of France, in the year 1780, at twenty-four millions six hundred and seventy thousand. But was this the probable ultimate term under the old establishment? Dr. Price is of opinion, that the growth of population in France was by no means at

---

1 Tæhmas Kouli Khân (1688–1747), known also as Nader Shah, ruled as shah of Persia from 1736 until his assassination in 1747. He was a brilliant and ferocious military leader who greatly expanded the territory of the Persian Empire; his final years of rule were marked by great cruelties.

2 Jacques Necker (1732–1804), Swiss financier and statesman, was Director-General of Finances in France in 1776–81 and 1788–90.

its *acmé* in that year. I certainly defer to Dr. Price's authority a good deal more in these speculations, than I do in his general politics. This gentleman, taking ground on Mr. Necker's data, is very confident, that since the period of that minister's calculation, the French population has encreased rapidly; so rapidly that in the year 1789 he will not consent to rate the people of that kingdom at a lower number than thirty millions. After abating much (and much I think ought to be abated) from the sanguine calculation of Dr. Price, I have no doubt that the population of France did encrease considerably during this later period: but supposing that it encreased to nothing more than will be sufficient to compleat the 24,670,000 to 25 millions, still a population of 25 millions, and that in an encreasing progress, on a space of about twenty-seven thousand square leagues, is immense. It is, for instance, a good deal more than the proportionable population of this island, or even than that of England, the best-peopled part of the united kingdom....

I do not attribute this population to the deposed government; because I do not like to compliment the contrivances of men, with what is due in a great degree to the bounty of Providence. But that decried government could not have obstructed, most probably it favoured, the operation of those causes (whatever they were) whether of nature in the soil, or in habits of industry among the people, which has produced so large a number of the species throughout that whole kingdom, and exhibited in some particular places such prodigies of population. I never will suppose that fabrick of a state to be the worst of all political institutions, which, by experience, is found to contain a principle favourable (however latent it may be) to the encrease of mankind.

The wealth of a country is another, and no contemptible standard, by which we may judge whether, on the whole, a government be protecting or destructive. France far exceeds England in the multitude of her people; but I apprehend that her comparative wealth is much inferior to ours; that it is not so equal in the distribution, nor so ready in the circulation. I believe the difference in the form of the two governments to be amongst the causes of this advantage on the side of England. I speak of England, not of the whole British dominions; which, if compared with those of France, will, in some degree, weaken the comparative rate of wealth upon our side. But that wealth, which will not endure a comparison with the riches of England, may constitute a very respectable degree of opulence. Mr. Necker's book published in 1785,[1] contains an accurate and interesting collection of facts relative to public œconomy and to political arithmetic; and his speculations on the subject are in general wise and liberal. In that work he gives an idea of the state of France, very remote from the portrait of a country whose government was a perfect grievance, an absolute evil, admitting no cure but through the violent and uncertain remedy of a total revolution. He affirms, that from the year 1726 to the year 1784, there was coined at the mint of France, in the species of gold and silver, to the amount of about one hundred millions of pounds sterling.[2] ...

Some adequate cause must have originally introduced all the money coined at its mint into that kingdom; and some cause as operative must have kept at home, or returned into its bosom, such a vast flood of treasure as Mr. Necker calculates to remain for domestic circulation. Suppose any reasonable deductions from M. Necker's computation; the remainder must still amount to an immense sum. Causes thus powerful to acquire and to retain, cannot be found in discouraged industry, insecure property, and a positively destructive government. Indeed, when I consider the face of the kingdom of France; the multitude and opulence of her cities; the useful magnificence of her spacious high roads and bridges; the opportunity of her artificial canals and navigations opening the conveniences of maritime communication through a solid continent of so immense an extent; when I turn my eyes to the stupendous works of her ports and harbours, and to her whole naval apparatus, whether for war or trade; when I bring before my view the number of her fortifications, constructed with so bold and masterly a skill, and made and maintained at so prodigious a charge, presenting an armed front and impenetrable barrier to her enemies upon every side; when I recollect how very small a part of that extensive region is without cultivation, and to what complete perfection the culture of many of the best productions of the earth have been brought in France; when I reflect on the excellence of her manufactures and fabrics, second to none but ours, and in some particulars not second; when I contemplate the grand foundations of charity, public and private; when I survey the state of all the arts that beautify and polish

---

1 [Burke's note:] De l'Administration des Finances de la France, par M. Necker.

2 [Burke's note:] Vol. iii. chap. 8. and chap. 9.

life; when I reckon the men she has bred for extending her fame in war, her able statesmen, the multitude of her profound lawyers and theologians, her philosophers, her critics, her historians and antiquaries, her poets, and her orators sacred and profane, I behold in all this something which awes and commands the imagination, which checks the mind on the brink of precipitate and indiscriminate censure, and which demands, that we should very seriously examine, what and how great are the latent vices that could authorise us at once to level so spacious a fabric with the ground. I do not recognize, in this view of things, the despotism of Turkey. Nor do I discern the character of a government, that has been, on the whole, so oppressive, or so corrupt, or so negligent, as to be utterly unfit *for all reformation.* I must think such a government well deserved to have its excellencies heightened; its faults corrected; and its capacities improved into a British constitution.

Whoever has examined into the proceedings of that deposed government for several years back, cannot fail to have observed, amidst the inconstancy and fluctuation natural to courts, an earnest endeavour towards the prosperity and improvement of the country; he must admit, that it had long been employed, in some instances, wholly to remove, in many considerably to correct, the abusive practices and usages that had prevailed in the state; and that even the unlimited power of the sovereign over the persons of his subjects, inconsistent, as undoubtedly it was, with law and liberty, had yet been every day growing more mitigated in the exercise. So far from refusing itself to reformation, that government was open, with a censurable degree of facility, to all sorts of projects and projectors on the subject. Rather too much countenance was given to the spirit of innovation, which soon was turned against those who fostered it, and ended in their ruin. It is but cold, and no very flattering justice to that fallen monarchy, to say, that, for many years, it trespassed more by levity and want of judgment in several of its schemes, than from any defect in diligence or in public spirit. To compare the government of France for the last fifteen or sixteen years with wise and well-constituted establishments, during that, or during any period, is not to act with fairness. But if in point of prodigality in the expenditure of money, or in point of rigour in the exercise of power, it be compared with any of the former reigns, I believe candid judges will give little credit to the good intentions of those who dwell perpetually on the donations to favourites, or on the expences of the court, or on the horrors of the Bastile in the reign of Louis the XVIth.[1]

Whether the system, if it deserves such a name, now built on the ruins of that antient monarchy, will be able to give a better account of the population and wealth of the country, which it has taken under its care, is a matter very doubtful. Instead of improving by the change, I apprehend that a long series of years must be told before it can recover in any degree the effects of this philosophic revolution, and before the nation can be replaced on its former footing. If Dr. Price should think fit, a few years hence, to favour us with an estimate of the population of France, he will hardly be able to make up his tale of thirty millions of souls, as computed in 1789, or the assembly's computation of twenty-six millions of that year; or even Mr. Necker's twenty-five millions in 1780. I hear that there are considerable emigrations from France; and that many quitting that voluptuous climate, and that seductive *Circean* liberty,[2] have taken refuge in the frozen regions, and under the British despotism, of Canada.

In the present disappearance of coin, no person could think it the same country, in which the present minister of the finances has been able to discover fourscore millions sterling in specie. From its general aspect one would conclude that it had been for some time past under the special direction of the learned academicians of Laputa and Balnibarbi.[3] Already the population of Paris has so declined, that Mr. Necker stated to the national assembly the provision to be made for its subsistence at a fifth less than what has formerly been found requisite. It is said (and I have never heard it contradicted) that an hundred thousand people are out of employment in that city, though it is become the seat of the imprisoned court and national assembly. Nothing, I am credibly informed, can exceed the shocking and disgusting spectacle

---

1 [Burke's note:] The world is obliged to Mr. de Calonne for the pains he has taken to refute the scandalous exaggerations relative to some of the royal expences, and to detect the fallacious account given of pensions, for the wicked purpose of provoking the populace to all sorts of crimes.

2 See Book X of Homer's *Odyssey*, in which the witch-goddess Circe captivates Odysseus and his crew, transforming some of them temporarily into swine and compelling them to live on her sumptuous island for a year before finally releasing them.

3 [Burke's note:] See [Swift's] Gulliver's Travels [1726] for the idea of countries governed by philosophers.

of mendicancy displayed in that capital. Indeed, the votes of the national assembly leave no doubt of the fact. They have lately appointed a standing committee of mendicancy. They are contriving at once a vigorous police on this subject, and, for the first time, the imposition of a tax to maintain the poor, for whose present relief great sums appear on the face of the public accounts of the year. In the mean time, the leaders of the legislative clubs and coffee-houses are intoxicated with admiration at their own wisdom and ability. They speak with the most sovereign contempt of the rest of the world. They tell the people, to comfort them in the rags with which they have cloathed them, that they are a nation of philosophers; and, sometimes, by all the arts of quackish parade, by shew, tumult, and bustle, sometimes by the alarms of plots and invasions, they attempt to drown the cries of indigence, and to divert the eyes of the observer from the ruin and wretchedness of the state. A brave people will certainly prefer liberty, accompanied with a virtuous poverty, to a depraved and wealthy servitude. But before the price of comfort and opulence is paid, one ought to be pretty sure it is real liberty which is purchased, and that she is to be purchased at no other price. I shall always, however, consider that liberty as very equivocal in her appearance, which has not wisdom and justice for her companions; and does not lead prosperity and plenty in her train.

The advocates for this revolution, not satisfied with exaggerating the vices of their antient government, strike at the fame of their country itself, by painting almost all that could have attracted the attention of strangers, I mean their nobility and their clergy, as objects of horror. If this were only a libel, there had not been much in it. But it has practical consequences. Had your nobility and gentry, who formed the great body of your landed men, and the whole of your military officers, resembled those of Germany, at the period when the Hanse-towns were necessitated to confederate against the nobles in defence of their property—had they been like the *Orsini* and *Vitelli* in Italy, who used to sally from their fortified dens to rob the trader and traveller—had they been such as the *Mamalukes* in Egypt, or the *Nayrs*[1] on the coast of Malabar, I do admit, that too critical an enquiry might not be adviseable into the means of freeing the world from such a nuisance. The

1   Orsini: a feuding Roman family; Vitelli: mercenary soldiers in fifteenth-century Italy; Mamalukes: slave-soldiers who seized power and established a dynasty in Egypt; Nayrs: a ferocious warrior caste in India.

statues of Equity and Mercy might be veiled for a moment. The tenderest minds, confounded with the dreadful exigence in which morality submits to the suspension of its own rules in favour of its own principles, might turn aside whilst fraud and violence were accomplishing the destruction of a pretended nobility which disgraced whilst it persecuted human nature. The persons most abhorrent from blood, and treason, and arbitrary confiscation, might remain silent spectators of this civil war between the vices.

But did the privileged nobility who met under the king's precept at Versailles, in 1789, or their constituents, deserve to be looked on as the *Nayres* or *Mamalukes* of this age, or as the *Orsini* and *Vitelli* of ancient times? If I had then asked the question, I should have passed for a madman. What have they since done that they were to be driven into exile, that their persons should be hunted about, mangled, and tortured, their families dispersed, their houses laid in ashes, that their order should be abolished, and the memory of it, if possible, extinguished, by ordaining them to change the very names by which they were usually known?[1] Read their instructions to their representatives. They breathe the spirit of liberty as warmly, and they recommend reformation as strongly, as any other order. Their privileges relative to contribution were voluntarily surrendered; as the king, from the beginning, surrendered all pretence to a right of taxation. Upon a free constitution there was but one opinion in France. The absolute monarchy was at an end. It breathed its last, without a groan, without struggle, without convulsion. All the struggle, all the dissension arose afterwards upon the preference of a despotic democracy to a government of reciprocal controul. The triumph of the victorious party was over the principles of a British constitution....

... I do not pretend to know France as correctly as some others; but I have endeavoured through my whole life to make myself acquainted with human nature: otherwise I should be unfit to take even my humble part in the service of mankind. In that study I could not pass by a vast portion of our nature, as it appeared modified in a country but twenty-four miles from the shore of this island. On my best observation, compared with my best enquiries, I found your nobility for the greater part composed of men of an high spirit, and of a delicate sense of honour,

---

1 On 20 June 1790, the National Assembly voted to abolish titles of nobility and forbid the display of hereditary coats of arms on the sides of carriages.

both with regard to themselves individually, and with regard to their whole corps, over whom they kept, beyond what is common in other countries, a censorial eye. They were tolerably well-bred; very officious, humane, and hospitable; in their conversation frank and open; with a good military tone; and reasonably tinctured with literature, particularly of the authors in their own language. Many had pretensions far above this description....

All this violent cry against the nobility I take to be a mere work of art. To be honoured and even privileged by the laws, opinions, and inveterate usages of our country, growing out of the prejudice of ages, has nothing to provoke horror and indignation in any man. Even to be too tenacious of those privileges, is not absolutely a crime. The strong struggle in every individual to preserve possession of what he has found to belong to him and to distinguish him, is one of the securities against injustice and despotism implanted in our nature. It operates as an instinct to secure property, and to preserve communities in a settled state. What is there to shock in this? Nobility is a graceful ornament to the civil order. It is the Corinthian capital of polished society. *Omnes boni nobilitati semper favemus*, was the saying of a wise and good man.[1] It is indeed one sign of a liberal and benevolent mind to incline to it with some sort of partial propensity. He feels no ennobling principle in his own heart who wishes to level all the artificial institutions which have been adopted for giving a body to opinion, and permanence to fugitive esteem. It is a sour, malignant, envious disposition, without taste for the reality, or for any image or representation of virtue, that sees with joy the unmerited fall of what had long flourished in splendour and in honour. I do not like to see any thing destroyed; any void produced in society; any ruin on the face of the land. It was therefore with no disappointment or dissatisfaction that my enquiries and observation did not present to me any incorrigible vices in the noblesse of France, or any abuse which could not be removed by a reform very short of abolition. Your noblesse did not deserve punishment; but to degrade is to punish.

It was with the same satisfaction I found that the result of my enquiry concerning your clergy was not dissimilar. It is no soothing news to my ears, that great bodies of men are incurably corrupt. It is not with much credulity I listen to any, when they speak evil of those whom they are going to plunder. I rather

---

1 "All good people always take the part of the highborn." Cicero, *Pro Sestio*, IX, 21.

suspect that vices are feigned or exaggerated, when profit is looked for in their punishment. An enemy is a bad witness: a robber is a worse. Vices and abuses there were undoubtedly in that order, and must be. It was an old establishment, and not frequently revised. But I saw no crimes in the individuals that merited confiscation of their substance, nor those cruel insults and degradations, and that unnatural persecution which have been substituted in the place of meliorating regulation.

If there had been any just cause for this new religious persecution, the atheistic libellers, who act as trumpeters to animate the populace to plunder, do not love any body so much as not to dwell with complacence on the vices of the existing clergy. This they have not done. They find themselves obliged to rake into the histories of former ages (which they have ransacked with a malignant and profligate industry) for every instance of oppression and persecution which has been made by that body or in its favour, in order to justify, upon very iniquitous, because very illogical principles of retaliation, their own persecutions, and their own cruelties. After destroying all other genealogies and family distinctions, they invent a sort of pedigree of crimes. It is not very just to chastise men for the offences of their natural ancestors; but to take the fiction of ancestry in a corporate succession, as a ground for punishing men who have no relation to guilty acts, except in names and general descriptions, is a sort of refinement in injustice belonging to the philosophy of this enlightened age. The assembly punishes men, many, if not most, of whom abhor the violent conduct of ecclesiastics in former times as much as their present persecutors can do, and who would be as loud and as strong in the expression of that sense, if they were not well aware of the purposes for which all this declamation is employed.

Corporate bodies are immortal for the good of the members, but not for their punishment. Nations themselves are such corporations. As well might we in England think of waging inexpiable war upon all Frenchmen for the evils which they have brought upon us in the several periods of our mutual hostilities. You might, on your part, think yourselves justified in falling upon all Englishmen on account of the unparalleled calamities brought upon the people of France by the unjust invasions of our Henries and our Edwards. Indeed we should be mutually justified in this exterminatory war upon each other, full as much as you are in the unprovoked persecution of your present countrymen, on account of the conduct of men of the same name in other times.

We do not draw the moral lessons we might from history. On the contrary, without care it may be used to vitiate our minds and to destroy our happiness. In history a great volume is unrolled for our instruction, drawing the materials of future wisdom from the past errors and infirmities of mankind. It may, in the perversion, serve for a magazine, furnishing offensive and defensive weapons for parties in church and state, and supplying the means of keeping alive, or reviving dissensions and animosities, and adding fuel to civil fury. History consists, for the greater part, of the miseries brought upon the world by pride, ambition, avarice, revenge, lust, sedition, hypocrisy, ungoverned zeal, and all the train of disorderly appetites, which shake the public with the same

———troublous storms that toss
The private state, and render life unsweet.[1]

These vices are the *causes* of those storms. Religion, morals, laws, prerogatives, privileges, liberties, rights of men, are the *pretexts*. The pretexts are always found in some specious appearance of a real good. You would not secure men from tyranny and sedition, by rooting out of the mind the principles to which these fraudulent pretexts apply? If you did, you would root out every thing that is valuable in the human breast. As these are the pretexts, so the ordinary actors and instruments in great public evils are kings, priests, magistrates, senates, parliaments, national assemblies, judges, and captains. You would not cure the evil by resolving, that there should be no more monarchs, nor ministers of state, nor of the gospel; no interpreters of law; no general officers; no public councils. You might change the names. The things in some shape must remain. A certain *quantum* of power must always exist in the community, in some hands, and under some appellation. Wise men will apply their remedies to vices, not to names; to the causes of evil which are permanent, not to the occasional organs by which they act, and the transitory modes in which they appear. Otherwise you will be wise historically, a fool in practice. Seldom have two ages the same fashion in their pretexts and the same modes of mischief. Wickedness is a little more inventive. Whilst you are discussing

---

1 Edmund Spenser (1552/53–99), *The Faerie Queene*, Book II, Canto VII, 14: "Long were to tell the troublous stormes, that tosse / The private state, and make the life unsweet."

fashion, the fashion is gone by. The very same vice assumes a new body. The spirit transmigrates; and, far from losing its principle of life by the change of its appearance, it is renovated in its new organs with the fresh vigour of a juvenile activity. It walks abroad; it continues its ravages; whilst you are gibbeting the carcass, or demolishing the tomb. You are terrifying yourself with ghosts and apparitions, whilst your house is the haunt of robbers. It is thus with all those, who, attending only to the shell and husk of history, think they are waging war with intolerance, pride, and cruelty, whilst, under colour of abhorring the ill principles of antiquated parties, they are authorizing and feeding the same odious vices in different factions, and perhaps in worse.

[*Burke here turns his attention to the expropriation of the French Church and argues strongly against the project of confiscation. He surveys the character of the French ecclesiastics, seeing them as "persons of moderate minds and decorous manners" and taking their side amid "the persecutions of oppressive power." The new arrangements in France are seen to be "preparatory to the utter abolition, under any of its forms, of the Christian religion," one of the principal aims of the "philosophical fanatics" at the helm of the revolution. Burke declares that the British thoroughly disapprove of the policy of confiscation: "we have never dreamt that Parliaments had any right whatever to violate property, [or] to override prescription."*]

It is not the confiscation of our church property from this example in France that I dread, though I think this would be no trifling evil. The great source of my solicitude is, lest it should ever be considered in England as the policy of a state, to seek a resource in confiscations of any kind; or that any one description of citizens should be brought to regard any of the others, as their proper prey.... Revolutions are favourable to confiscation; and it is impossible to know under what obnoxious names the next confiscations will be authorised. I am sure that the principles predominant in France extend to very many persons and descriptions of persons in all countries who think their innoxious indolence their security. This kind of innocence in proprietors may be argued into inutility; and inutility into an unfitness for their estates. Many parts of Europe are in open disorder. In many others there is a hollow murmuring under ground; a confused movement is felt, that threatens a general earthquake in the political world. Already confederacies and correspondences of the most extraordinary nature are forming, in several countries. In such a state of things we ought to hold ourselves upon our guard. In all mutations (if mutations must be) the circumstance which will serve most to blunt the edge of their mischief, and to promote what good may be in them, is, that they should find us with our minds tenacious of justice, and tender of property.

But it will be argued, that this confiscation in France ought not to alarm other nations. They say it is not made from wanton rapacity; that it is a great measure of national policy, adopted to remove an extensive, inveterate, superstitious mischief. It is with the greatest difficulty that I am able to separate policy from justice. Justice is itself the great standing policy of civil society; and any eminent departure from it, under any circumstances, lies under the suspicion of being no policy at all.

When men are encouraged to go into a certain mode of life by the existing laws, and protected in that mode as in a lawful occupation—when they have accommodated all their ideas, and all their habits to it—when the law had long made their adherence to its rules a ground of reputation, and their departure from them a ground of disgrace and even of penalty—I am sure it is unjust in legislature, by an arbitrary act, to offer a sudden violence to their minds and their feelings; forcibly to degrade them from their state and condition, and to stigmatize with shame and infamy that character and those customs which before had been made the measure of their happiness and honour. If to this be added an expulsion from their habitations, and a confiscation of all their goods, I am not sagacious enough to discover how this despotic sport, made of the feelings, consciences, prejudices, and properties of men, can be discriminated from the rankest tyranny.

If the injustice of the course pursued in France be clear, the policy of the measure, that is, the public benefit to be expected from it, ought to be at least as evident, and at least as important. To a man who acts under the influence of no passion, who has nothing in view in his projects but the public good, a great difference will immediately strike him, between what policy would dictate on the original introduction of such institutions, and on a question of their total abolition, where they have cast their roots wide and deep, and where by long habit things more valuable than themselves are so adapted to them, and in a manner interwoven with them, that the one cannot be destroyed without notably impairing the other. He might be embarrassed, if the case were really such as sophisters represent it in their paltry style of debating. But in this, as in most questions of state, there is a middle. There is something else than the mere alternative of absolute destruction, or unreformed existence. *Spartam nactus es; hanc exorna.*[1] This is, in my opinion, a rule of profound sense, and ought never to depart from the mind of an honest reformer. I cannot conceive how any man can have brought himself to that pitch of presumption, to consider his country as nothing but *carte blanche*, upon which he may scribble whatever he pleases. A man full of warm speculative benevolence may wish his society otherwise constituted than he finds it; but a good patriot, and a true politician, always considers how he shall make the most of the existing materials of his country. A disposition to preserve, and an ability to improve, taken together, would be my standard of a statesman. Every thing else is vulgar in the conception, perilous in the execution....

This letter is grown to a great length,[2] though it is indeed short with regard to the infinite extent of the subject. Various avocations have from time to time called my mind from the subject. I was not sorry to give myself leisure to observe whether, in the proceedings of the national assembly, I might not find reasons to change or to qualify some of my first sentiments. Every thing has confirmed me more strongly in my first opinions. It was my original purpose to take a view of the principles of the national assembly with regard to the great and fundamental establishments; and to compare the whole of what you have substituted in the place of what you have destroyed, with the several members of our British constitution. But this plan is of greater extent than at first I computed, and I find that you have little desire to take the advantage of any examples. At present I must content myself with some remarks upon your establishments;

---

1   "Your lot is cast in Sparta; adorn it." Cicero, *Letters to Atticus*, Book IV, 6, quoting a line, spoken by Agamemnon to Menelaus, in Euripides' *Telephus* (438 BCE). The meaning is that one should make the best of what one has, and of the actual institutions at hand, a frequent theme in Burke's writings: "it is a settled rule with me, to make the most of my *actual situation*; and not to refuse to do a proper thing, because there is something else more proper, which I am not able to do" (Edmund Burke, "Two Letters to Gentlemen in Bristol," *Works* III, 336).

2   J.C.D. Clark suggests, plausibly, that this paragraph marks a division in the *Reflections*, and that it recommences work that had been interrupted by the parliamentary session in early 1790.

reserving for another time what I proposed to say concerning the spirit of our British monarchy, aristocracy, and democracy, as practically they exist.

I have taken a review of what has been done by the governing power in France. I have certainly spoke of it with freedom. Those whose principle it is to despise the antient permanent sense of mankind, and to set up a scheme of society on new principles, must naturally expect that such of us who think better of the judgment of the human race than of theirs, should consider both them and their devices, as men and schemes upon their trial. They must take it for granted that we attend much to their reason, but not at all to their authority. They have not one of the great influencing prejudices of mankind in their favour. They avow their hostility to opinion. Of course they must expect no support from that influence, which, with every other authority, they have deposed from the seat of its jurisdiction.

I can never consider this assembly as any thing else than a voluntary association of men, who have availed themselves of circumstances, to seize upon the power of the state. They have not the sanction and authority of the character under which they first met. They have assumed another of a very different nature; and have completely altered and inverted all the relations in which they originally stood. They do not hold the authority they exercise under any constitutional law of the state. They have departed from the instructions of the people by whom they were sent; which instructions, as the assembly did not act in virtue of any antient usage or settled law, were the sole source of their authority. The most considerable of their acts have not been done by great majorities; and in this sort of near divisions, which carry only the constructive authority of the whole, strangers will consider reasons as well as resolutions.

If they had set up this new experimental government as a necessary substitute for an expelled tyranny, mankind would anticipate the time of prescription, which, through long usage, mellows into legality governments that were violent in their commencement. All those who have affections which lead them to the conservation of civil order would recognize, even in its cradle, the child as legitimate, which has been produced from those principles of cogent expediency to which all just governments owe their birth, and on which they justify their continuance. But they will be late and reluctant in giving any sort of countenance to the operations of a power, which has derived its birth from no law and no necessity; but which on the contrary has had its origin in those vices and sinister practices by which the social union is often disturbed and sometimes destroyed. This assembly has hardly a year's prescription. We have their own word for it that they have made a revolution. To make a revolution is a measure which, *prima fronte*, requires an apology. To make a revolution is to subvert the antient state of our country; and no common reasons are called for to justify so violent a proceeding. The sense of mankind authorizes us to examine into the mode of acquiring new power, and to criticise on the use that is made of it with less awe and reverence than that which is usually conceded to a settled and recognized authority.

In obtaining and securing their power, the assembly proceeds upon principles the most opposite from those which appear to direct them in the use of it. An observation on this difference will let us into the true spirit of their conduct. Every thing which they have done, or continue to do, in order to obtain and keep their power, is by the most common arts. They proceed exactly as their ancestors of ambition have done before them. Trace them through all their artifices, frauds, and violences, you can find nothing at all that is new. They follow precedents and examples with the punctilious exactness of a pleader. They never depart an iota from the authentic formulas of tyranny and usurpation. But in all the regulations relative to the public good, the spirit has been the very reverse of this. There they commit the whole to the mercy of untried speculations; they abandon the dearest interests of the public to those loose theories, to which none of them would chuse to trust the slightest of his private concerns. They make this difference, because in their desire of obtaining and securing power they are thoroughly in earnest; there they travel in the beaten road. The public interests, because about them they have no real solicitude, they abandon wholly to chance; I say to chance, because their schemes have nothing in experience to prove their tendency beneficial.

We must always see with a pity not unmixed with respect, the errors of those who are timid and doubtful of themselves with regard to points wherein the happiness of mankind is concerned. But in these gentlemen there is nothing of the tender parental solicitude which fears to cut up the infant for the sake of an experiment. In the vastness of their promises, and the confidence of their predictions, they far outdo all the boasting of empirics. The arrogance of their pretensions, in a manner provokes, and challenges us to an enquiry into their foundation.

I am convinced that there are men of considerable parts among the popular leaders in the national assembly. Some of them display eloquence in their speeches and their writings. This cannot be without powerful and cultivated talents. But eloquence may exist without a proportionable degree of wisdom. When I speak of ability, I am obliged to distinguish. What they have done towards the support of their system bespeaks no ordinary men. In the system itself, taken as the scheme of a republic constructed for procuring the prosperity and security of the citizen, and for promoting the strength and grandeur of the state, I confess myself unable to find out any thing which displays, in a single instance, the work of a comprehensive and disposing mind, or even the provisions of a vulgar prudence. Their purpose every where seems to have been to evade and slip aside from *difficulty*. This it has been the glory of the great masters in all the arts to confront, and to overcome; and when they had overcome the first difficulty, to turn it into an instrument for new conquests over new difficulties; thus to enable them to extend the empire of their science; and even to push forward beyond the reach of their original thoughts, the land marks of the human understanding itself. Difficulty is a severe instructor, set over us by the supreme ordinance of a parental guardian and legislator, who knows us better than we know ourselves, as he loves us better too. *Pater ipse colendi haud facilem esse viam voluit.*[1] He that wrestles with us strengthens our nerves, and sharpens our skill. Our antagonist is our helper. This amicable conflict with difficulty obliges us to an intimate acquaintance with our object, and compels us to consider it in all its relations. It will not suffer us to be superficial. It is the want of nerves of understanding for such a task; it is the degenerate fondness for tricking short-cuts, and little fallacious facilities, that has in so many parts of the world created governments with arbitrary powers. They have created the late arbitrary monarchy of France. They have created the arbitrary republic of Paris. With them defects in wisdom are to be supplied by the plenitude of force. They get nothing by it. Commencing their labours on a principle of sloth, they have the common fortune of slothful men. The difficulties which they rather had eluded than escaped, meet them again in their course; they multiply and thicken on them; they are involved, through a labyrinth of confused detail, in an industry

---

1   "The great Father himself willed it, that the ways of farming should not be easy." Virgil, *Georgics*, Book I, 121–22.

without limit, and without direction; and, in conclusion, the whole of their work becomes feeble, vitious, and insecure.

It is this inability to wrestle with difficulty which has obliged the arbitrary assembly of France to commence their schemes of reform with abolition and total destruction.[1] But is it in destroying and pulling down that skill is displayed? Your mob can do this as well at least as your assemblies. The shallowest understanding, the rudest hand, is more than equal to that task. Rage and phrenzy will pull down more in half an hour, than prudence, deliberation, and foresight can build up in an hundred years. The errors and defects of old establishments are visible and palpable. It calls for little ability to point them out; and where absolute power is given, it requires but a word wholly to abolish the vice and the establishment together. The same lazy but restless disposition, which loves sloth and hates quiet, directs these politicians, when they come to work, for supplying the place of what they have destroyed. To make every thing the reverse of what they have seen is quite as easy as to destroy. No difficulties occur in what has never been tried. Criticism is almost baffled in discovering the defects of what has not existed; and eager enthusiasm, and cheating hope, have all the wide field of imagination in which they may expatiate with little or no opposition.

At once to preserve and to reform is quite another thing. When the useful parts of an old establishment are kept, and what

---

1   [Burke's note:] A leading member of the assembly, M. Rabaud de St. Etienne [1743–93], has expressed the principle of all their proceedings as clearly as possible. Nothing can be more simple:—*"Tous les établissemens en France couronnent le malheur du peuple: pour le rendre heureux il faut le renouveler; changer ses idées; changer ses loix; changer ses moeurs; ... changer les hommes; changer les choses; changer les mots ... tout détruire; oui, tout détruire; puisque tout est à recréer."* ["All the institutions in France crown the unhappiness of the people: to make them happy they must be renewed; their ideas changed; their laws changed; their manners changed ... men changed; things changed; words changed ... destroy everything; yes, destroy everything; since everything is to be recreated."] This gentleman was chosen president in an assembly not sitting at the *Quinze vingt*, or the *Petites Maisons*; and composed of persons giving themselves out to be rational beings; but neither his ideas, language, or conduct, differ in the smallest degree from the discourses, opinions, and actions of those within and without the assembly, who direct the operations of the machine now at work in France.

is superadded is to be fitted to what is retained, a vigorous mind, steady persevering attention, various powers of comparison and combination, and the resources of an understanding fruitful in expedients are to be exercised; they are to be exercised in a continued conflict with the combined force of opposite vices; with the obstinacy that rejects all improvement, and the levity that is fatigued and disgusted with every thing of which it is in possession. But you may object—"A process of this kind is slow. It is not fit for an assembly, which glories in performing in a few months the work of ages. Such a mode of reforming, possibly might take up many years." Without question it might; and it ought. It is one of the excellencies of a method in which time is amongst the assistants, that its operation is slow, and in some cases almost imperceptible. If circumspection and caution are a part of wisdom, when we work only upon inanimate matter, surely they become a part of duty too, when the subject of our demolition and construction is not brick and timber, but sentient beings, by the sudden alteration of whose state, condition, and habits, multitudes may be rendered miserable. But it seems as if it were the prevalent opinion in Paris, that an unfeeling heart, and an undoubting confidence, are the sole qualifications for a perfect legislator. Far different are my ideas of that high office. The true lawgiver ought to have an heart full of sensibility. He ought to love and respect his kind, and to fear himself. It may be allowed to his temperament to catch his ultimate object with an intuitive glance; but his movements towards it ought to be deliberate. Political arrangement, as it is a work for social ends, is to be only wrought by social means. There mind must conspire with mind. Time is required to produce that union of minds which alone can produce all the good we aim at. Our patience will atchieve more than our force. If I might venture to appeal to what is so much out of fashion in Paris, I mean to experience, I should tell you, that in my course I have known, and, according to my measure, have co-operated with great men; and I have never yet seen any plan which has not been mended by the observations of those who were much inferior in understanding to the person who took the lead in the business. By a slow but well-sustained progress, the effect of each step is watched; the good or ill success of the first, gives light to us in the second; and so, from light to light, we are conducted with safety through the whole series. We see, that the parts of the system do not clash. The evils latent in the most promising contrivances are provided for as they arise. One advantage is as little as possible sacrificed to another. We compensate, we reconcile, we balance. We are enabled to unite into a consistent whole the various anomalies and contending principles that are found in the minds and affairs of men. From hence arises, not an excellence in simplicity, but one far superior, an excellence in composition. Where the great interests of mankind are concerned through a long succession of generations, that succession ought to be admitted into some share in the councils which are so deeply to affect them. If justice requires this, the work itself requires the aid of more minds than one age can furnish. It is from this view of things that the best legislators have been often satisfied with the establishment of some sure, solid, and ruling principle in government; a power like that which some of the philosophers have called a plastic nature; and having fixed the principle, they have left it afterwards to its own operation.

To proceed in this manner, that is, to proceed with a presiding principle, and a prolific energy, is with me the criterion of profound wisdom. What your politicians think the marks of a bold, hardy genius, are only proofs of a deplorable want of ability. By their violent haste, and their defiance of the process of nature, they are delivered over blindly to every projector and adventurer, to every alchymist and empiric. They despair of turning to account any thing that is common. Diet is nothing in their system of remedy. The worst of it is, that this their despair of curing common distempers by regular methods, arises not only from defect of comprehension, but, I fear, from some malignity of disposition. Your legislators seem to have taken their opinions of all professions, ranks, and offices, from the declamations and buffooneries of satirists; who would themselves be astonished if they were held to the letter of their own descriptions. By listening only to these, your leaders regard all things only on the side of their vices and faults, and view those vices and faults under every colour of exaggeration. It is undoubtedly true, though it may seem paradoxical; but in general, those who are habitually employed in finding and displaying faults, are unqualified for the work of reformation: because their minds are not only unfurnished with patterns of the fair and good, but by habit they come to take no delight in the contemplation of those things. By hating vices too much, they come to love men too little. It is therefore not wonderful, that they should be indisposed and unable to serve them. From hence arises the complexional disposition of some of your guides to pull every thing in pieces. At this malicious game they display the whole of their *quadrima-nous*[1] activity. As to the rest, the paradoxes of eloquent writers, brought forth purely as a sport of fancy, to try their talents, to rouze attention, and excite surprize, are taken up by these gentlemen, not in the spirit of the original authors, as means of cultivating their taste and improving their style. These paradoxes become with them serious grounds of action, upon which they proceed in regulating the most important concerns of the state. Cicero ludicrously describes Cato as endeavouring to act in the commonwealth upon the school paradoxes which exercised the wits of the junior students in the stoic philosophy. If this was true of Cato, these gentlemen copy after him in the manner of some persons who lived about his time—*pede nudo Catonem.*[2] Mr. Hume[3] told me, that he had from Rousseau himself the secret of his principles of composition. That acute, though eccentric, observer had perceived, that to strike and interest the public, the marvellous must be produced; that the marvellous of the heathen mythology had long since lost its effect; that giants, magicians, fairies, and heroes of romance which succeeded, had exhausted the portion of credulity which belonged to their age; that now nothing was left to a writer but that species of the marvellous, which might still be produced, and with as great an effect as ever, though in another way; that is, the marvellous in life, in manners, in characters, and in extraordinary situations, giving rise to new and unlooked-for strokes in politics and morals. I believe, that were Rousseau alive, and in one of his lucid intervals, he would be shocked at the practical phrenzy of his scholars, who in their paradoxes are servile imitators; and even in their incredulity discover an implicit faith.

Men who undertake considerable things, even in a regular way, ought to give us ground to presume ability. But the physician of the state, who, not satisfied with the cure of distempers, undertakes to regenerate constitutions, ought to shew uncommon powers. Some very unusual appearances of wisdom ought to display themselves on the face of the designs of those who appeal to no practice, and who copy after no model. Has any

---

1　Having all four feet adapted to function as hands, like a monkey.
2　"With the bare feet of Cato." From a line in Horace, *Epistles*, Book I, xix, 12–14: "If someone looks fierce and goes round with bare feet and poor clothes to be like Cato, does he really display the virtue and morality of Cato?"
3　David Hume (1711–76), Scottish philosopher and historian.

such been manifested? I shall take a view (it shall for the subject be a very short one) of what the assembly has done....

It is in the model of the sovereign and presiding part of this new republic, that we should expect their grand display. Here they were to prove their title to their proud demands. For the plan itself at large, and for the reasons on which it is grounded, I refer to the journals of the assembly of the 29th of September 1789, and to the subsequent proceedings which have made any alterations in the plan. So far as in a matter somewhat confused I can see light, the system remains substantially as it has been originally framed. My few remarks will be such as regard its spirit, its tendency, and its fitness for framing a popular commonwealth, which they profess theirs to be, suited to the ends for which any commonwealth, and particularly such a commonwealth, is made. At the same time, I mean to consider its consistency with itself, and its own principles.

Old establishments are tried by their effects. If the people are happy, united, wealthy, and powerful, we presume the rest. We conclude that to be good from whence good is derived. In old establishments various correctives have been found for their aberrations from theory. Indeed they are the results of various necessities and expediences. They are not often constructed after any theory; theories are rather drawn from them. In them we often see the end best obtained, where the means seem not perfectly reconcileable to what we may fancy was the original scheme. The means taught by experience may be better suited to political ends than those contrived in the original project. They again re-act upon the primitive constitution, and sometimes improve the design itself from which they seem to have departed. I think all this might be curiously exemplified in the British constitution. At worst, the errors and deviations of every kind in reckoning are found and computed, and the ship proceeds in her course. This is the case of old establishments; but in a new and merely theoretic system, it is expected that every contrivance shall appear, on the face of it, to answer its end; especially where the projectors are no way embarrassed with an endeavour to accommodate the new building to an old one, either in the walls or on the foundations.

The French builders, clearing away as mere rubbish whatever they found, and, like their ornamental gardeners, forming every thing into an exact level, propose to rest the whole local and general legislature on three bases of three different kinds; one geometrical, one arithmetical, and the third financial; the first of which they call the *basis of territory*; the second, the *basis of population*; and the third, the *basis of contribution*. For the accomplishment of the first of these purposes they divide the area of their country into eighty-three pieces, regularly square, of eighteen leagues by eighteen. These large divisions are called *Departments*. These they portion, proceeding by square measurement, into seventeen hundred and twenty districts called *Communes*. These again they subdivide, still proceeding by square measurement, into smaller districts called *Cantons*, making in all 6,400.

At first view this geometrical basis of theirs presents not much to admire or to blame. It calls for no legislative talents. Nothing more than an accurate land surveyor, with his chain, sight, and theodolite, is requisite for such a plan as this....

It is impossible not to observe, that in the spirit of this geometrical distribution, and arithmetical arrangement, these pretended citizens treat France exactly like a country of conquest. Acting as conquerors, they have imitated the policy of the harshest of that harsh race. The policy of such barbarous victors, who contemn a subdued people, and insult their feelings, has ever been, as much as in them lay, to destroy all vestiges of the antient country, in religion, in polity, in laws, and in manners; to confound all territorial limits; to produce a general poverty; to put up their properties to auction; to crush their princes, nobles, and pontiffs; to lay low every thing which had lifted its head above the level, or which could serve to combine or rally, in their distresses, the disbanded people, under the standard of old opinion....

... It is boasted, that the geometrical policy has been adopted, that all local ideas should be sunk, and that the people should be no longer Gascons, Picards, Bretons, Normans, but Frenchmen, with one country, one heart, and one assembly. But instead of being all Frenchmen, the greater likelihood is, that the inhabitants of that region will shortly have no country. No man ever was attached by a sense of pride, partiality, or real affection, to a description of square measurement. He never will glory in belonging to the Checquer, N° 71, or to any other badge-ticket. We begin our public affections in our families. No cold relation is a zealous citizen. We pass on to our neighbourhoods, and our habitual provincial connections. These are inns and resting-places. Such divisions of our country as have been formed by habit, and not by a sudden jerk of authority, were so many little images of the great country in which the heart found something which it could fill. The love to the whole is not extinguished by this subordinate partiality. Perhaps it is a sort of elemental training to those higher and more large regards, by which alone men come to be affected, as with their own concern, in the prosperity of a kingdom so extensive as that of France. In that general territory itself, as in the old name of provinces, the citizens are interested from old prejudices and unreasoned habits, and not on account of the geometric properties of its figure....

Has more wisdom been displayed in the constitution of your army ...? ...

The minister and secretary of state for the war department is M. de la Tour du Pin.[1] This gentleman, like his colleagues in administration, is a most zealous assertor of the revolution, and a sanguine admirer of the new constitution, which originated in that event. His statement of facts, relative to the military of France, is important, not only from his official and personal authority, but because it displays very clearly the actual condition of the army in France, and because it throws light on the principles upon which the assembly proceeds in the administration of this critical object. It may enable us to form some judgment how far it may be expedient in this country to imitate the martial policy of France.

M. de la Tour du Pin, on the 4th of last June, comes to give an account of the state of his department, as it exists under the auspices of the national assembly. No man knows it so well; no man can express it better. Addressing himself to the National Assembly, he says, "His Majesty has *this day* sent me to apprize you of the multiplied disorders of which *every day* he receives the most distressing intelligence. The army (le corps militaire) threatens to fall into the most turbulent anarchy. Entire regiments have dared to violate at once the respect due to the laws, to the King, to the order established by your decrees, and to the oaths which they have taken with the most awful solemnity. Compelled by my duty to give you information of these excesses, my heart bleeds when I consider who they are that have committed them. Those, against whom it is not in my power to withhold the most grievous complaints, are a part of that very soldiery which to this day have been so full of honour and loyalty, and with whom, for fifty years, I have lived the comrade and the friend.

"What incomprehensible spirit of delirium and delusion has all at once led them astray? Whilst you are indefatigable in

---

1 Jean-Frédéric de La Tour du Pin Gouvernet (1727–94), Minister of War from August 1789 until November 1790, guillotined in 1794.

establishing uniformity in the empire, and moulding the whole into one coherent and consistent body; whilst the French are taught by you, at once the respect which the laws owe to the rights of man, and that which the citizens owe to the laws, the administration of the army presents nothing but disturbance and confusion. I see in more than one corps the bonds of discipline relaxed or broken; the most unheard-of pretensions avowed directly and without any disguise; the ordinances without force; the chiefs without authority; the military chest and the colours carried off; the authority of the King himself [*risum teneatis*][1] proudly defied; the officers despised, degraded, threatened, driven away, and some of them prisoners in the midst of their corps, dragging on a precarious life in the bosom of disgust and humiliation. To fill up the measure of all these horrors, the commandants of places have had their throats cut, under the eyes, and almost in the arms of their own soldiers.

"These evils are great; but they are not the worst consequences which may be produced by such military insurrections. Sooner or later they may menace the nation itself. *The nature of things requires*, that the army should never act but as *an instrument*. The moment that, erecting itself into a deliberative body, it shall act according to its own resolutions, the *government, be it what it may, will immediately degenerate into a military democracy*; a species of political monster, which has always ended by devouring those who have produced it.

"After all this, who must not be alarmed at the irregular consultations, and turbulent committees, formed in some regiments by the common soldiers and non-commissioned officers, without the knowledge, or even in contempt of the authority of their superiors; although the presence and concurrence of those superiors could give no authority to such monstrous democratic assemblies [comices]." ...

I cannot help pausing here for a moment, to reflect upon the expressions of surprise which this Minister has let fall, relative to the excesses he relates. To him the departure of the troops from their antient principles of loyalty and honour seems quite inconceivable. Surely those to whom he addresses himself know the causes of it but too well. They know the doctrines which they have preached, the decrees which they have passed, the practices which they have countenanced. The soldiers remember the 6th of

---

1 "Can you help but laugh?" (Burke inserted this sardonic parenthetical remark).

October. They recollect the French guards. They have not forgot the taking of the King's castles in Paris, and at Marseilles. That the governors in both places, were murdered with impunity, is a fact that has not passed out of their minds. They do not abandon the principles laid down so ostentatiously and laboriously of the equality of men. They cannot shut their eyes to the degradation of the whole noblesse of France; and the suppression of the very idea of a gentleman. The total abolition of titles and distinctions is not lost upon them. But Mr. du Pin is astonished at their disloyalty, when the doctors of the assembly have taught them at the same time the respect due to laws. It is easy to judge which of the two sorts of lessons men with arms in their hands are likely to learn. As to the authority of the King, we may collect from the minister himself (if any argument on that head were not quite superfluous) that it is not of more consideration with these troops, than it is with every body else. "The King," says he, "has over and over again repeated his orders to put a stop to these excesses: but, in so terrible a crisis *your* [the assembly's] concurrence is become indispensably necessary to prevent the evils which menace the state. *You* unite to the force of the legislative power, *that of opinion* still more important." To be sure the army can have no opinion of the power or authority of the king. Perhaps the soldier has by this time learned, that the assembly itself does not enjoy a much greater degree of liberty than that royal figure.

It is now to be seen what has been proposed in this exigency, one of the greatest that can happen in a state. The Minister requests the assembly to array itself in all its terrors, and to call forth all its majesty. He desires that the grave and severe principles announced by them may give vigour to the King's proclamation. After this we should have looked for courts civil and martial; breaking of some corps, decimating others, and all the terrible means which necessity has employed in such cases to arrest the progress of the most terrible of all evils; particularly, one might expect, that a serious inquiry would be made into the murder of commandants in the view of their soldiers. Not one word of all this, or of any thing like it. After they had been told that the soldiery trampled upon the decrees of the assembly promulgated by the King, the assembly pass new decrees; and they authorise the King to make new proclamations. After the Secretary at War had stated that the regiments had paid no regard to oaths *prêtés avec la plus imposante solemnité*[1]—they propose—

---

1 "Sworn with the most imposing solemnity."

what? More oaths. They renew decrees and proclamations as they experience their insufficiency, and they multiply oaths in proportion as they weaken, in the minds of men, the sanctions of religion. I hope that handy abridgments of the excellent sermons of Voltaire, d'Alembert, Diderot, and Helvetius, on the Immortality of the Soul, on a particular superintending Providence, and on a Future State of Rewards and Punishments, are sent down to the soldiers along with their civic oaths.[1] Of this I have no doubt; as I understand, that a certain description of reading makes no inconsiderable part of their military exercises, and that they are full as well supplied with the ammunition of pamphlets as of cartridges....

What you may do finally, does not appear; nor is it of much moment, whilst the strange and contradictory relation between your army and all the parts of your republic, as well as the puzzled relation of those parts to each other and to the whole, remain as they are. You seem to have given the provisional nomination of the officers, in the first instance, to the king, with a reserve of approbation by the National Assembly. Men who have an interest to pursue are extremely sagacious in discovering the true seat of power. They must soon perceive that those who can negative indefinitely, in reality appoint. The officers must therefore look to their intrigues in that assembly, as the sole certain road to promotion. Still, however, by your new constitution they must begin their solicitation at court. This double negotiation for military rank seems to me a contrivance as well adapted, as if it were studied for no other end, to promote faction in the assembly itself, relative to this vast military patronage; and then to poison the corps of officers with factions of a nature still more dangerous to the safety of government, upon any bottom on which it can be placed, and destructive in the end to the efficiency of the army itself. Those officers, who lose the promotions intended for them by the crown, must become of a faction opposite to that of the assembly which has rejected their claims, and must nourish discontents in the heart of the army against the ruling powers. Those officers, on the other hand, who, by carrying their point through an interest in the assembly, feel themselves to be

---

1 A sentence dripping with sarcasm: the fashionable works of the French philosophers Voltaire (1694–1778), Jean-Baptiste le Rond d'Alembert (1717–83), Denis Diderot (1713–84), and Claude Adrien Helvetius (1715–71) had cast doubt on an afterlife and had accordingly weakened "the sanctions of religion."

at best only second in the good-will of the crown, though first in that of the assembly, must slight an authority which would not advance, and could not retard their promotion. If to avoid these evils you will have no other rule for command or promotion than seniority, you will have an army of formality; at the same time it will become more independent, and more of a military republic. Not they but the king is the machine. A king is not to be deposed by halves. If he is not every thing in the command of an army, he is nothing. What is the effect of a power placed nominally at the head of the army, who to that army is no object of gratitude, or of fear? Such a cypher is not fit for the administration of an object, of all things the most delicate, the supreme command of military men. They must be constrained (and their inclinations lead them to what their necessities require) by a real, vigorous, effective, decided, personal authority. The authority of the assembly itself suffers by passing through such a debilitating channel as they have chosen. The army will not long look to an assembly acting through the organ of false shew, and palpable imposition. They will not seriously yield obedience to a prisoner. They will either despise a pageant, or they will pity a captive king. The relation of your army to the crown will, if I am not greatly mistaken, become a serious dilemma in your politics.

It is besides to be considered, whether an assembly like yours, even supposing that it was in possession of another sort of organ through which its orders were to pass, is fit for promoting the obedience and discipline of an army. It is known, that armies have hitherto yielded a very precarious and uncertain obedience to any senate, or popular authority; and they will least of all yield it to an assembly which is to have only a continuance of two years.[1] The officers must totally lose the characteristic disposition of military men, if they see with perfect submission and due admiration, the dominion of pleaders; especially when they find, that they have a new court to pay to an endless succession of those pleaders, whose military policy, and the genius of whose command (if they should have any) must be as uncertain as their duration is transient. In the weakness of one kind of authority, and in the fluctuation of all, the officers of an army will remain

---

1 Burke was highly critical of the term limits set for assembly members: "Every man who has served in an assembly is ineligible for two years after. Just as these magistrates begin to learn their trade, like chimney-sweepers, they are disqualified for exercising it." *Reflections* 278–79.

for some time mutinous and full of faction, until some popular general, who understands the art of conciliating the soldiery, and who possesses the true spirit of command, shall draw the eyes of all men upon himself. Armies will obey him on his personal account. There is no other way of securing military obedience in this state of things. But the moment in which that event shall happen, the person who really commands the army is your master; the master (that is little) of your king, the master of your assembly, the master of your whole republic.[1]

How came the assembly by their present power over the army? Chiefly, to be sure, by debauching the soldiers from their officers. They have begun by a most terrible operation. They have touched the central point, about which the particles that compose armies are at repose. They have destroyed the principle of obedience in the great essential critical link between the officer and the soldier, just where the chain of military subordination commences, and on which the whole of that system depends. The soldier is told, he is a citizen, and has the rights of man and citizen. The right of a man, he is told, is to be his own governor, and to be ruled only by those to whom he delegates that self-government. It is very natural he should think, that he ought most of all to have his choice where he is to yield the greatest degree of obedience. He will therefore, in all probability, systematically do, what he does at present occasionally; that is, he will exercise at least a negative in the choice of his officers. At present the officers are known at best to be only permissive, and on their good behaviour. In fact, there have been many instances in which they have been cashiered by their corps. Here is a second negative on the choice of the king; a negative as effectual at least as the other of the assembly. The soldiers know already that it has been a question, not ill received in the national assembly, whether they ought not to have the direct choice of their officers, or some proportion of them? When such matters are in deliberation, it is no extravagant supposition that they will incline to the opinion most favourable to their pretensions. They will not bear to be deemed the army of an imprisoned king, whilst another army in the same country, with whom too they are to feast and confederate, is to be considered as the free army of a free constitution. They will cast their eyes on the other and

---

1 This most famous of Burke's prognostications came to pass on 9 November 1799, when the coup of the 18th Brumaire brought Napoleon Bonaparte (1769–1821) to power.

more permanent army; I mean the municipal. That corps, they well know, does actually elect its own officers. They may not be able to discern the grounds of distinction on which they are not to elect a Marquis de la Fayette (or what is his new name?)[1] of their own. If this election of a commander in chief be a part of the rights of men, why not of theirs? They see elective justices of peace, elective judges, elective curates, elective bishops, elective municipalities, and elective commanders of the Parisian army.—Why should they alone be excluded? Are the brave troops of France the only men in that nation who are not the fit judges of military merit, and of the qualifications necessary for a commander in chief? Are they paid by the state, and do they therefore lose the rights of men? They are a part of that nation themselves, and contribute to that pay. And is not the king, is not the national assembly, and are not all who elect the national assembly, likewise paid? Instead of seeing all these forfeit their rights by their receiving a salary, they perceive that in all these cases a salary is given for the exercise of those rights. All your resolutions, all your proceedings, all your debates, all the works of your doctors in religion and politics, have industriously been put into their hands; and you expect that they will apply to their own case just as much of your doctrines and examples as suits your pleasure.

Every thing depends upon the army in such a government as yours; for you have industriously destroyed all the opinions, and prejudices, and, as far as in you lay, all the instincts which support government. Therefore the moment any difference arises between your national assembly and any part of the nation, you must have recourse to force. Nothing else is left to you; or rather you have left nothing else to yourselves. You see by the report of your war minister, that the distribution of the army is in a

---

1 Marie-Joseph Paul Yves Roch Gilbert du Motier, Marquis de La Fayette (1757–1834), fought against the British in the American War of Independence and became commander of France's National Guard from 1789 until 1791. Denounced by the National Assembly in 1792, he fled to Austria, returning to France in 1797 and remaining an active figure in French political life until his death in 1834. Burke is having fun with the name of the Marquis here: when, on 20 June 1790, the National Assembly abolished hereditary titles, La Fayette's elaborate and high-flown name would properly have been reduced to the very plain Monsieur Motier.

great measure made with a view of internal coercion.[1] You must rule by an army; and you have infused into that army by which you rule, as well as into the whole body of the nation, principles which after a time must disable you in the use you resolve to make of it. The king is to call out troops to act against his people, when the world has been told, and the assertion is still ringing in our ears, that troops ought not to fire on citizens. The colonies assert to themselves an independent constitution and a free trade. They must be constrained by troops. In what chapter of your code of the rights of men are they able to read, that it is a part of the rights of men to have their commerce monopolized and restrained for the benefit of others. As the colonists rise on you, the negroes rise on them. Troops again—Massacre, torture, hanging! These are your rights of men! These are the fruits of metaphysic declarations wantonly made, and shamefully retracted![2] ...

... The assembly keep a school where, systematically, and with unremitting perseverance, they teach principles, and form regulations destructive to all spirit of subordination, civil and military—and then they expect that they shall hold in obedience an anarchic people by an anarchic army....

The effects of the incapacity shewn by the popular leaders in all the great members of the commonwealth are to be covered with the "all-atoning name" of liberty. In some people I see great liberty indeed; in many, if not in the most, an oppressive degrading servitude. But what is liberty without wisdom, and without virtue? It is the greatest of all possible evils; for it is folly, vice, and madness, without tuition or restraint. Those who know what virtuous liberty is, cannot bear to see it disgraced by incapable heads, on account of their having high-sounding words in their mouths. Grand, swelling sentiments of liberty, I am sure I do not despise. They warm the heart; they enlarge and liberalise our minds; they animate our courage in a time of conflict. Old as I am, I read the fine raptures of Lucan and Corneille[3] with pleasure. Neither do I wholly condemn the little arts and devices of popularity. They facilitate the carrying

---

1 [Burke's note:] Courier François, 30 July, 1790. Assemblée Nationale, Numero 210.

2 This passage refers to agitations in France's colonial possessions in the West Indies.

3 Marcus Annaeus Lucanus (AD 39–65), Roman poet; Pierre Corneille (1606–84), French dramatist.

of many points of moment; they keep the people together; they refresh the mind in its exertions; and they diffuse occasional gaiety over the severe brow of moral freedom. Every politician ought to sacrifice to the graces; and to join compliance with reason. But in such an undertaking as that in France, all these subsidiary sentiments and artifices are of little avail. To make a government requires no great prudence. Settle the seat of power; teach obedience: and the work is done. To give freedom is still more easy. It is not necessary to guide; it only requires to let go the rein. But to form a *free government*; that is, to temper together these opposite elements of liberty and restraint in one consistent work, requires much thought, deep reflection, a sagacious, powerful, and combining mind. This I do not find in those who take the lead in the national assembly. Perhaps they are not so miserably deficient as they appear. I rather believe it. It would put them below the common level of human understanding. But when the leaders choose to make themselves bidders at an auction of popularity, their talents, in the construction of the state, will be of no service. They will become flatterers instead of legislators; the instruments, not the guides of the people. If any of them should happen to propose a scheme of liberty, soberly limited, and defined with proper qualifications, he will be immediately outbid by his competitors, who will produce something more splendidly popular. Suspicions will be raised of his fidelity to his cause. Moderation will be stigmatized as the virtue of cowards; and compromise as the prudence of traitors; until, in hopes of preserving the credit which may enable him to temper and moderate on some occasions, the popular leader is obliged to become active in propagating doctrines, and establishing powers, that will afterwards defeat any sober purpose at which he ultimately might have aimed.

But am I so unreasonable as to see nothing at all that deserves commendation in the indefatigable labours of this assembly? I do not deny that among an infinite number of acts of violence and folly, some good may have been done. They who destroy every thing certainly will remove some grievance. They who make every thing new, have a chance that they may establish something beneficial. To give them credit for what they have done in virtue of the authority they have usurped, or which can excuse them in the crimes by which that authority has been acquired, it must appear, that the same things could not have been accomplished without producing such a revolution. Most assuredly they might; because almost every one of the regulations made by them, which is not very equivocal, was either in the cession of the king, voluntarily made at the meeting of the states, or in the concurrent instructions to the orders. Some usages have been abolished on just grounds; but they were such that if they had stood as they were to all eternity, they would little detract from the happiness and prosperity of any state. The improvements of the national assembly are superficial, their errors fundamental.

Whatever they are, I wish my countrymen rather to recommend to our neighbours the example of the British constitution, than to take models from them for the improvement of our own. In the former they have got an invaluable treasure. They are not, I think, without some causes of apprehension and complaint; but these they do not owe to their constitution, but to their own conduct. I think our happy situation owing to our constitution; but owing to the whole of it, and not to any part singly; owing in a great measure to what we have left standing in our several reviews and reformations, as well as to what we have altered or superadded. Our people will find employment enough for a truly patriotic, free, and independent spirit, in guarding what they possess, from violation. I would not exclude alteration neither; but even when I changed, it should be to preserve. I should be led to my remedy by a great grievance. In what I did, I should follow the example of our ancestors. I would make the reparation as nearly as possible in the style of the building. A politic caution, a guarded circumspection, a moral rather than a complexional timidity were among the ruling principles of our forefathers in their most decided conduct. Not being illuminated with the light of which the gentlemen of France tell us they have got so abundant a share, they acted under a strong impression of the ignorance and fallibility of mankind. He that had made them thus fallible, rewarded them for having in their conduct attended to their nature. Let us imitate their caution, if we wish to deserve their fortune, or to retain their bequests. Let us add, if we please, but let us preserve what they have left; and, standing on the firm ground of the British constitution, let us be satisfied to admire rather than attempt to follow in their desperate flights the aëronauts of France.

I have told you candidly my sentiments. I think they are not likely to alter yours. I do not know that they ought. You are young; you cannot guide, but must follow the fortune of your country. But hereafter they may be of some use to you, in some future form which your commonwealth may take. In the present it can hardly remain; but before its final settlement it may be obliged to pass, as one of our poets says, "through great varieties of untried being,"[1] and in all its transmigrations to be purified by fire and blood.

I have little to recommend my opinions, but long observation and much impartiality. They come from one who has been no tool of power, no flatterer of greatness; and who in his last acts does not wish to belye the tenour of his life. They come from one, almost the whole of whose public exertion has been a struggle for the liberty of others; from one in whose breast no anger durable or vehement has ever been kindled, but by what he considered as tyranny; and who snatches from his share in the endeavours which are used by good men to discredit opulent oppression, the hours he has employed on your affairs; and who in so doing persuades himself he has not departed from his usual office: they come from one who desires honours, distinctions, and emoluments, but little; and who expects them not at all; who has no contempt for fame, and no fear of obloquy; who shuns contention, though he will hazard an opinion: from one who wishes to preserve consistency; but who would preserve consistency by varying his means to secure the unity of his end; and, when the equipoise of the vessel in which he sails, may be endangered by overloading it upon one side, is desirous of carrying the small weight of his reasons to that which may preserve its equipoise.

F I N I S .

---

1   Joseph Addison (1672–1719), *Cato*, 5.1.11: "Eternity! thou pleasing, dreadful thought! / Through what variety of untried being, / Through what new scenes and changes must we pass!"

Appendix A: Background Materials

[The background materials assembled in this appendix are of two kinds. Four of the selections present material explicitly discussed by Burke in *Reflections on the Revolution in France*: The Bill of Rights of 1689 (A2); the National Assembly's "Declaration of the Rights of Man and of Citizens" (A4); selections from *A Discourse on the Love of Our Country* by Richard Price (1723–91) (A5); and the "Congratulatory Address from the Revolution Society to the National Assembly of France" (A6). The two remaining selections aim to illuminate aspects of Burke's political thinking and are discussed in the introduction to this edition. First, some brief selections are extracted from *The Character of a Trimmer* (A1), a political pamphlet written by Sir George Savile, Marquis of Halifax (1633–95): Halifax's thinking, and his maritime imagery, bears fruitful comparison both with the closing paragraph of the *Reflections* and with Burke's overall desire in politics to emphasize "the middle." The selections drawn from Burke's *Philosophical Enquiry into the Origin of Our Ideas of the Sublime and Beautiful* (A3) are intended to throw light on the difference between the smooth, non-revolutionary politics of the English and the jolting, terrifying politics of the revolutionary French.]

1. From Sir George Savile, Marquis of Halifax, *The Character of a Trimmer* (1688), *Miscellanies by the Right Noble Lord, the Late Lord Marquis of Halifax* (W. Rogers, 1704), 87–89, 187

It must be more than an ordinary provocation that can tempt a Man to write in an Age over-run with Scribblers, as *Egypt* was with Flies and Locusts: That worst Vermin of small Authors has given the World such a Surfeit, that instead of desiring to Write, a Man would be more inclin'd to wish, for his own ease, that he could not Read; but there are some things which do so raise our Passions, that our Reason can make no Resistance; and when Madmen, in two Extremes, shall agree to make common Sense Treason, and joyn to fix an ill Character upon the only Men in the Nation who deserve a good one; I am no longer Master of my better Resolution to let the World alone, and must break loose from my more reasonable Thoughts, to expose these false Coyners, who would make their Copper Wares pass upon us for good Payment.

Amongst all the Engines of Dissention, there has been none more powerfull in all Times, than the fixing Names upon one another of Contumely and Reproach, and the reason is plain, in respect of the People, who tho' generally they are uncapable of making a Syllogism, or forming an Argument, yet they can pronounce a word; and that serves their turn to throw it with their dull malice at the Head of those they do not like; such things ever begin in Jest, and end in Blood, and the same word which at first makes the Company merry, grows in time to a Military Signal to cut one another's Throat.

These Mistakes are to be lamented, tho' not easily cured, being suitable enough to the corrupted Nature of Mankind; but 'tis hard, that Men will not only invent ill Names, but they will wrest and misinterpret good ones; so afraid some are even of a reconciling sound, that they raise another noise to keep it from being heard, lest it should set up, and encourage a dangerous sort of Men, who prefer Peace and Agreement, before Violence and Confusion.

Were it not for this, why, after we have played the Fool with throwing *Whig* and *Tory* at one another, as Boys do Snow-Balls, do we grow angry at a new Name, which by its true signification might do as much to put us into our Wits, as the other has done to put us out of them?

This innocent word *Trimmer* signifies no more than this, That if Men are together in a Boat, and one part of the Company would weigh it down on one side, another would make it lean as much to the contrary; it happens there is a third Opinion of those, who conceive it would do as well, if the Boat went even, without endangering the Passengers; now 'tis hard to imagine by what Figure in Language, or by what Rule in Sense this comes to be a Fault, and it is much more a Wonder it should be thought a Heresy....

... Our *Trimmer* ... thinks fit to conclude with these assertions, That our Climate is a *Trimmer*, between that part of the World, where Men are Roasted, and the other where they are Frozen; That our Church is a *Trimmer* between the Phrenzy of Platonick Visions, and the Lethargick Ignorance of Popish Dreams; That our Laws are *Trimmers*, between the Excess of unbounded Power, and the Extravagance of Liberty not enough restrained; That true Virtue has ever been thought a *Trimmer*, and to have its dwelling in the middle between two Extreams;

That even God Almighty himself is divided between his two great Attributes, his Mercy and his Justice.

In such Company, our *Trimmer* is not ashamed of his Name, and willingly leaves to the bold Champions of either Extream, the honour of contending with no less Adversaries than Nature, Religion, Liberty, Prudence, Humanity and Common Sense.

2. The Bill of Rights (1689), *English Historical Documents 1660–1714*, edited by Andrew Browning (Oxford UP, 1953), 122–28

AN ACT DECLARING THE RIGHTS AND LIBERTIES OF THE SUBJECT AND SETTLING THE SUCCESSION OF THE CROWN
(1 Gul. & Mar. sess. 2, cap. 2)

Whereas the Lords Spiritual and Temporal and Commons assembled at Westminster, lawfully, fully and freely representing all the estates of the people of this realm, did upon the thirteenth day of February in the year of our Lord one thousand six hundred eighty-eight[1] present unto their Majesties, then called and known by the names and style of William and Mary, prince and princess of Orange, being present in their proper persons, a certain declaration in writing made by the said Lords and Commons in the words following, viz.:

Whereas the late King James the Second, by the assistance of divers evil counsellors, judges and ministers employed by him, did endeavour to subvert and extirpate the Protestant religion and the laws and liberties of this kingdom;

By assuming and exercising a power of dispensing with and suspending of laws and the execution of laws without consent of Parliament;

By committing and prosecuting divers worthy prelates for humbly petitioning to be excused concurring to the said assumed power;

By issuing and causing to be executed a commission under the great seal for erecting a court called the Court of Commissioners for Ecclesiastical Causes;

By levying money for and to the use of the Crown by pretence of prerogative for other time and in other manner than the same was granted by Parliament;

---

1 1688/89.

By raising and keeping a standing army within this kingdom in time of peace without consent of Parliament, and quartering soldiers contrary to law;

By causing several good subjects being Protestants to be disarmed at the same time when papists were both armed and employed contrary to law;

By violating the freedom of election of members to serve in Parliament;

By prosecutions in the Court of King's Bench for matters and causes cognizable only in Parliament, and by divers other arbitrary and illegal courses;

And whereas of late years partial, corrupt and unqualified persons have been returned and served on juries in trials, and particularly divers jurors in trials for high treason which were not freeholders;

And excessive bail hath been required of persons committed in criminal cases to elude the benefit of the laws made for the liberty of the subjects;

And excessive fines have been imposed;

And illegal and cruel punishments inflicted;

And several grants and promises made of fines and forfeitures before any conviction or judgment against the persons upon whom the same were to be levied;

All of which are utterly and directly contrary to the known laws and statutes and freedom of this realm;

And whereas the said late King James the Second having abdicated the government and the throne being thereby vacant, his Highness the prince of Orange (whom it hath pleased Almighty God to make the glorious instrument of delivering this kingdom from popery and arbitrary power) did (by the advice of the Lords Spiritual and Temporal and divers principal persons of the Commons) cause letters to be written to the Lords Spiritual and Temporal being Protestants, and other letters to the several counties, cities, universities, boroughs and cinque ports, for the choosing of such persons to represent them as were of right to be sent to Parliament, to meet and sit at Westminster upon the two and twentieth day of January in this year one thousand six hundred eighty and eight,[1] in order to such an establishment as that their religion, laws and liberties might not again be in danger of being subverted, upon which letters elections have been accordingly made;

---

1 1688/89.

And thereupon the said Lords Spiritual and Temporal and Commons, pursuant to their respective letters and elections, being now assembled in a full and free representative of this nation, taking into their most serious consideration the best means for attaining the ends aforesaid, do in the first place (as their ancestors in like case have usually done) for the vindicating and asserting their ancient rights and liberties declare

That the pretended power of suspending of laws or the execution of laws by regal authority without consent of Parliament is illegal;

That the pretended power of dispensing with laws or the execution of laws by regal authority, as it hath been assumed and exercised of late, is illegal;

That the commission for erecting the late Court of Commissioners for Ecclesiastical Causes, and all other commissions and courts of like nature, are illegal and pernicious;

That levying money for or to the use of the Crown by pretence of prerogative, without grant of Parliament, for longer time, or in other manner than the same is or shall be granted, is illegal;

That it is the right of the subjects to petition the king, and all commitments and prosecutions for such petitioning are illegal;

That the raising or keeping a standing army within the kingdom in time of peace, unless it be with consent of Parliament, is against law;

That the subjects which are Protestants may have arms for their defence suitable to their conditions and as allowed by law;

That election of members of Parliament ought to be free;

That the freedom of speech and debates or proceedings in Parliament ought not to be impeached or questioned in any court or place out of Parliament;

That excessive bail ought not to be required, nor excessive fines imposed, nor cruel and unusual punishments inflicted;

That jurors ought to be duly impanelled and returned, and jurors which pass upon men in trials of high treason ought to be freeholders;

That all grants and promises of fines and forfeitures of particular persons before conviction are illegal and void;

And that for redress of all grievances, and for the amending, strengthening and preserving of the laws, Parliaments ought to be held frequently.

And they do claim, demand and insist upon all and singular the premises as their undoubted rights and liberties, and that no declarations, judgments, doings or proceedings to the prejudice of the people in any of the said premises ought in any wise to be drawn hereafter into consequence or example; to which demand of their rights they are particularly encouraged by the declaration of his Highness the prince of Orange as being the only means for obtaining a full redress and remedy therein. Having therefore an entire confidence that his said Highness the prince of Orange will perfect the deliverance so far advanced by him, and will still preserve them from the violation of their rights which they have here asserted, and from all other attempts upon their religion, rights and liberties, the said Lords Spiritual and Temporal and Commons assembled at Westminster do resolve that William and Mary, prince and princess of Orange, be and be declared king and queen of England, France and Ireland and the dominions thereunto belonging, to hold the crown and royal dignity of the said kingdoms and dominions to them, the said prince and princess, during their lives and the life of the survivor of them, and that the sole and full exercise of the regal power be only in and executed by the said prince of Orange in the names of the said prince and princess during their joint lives, and after their deceases the said crown and royal dignity of the said kingdoms and dominions to be to the heirs of the body of the said princess, and for default of such issue to the Princess Anne of Denmark and the heirs of her body, and for default of such issue to the heirs of the body of the said prince of Orange. And the Lords Spiritual and Temporal and Commons do pray the said prince and princess to accept the same accordingly.

And that the oaths hereafter mentioned be taken by all persons of whom the oaths of allegiance and supremacy might be required by law, instead of them; and that the said oaths of allegiance and supremacy may be abrogated.

I, A.B., do sincerely promise and swear that I will be faithful and bear true allegiance to their Majesties King William and Queen Mary. So help me God.

I, A.B., do swear that I from my heart abhor, detest and abjure as impious and heretical this damnable doctrine and position, that princes excommunicated or deprived by the Pope or any authority of the see of Rome may be deposed or murdered by their subjects or any other whatsoever. And I do declare that no foreign prince, person, prelate, state or potentate hath or ought to have any jurisdiction, power, superiority, pre-eminence or authority, ecclesiastical or spiritual, within this realm. So help me God.

Upon which their said Majesties did accept the crown and royal dignity of the kingdoms of England, France, and Ireland,

and the dominions thereunto belonging, according to the resolution and desire of the said Lords and Commons contained in the said declaration. And thereupon their Majesties were pleased that the said Lords Spiritual and Temporal and Commons, being the two Houses of Parliament, should continue to sit, and with their Majesties' royal concurrence make effectual provision for the settlement of the religion, laws and liberties of this kingdom, so that the same for the future might not be in danger again of being subverted, to which the said Lords Spiritual and Temporal and Commons did agree, and proceed to act accordingly. Now in pursuance of the premises the said Lords Spiritual and Temporal and Commons in Parliament assembled, for the ratifying, confirming and establishing the said declaration and the articles, clauses, matters and things therein contained by the force of a law made in due form by authority of Parliament, do pray that it may be declared and enacted that all and singular the rights and liberties asserted and claimed in the said declaration are the true, ancient and indubitable rights and liberties of the people of this kingdom, and so shall be esteemed, allowed, adjudged, deemed and taken to be; and that all and every the particulars aforesaid shall be firmly and strictly holden and observed as they are expressed in the said declaration, and all officers and ministers whatsoever shall serve their Majesties and their successors according to the same in all times to come. And the said Lords Spiritual and Temporal and Commons, seriously considering how it hath pleased Almighty God in his marvellous providence and merciful goodness to this nation to provide and preserve their said Majesties' royal persons most happily to reign over us upon the throne of their ancestors, for which they render unto him from the bottom of their hearts their humblest thanks and praises, do truly, firmly, assuredly and in the sincerity of their hearts think, and do hereby recognize, acknowledge and declare, that King James the Second having abdicated the government, and their Majesties having accepted the crown and royal dignity as aforesaid, their said Majesties did become, were, are and of right ought to be by the laws of this realm our sovereign liege lord and lady, king and queen of England, France and Ireland and the dominions thereunto belonging, in and to whose princely persons the royal state, crown and dignity of the said realms with all honours, styles, titles, regalities, prerogatives, powers, jurisdictions and authorities to the same belonging and appertaining are most fully, rightfully and entirely invested and incorporated, united and annexed. And for preventing all questions and divisions in this realm by reason of any pretended titles to the crown, and for preserving a certainty in the succession thereof, in and upon which the unity, peace, tranquillity and safety of this nation doth under God wholly consist and depend, the said Lords Spiritual and Temporal and Commons do beseech their Majesties that it may be enacted, established and declared, that the crown and regal government of the said kingdoms and dominions, with all and singular the premises thereunto belonging and appertaining, shall be and continue to their said Majesties and the survivor of them during their lives and the life of the survivor of them, and that the entire, perfect and full exercise of the regal power and government be only in and executed by his Majesty in the names of both their Majesties during their joint lives; and after their deceases the said crown and premises shall be and remain to the heirs of the body of her Majesty, and for default of such issue to her Royal Highness the Princess Anne of Denmark and the heirs of her body, and for default of such issue to the heirs of the body of his said Majesty; and thereunto the said Lords Spiritual and Temporal and Commons do in the name of all the people aforesaid most humbly and faithfully submit themselves, their heirs and posterities for ever, and do faithfully promise that they will stand to, maintain and defend their said Majesties, and also the limitation and succession of the crown herein specified and contained, to the utmost of their powers with their lives and estates against all persons whatsoever that shall attempt anything to the contrary. And whereas it hath been found by experience that it is inconsistent with the safety and welfare of this Protestant kingdom to be governed by a popish prince, or by any king or queen marrying a papist, the said Lords Spiritual and Temporal and Commons do further pray that it may be enacted, that all and every person and persons that is, are or shall be reconciled to or shall hold communion with the see or Church of Rome, or shall profess the popish religion, or shall marry a papist, shall be excluded, and be for ever incapable to inherit, possess or enjoy the crown and government of this realm and Ireland and the dominions thereunto belonging or any part of the same, or to have, use or exercise any regal power, authority or jurisdiction within the same; and in all and every such case or cases the people of these realms shall be and are hereby absolved of their allegiance; and the said crown and government shall from time to time descend to and be enjoyed by such person or persons being Protestants as should have inherited and enjoyed the same in case the said person or persons so reconciled, holding communion or professing or marrying as aforesaid were naturally dead; and that every king and queen of this realm who at any time hereafter shall come to and succeed in the imperial crown of this kingdom shall on the first day of the meeting of the first Parliament next after his or her coming to the crown, sitting in his or her throne in the House of Peers in the presence of the Lords and Commons therein assembled, or at his or her coronation before such person or persons who shall administer the coronation oath to him or her at the time of his or her taking the said oath (which shall first happen), make, subscribe and audibly repeat the declaration mentioned in the statute made in the thirtieth year of the reign of King Charles the Second, entituled, *An Act for the more effectual preserving the king's person and government by disabling papists from sitting in either House of Parliament.* But if it shall happen, that such king or queen upon his or her succession to the crown of this realm shall be under the age of twelve years, then every such king or queen shall make, subscribe and audibly repeat the said declaration at his or her coronation or the first day of the meeting of the first Parliament as aforesaid which shall first happen after such king or queen shall have attained the said age of twelve years. All which their Majesties are contented and pleased shall be declared, enacted and established by authority of this present Parliament, and shall stand, remain and be the law of this realm for ever; and the same are by their said Majesties, by and with the advice and consent of the Lords Spiritual and Temporal and Commons in Parliament assembled and by the authority of the same, declared, enacted and established accordingly.

II. And be it further declared and enacted by the authority aforesaid, that from and after this present session of Parliament no dispensation by *non obstante* of or to any statute or any part thereof shall be allowed, but that the same shall be held void and of no effect, except a dispensation be allowed of in such a statute, and except in such cases as shall be specially provided for by one or more bill or bills to be passed during this present session of Parliament.

III. Provided that no charter or grant or pardon granted before the three and twentieth day of October in the year of our Lord one thousand six hundred eighty-nine shall be any ways impeached or invalidated by this Act, but that the same shall be and remain of the same force and effect in law and no other than as if this Act had never been made.

3. From Edmund Burke, *A Philosophical Enquiry into the Origin of Our Ideas of the Sublime and Beautiful* (1757) (*Works* II, 598–600, 617, 621, 638–39, 646, 667–68)

The passion caused by the great and sublime in *nature*, when those causes operate most powerfully, is astonishment: and astonishment is that state of the soul in which all its motions are suspended, with some degree of horror. In this case the mind is so entirely filled with its object, that it cannot entertain any other, nor by consequence reason on that object which employs it. Hence arises the great power of the sublime, that, far from being produced by them, it anticipates our reasonings, and hurries us on by an irresistible force. Astonishment, as I have said, is the effect of the sublime in its highest degree; the inferior effects are admiration, reverence, and respect....

To make any thing very terrible, obscurity seems in general to be necessary. When we know the full extent of any danger, when we can accustom our eyes to it, a great deal of the apprehension vanishes. Every one will be sensible of this, who considers how greatly night adds to our dread, in all cases of danger, and how much the notions of ghosts and goblins, of which none can form clear ideas, affect minds which give credit to the popular tales concerning such sorts of beings. Those despotic governments, which are founded on the passions of men, and principally upon the passion of fear, keep their chief as much as may be from the public eye. The policy has been the same in many cases of religion. Almost all the heathen temples were dark. Even in the barbarous temples of the Americans at this day, they keep their idol in a dark part of the hut, which is consecrated to his worship. For this purpose too the Druids performed all their ceremonies in the bosom of the darkest woods, and in the shade of the oldest and most spreading oaks. No person seems better to have understood the secret of heightening, or of setting terrible things, if I may use the expression, in their strongest light, by the force of a judicious obscurity, than Milton. His description of death in the second book is admirably studied; it is astonishing with what a gloomy pomp, with what a significant and expressive uncertainty of strokes and colouring, he has finished the portrait of the king of terrors:

> "The other shape,
> If shape it might be call'd that shape had none
> Distinguishable, in member, joint, or limb;

> Or substance might be call'd that shadow seem'd;
> For each seem'd either; black he stood as night;
> Fierce as ten furies; terrible as hell;
> And shook a deadly dart. What seem'd his head
> The likeness of a kingly crown had on."[1]

In this description all is dark, uncertain, confused, terrible, and sublime to the last degree....

A sudden beginning, or sudden cessation of sound of any considerable force, has the same power. The attention is roused by this; and the faculties driven forward, as it were, on their guard. Whatever, either in sights or sounds, makes the transition from one extreme to the other easy, causes no terror, and consequently can be no cause of greatness. In every thing sudden and unexpected, we are apt to start; that is, we have a perception of danger, and our nature rouses us to guard against it....

... It is my design to consider beauty as distinguished from the sublime.... By beauty, I mean that quality, or those qualities in bodies, by which they cause love, or some passion similar to it....

The next property constantly observable in such objects is *smoothness*; a quality so essential to beauty, that I do not now recollect any thing beautiful that is not smooth. In trees and flowers, smooth leaves are beautiful; smooth slopes of earth in gardens; smooth streams in the landscape; smooth coats of birds and beasts in animal beauties; in fine women, smooth skins; and in several sorts of ornamental furniture, smooth and polished surfaces. A very considerable part of the effect of beauty is owing to this quality; indeed the most considerable. For, take any beautiful object, and give it a broken and rugged surface; and, however well formed it may be in other respects, it pleases no longer.... For, indeed, any ruggedness, any sudden projection, any sharp angle, is in the highest degree contrary to that idea....

But as perfectly beautiful bodies are not composed of angular parts, so their parts never continue long in the same right line. They vary their direction every moment, and they change under the eye by a deviation continually carrying on, but for whose beginning or end you will find it difficult to ascertain a point. The view of a beautiful bird will illustrate this observation. Here we see the head increasing insensibly to the middle, from

---

1 John Milton (1608–74), *Paradise Lost*, Book II, 666–73.

whence it lessens gradually until it mixes with the neck; the neck loses itself in a larger swell, which continues to the middle of the body, when the whole decreases again to the tail, the tail takes a new direction, but it soon varies its new course, it blends again with the other parts, and the line is perpetually changing, above, below, upon every side. In this description I have before me the idea of a dove; it agrees very well with most of the conditions of beauty. It is smooth and downy; its parts are (to use that expression) melted into one another; you are presented with no sudden protuberance through the whole, and yet the whole is continually changing. Observe that part of a beautiful woman where she is perhaps the most beautiful, about the neck and breasts; the smoothness, the softness, the easy and insensible swell; the variety of the surface, which is never for the smallest space the same; the deceitful maze, through which the unsteady eye slides giddily, without knowing where to fix, or whither it is carried. Is not this a demonstration of that change of surface, continual, and yet hardly perceptible at any point, which forms one of the great constituents of beauty? ...

On closing this general view of beauty, it naturally occurs that we should compare it with the sublime; and in this comparison there appears a remarkable contrast. For sublime objects are vast in their dimensions, beautiful ones comparatively small: beauty should be smooth and polished; the great, rugged, and negligent; beauty should shun the right line, yet deviate from it insensibly; the great in many cases loves the right line; and when it deviates, it often makes a strong deviation: beauty should not be obscure; the great ought to be dark and gloomy: beauty should be light and delicate; the great ought to be solid, and even massive. They are indeed ideas of a very different nature, one being founded on pain, the other on pleasure....

... Another principal property of beautiful objects is, that the line of their parts is continually varying its direction; but it varies it by a very insensible deviation; it never varies it so quickly as to surprise, or by the sharpness of its angle to cause any twitching or convulsion of the optic nerve. Nothing long continued in the same manner, nothing very suddenly varied, can be beautiful; because both are opposite to that agreeable relaxation which is the characteristic effect of beauty. It is thus in all the senses. A motion in a right line is that manner of moving, next to a very gentle descent, in which we meet the least resistance; yet it is not that manner of moving, which next to a descent, wearies us the least. Rest certainly tends to relax: yet there is a species of motion which relaxes more than rest; a gentle oscillatory motion, a rising and falling. Rocking sets children to sleep better than absolute rest; there is indeed scarcely any thing at that age, which gives more pleasure than to be gently lifted up and down; the manner of playing which their nurses use with children, and the weighing and swinging used afterwards by themselves as a favourite amusement, evince this very sufficiently. Most people must have observed the sort of sense they have had on being swiftly drawn in an easy coach on a smooth turf, with gradual ascents and declivities. This will give a better idea of the beautiful, and point out its probable cause better than almost any thing else. On the contrary, when one is hurried over a rough, rocky, broken road, the pain felt by these sudden inequalities shows why similar sights, feelings, and sounds, are so contrary to beauty: and with regard to the feeling, it is exactly the same in its effect, or very nearly the same, whether, for instance, I move my hand along the surface of a body of a certain shape, or whether such a body is moved along my hand. But to bring this analogy of the senses home to the eye: if a body presented to that sense has such a waving surface, that the rays of light reflected from it are in a continual insensible deviation from the strongest to the weakest (which is always the case in a surface gradually unequal), it must be exactly similar in its effects on the eye and touch; upon the one of which it operates directly, on the other indirectly. And this body will be beautiful if the lines which compose its surface are not continued, even so varied, in a manner that may weary or dissipate the attention. The variation itself must be continually varied.

4. Declaration of the Rights of Man and of Citizens, By the National Assembly of France (26 August 1789), in Richard Price, A Discourse on the Love of Our Country (T. Cadell, 1790), Appendix 5–8

The Representatives of the people of FRANCE formed into a National Assembly, considering that ignorance, neglect, or contempt of human rights, are the sole causes of public misfortunes and corruptions of government, have resolved to set forth, in a solemn declaration, these natural, imprescriptible, and unalienable rights: that this declaration being constantly present to the minds of the members of the body social, they may be ever kept attentive to their rights and their duties: That the acts of the legislative and executive powers of government being capable of being every moment compared with the end of political institutions, may be more respected: and also, that the future claims of the citizens, being directed by simple and incontestable principles, may tend to the maintenance of the Constitution, and the general happiness.

For these reasons, the NATIONAL ASSEMBLY doth recognize and declare, in the presence of the Supreme Being and with the hope of his blessing and favour, the following *sacred* rights of men and of citizens.

I. Men were born and always continue free, and equal in respect of their rights. Civil distinctions, therefore, can be founded only on public utility.

II. The end of all political associations is the preservation of the natural and imprescriptible rights of man; and these rights are liberty, property, security, and resistance of oppression.

III. The nation is essentially the source of all sovereignty; nor can any individual, or any body of men, be entitled to any authority which is not expressly derived from it.

IV. Political liberty consists in the power of doing whatever does not injure another. The exercise of the natural rights of every man, has no other limits than those which are necessary to secure to every *other* man the free exercise of the same rights; and these limits are determinable only by the law.

V. The law ought to prohibit only actions hurtful to society. What is not prohibited by the law should not be hindered; nor should any one be compelled to that which the law does not require.

VI. The law is an expression of the will of the community. All citizens have a right to concur, either personally or by their representatives, in its formation. It should be the same to all, whether it protects or punishes; and all being equal in its sight, are equally eligible to all honours, places, and employments, according to their different abilities, without any other distinction than that created by their virtues and talents.

VII. No man should be accused, arrested, or held in confinement, except in cases determined by the law, and according to the forms which it has prescribed. All who promote, solicit, execute, or cause to be executed arbitrary orders, ought to be punished; and every citizen called upon or apprehended by virtue of the law, ought immediately to obey, and renders himself culpable by resistance.

VIII. The law ought to impose no other penalties but such as are absolutely and evidently necessary: and no one ought to be punished but in virtue of a law promulgated before the offence, and legally applied.

IX. Every man being presumed innocent till he has been convicted, whenever his detention becomes indispensable, all rigour to him, more than is necessary to secure his person, ought to be provided against by the law.

X. No man ought to be molested on account of his opinions, not even on account of his *religious* opinions, provided his avowal of them does not disturb the public order established by the law.

XI. The unrestrained communication of thoughts and opinions being one of the most precious rights of man, every citizen may speak, write, and publish freely, provided he is responsible for the abuse of this liberty in cases determined by the law.

XII. A public force being necessary to give security to the rights of men and of citizens, that force is instituted for the benefit of the community, and not for the particular benefit of the persons with whom it is entrusted.

XIII. A common contribution being necessary for the support of the public force, and for defraying the other expenses of government, it ought to be divided equally among the members of the community, according to their abilities.

XIV. Every citizen has a right, either by himself or his representative, to a free voice in determining the necessity of public contributions, the appropriation of them, and their amount, mode of assessment, and duration.

XV. Every community has a right to demand of all its agents an account of their conduct.

XVI. Every community in which a separation of powers and a security of rights is not provided for, wants a constitution.

XVII. The right to property being inviolable and sacred, no one ought to be deprived of it, except in cases of evident public necessity legally ascertained, and on condition of a previous just indemnity.

5. From Richard Price, *A Discourse on the Love of Our Country, Delivered on Nov. 4, 1789, at the Meeting-House in the Old Jewry, to the Society for Commemorating the Revolution in Great Britain* (T. Cadell, 1790), 2–6, 9–15, 19–26, 31–35, 48–51

The love of our country has in all times been a subject of warm commendations; and it is certainly a noble passion; but, like all other passions, it requires regulation and direction. There are mistakes and prejudices by which, in this instance, we are in particular danger of being misled.—I will briefly mention some of these to you, and observe,

First, That by our country is meant, in this case, not the soil or the spot of earth on which we happen to have been born; not the forests and fields, but that community of which we are members; or that body of companions and friends and kindred who are associated with us under the same constitution of government, protected by the same laws, and bound together by the same civil polity.

Secondly, It is proper to observe that even in this sense of our country, that love of it which is our duty, does not imply any conviction of the superior value of it to other countries, or any particular preference of its laws and constitution of government. Were this implied, the love of their country would be the duty of only a very small part of mankind; for there are few countries that enjoy the advantage of laws and governments which deserve to be preferred. To found, therefore, this duty on such a preference, would be to found it on error and delusion. It is, however, a common delusion. There is the same partiality in countries, to themselves, that there is in individuals. All our attachments should be accompanied, as far as possible, with right opinions.— We are too apt to confine wisdom and virtue within the circle of our own acquaintance and party. Our friends, our country, and, in short, every thing related to us, we are disposed to overvalue. A wise man will guard himself against this delusion. He will study to think of all things as they are, and not suffer any partial affections to blind his understanding. In other families there may be as much worth as in our own. In other circles of friends there may be as much wisdom; and in other countries as much of all that deserves esteem; but, notwithstanding this, our obligation to love our own families, friends, and country, and to seek, in the first place, their good, will remain the same.

Thirdly, It is proper I should desire you particularly to distinguish between the love of our country and that spirit of rivalship and ambition which has been common among nations.—What has the love of their country hitherto been among mankind? What has it been but a love of domination; a desire of conquest, and a thirst for grandeur and glory, by extending territory, and enslaving surrounding countries? What has it been but a blind and narrow principle, producing in every country a contempt of other countries, and forming men into combinations and factions against their common rights and liberties? This is the principle that has been too often cried up as a virtue of the first rank: a principle of the same kind with that which governs clans of *Indians* or tribes of *Arabs*, and leads them out to plunder and massacre. As most of the evils which have taken place in private life, and among individuals, have been occasioned by the desire of private interest overcoming the public affections; so most of the evils which have taken place among bodies of men have been occasioned by the desire of their own interest overcoming the principle of universal benevolence: and leading them to attack one another's territories, to encroach on one another's rights, and to endeavour to build their own advancement on the degradation of all within the reach of their power....

But I am digressing from what I had chiefly in view; which was, after noticing that love of our country which is false and spurious, to explain the nature and effects of that which is just and reasonable. With this view I must desire you to recollect that we are so constituted that our affections are more drawn to some among mankind than to others, in proportion to their degrees of nearness to us, and our power of being useful to them. It is obvious that this is a circumstance in the constitution of our natures which proves the wisdom and goodness of our Maker; for had our affections been determined alike to all our fellow-creatures, human life would have been a scene of embarrassment and distraction. Our regards, according to the order of nature, begin with ourselves; and every man is charged primarily with the care of himself. Next come our families, and benefactors, and friends; and after them our country. We can do little for the interest of mankind at large. To this interest, however, all other interests are subordinate. The noblest principle in our nature is the regard to general justice, and that good-will which embraces all the world.—I have already observed this; but it cannot be too often repeated. Though our immediate attention must be employed in promoting our own interest and that of our nearest connexions; yet we must remember, that a narrower interest ought always to give way to a more extensive interest. In pursuing particularly the interest of our country, we ought to carry our views beyond it. We should love it ardently, but not exclusively. We ought to seek its good, by all the means that our different circumstances and abilities will allow; but at the same time we ought to consider ourselves as citizens of the world, and take care to maintain a just regard to the rights of other countries.

The enquiry by what means (subject to this limitation) we may best promote the interests of our country is very important;

and all that remains of this discourse shall be employed in answering it, and in exhorting you to manifest your love to your country, by the means I shall mention.

The chief blessings of human nature are the three following:—TRUTH—VIRTUE—and LIBERTY.—These are, therefore, the blessings in the possession of which the interest of our country lies, and to the attainment of which our love of it ought to direct our endeavours. By the diffusion of KNOWLEDGE it must be distinguished from a country of *Barbarians*: by the practice of religious VIRTUE, it must be distinguished from a country of *gamblers, Atheists,* and *libertines*: and by the possession of LIBERTY, it must be distinguished from a country of *slaves*.—I will dwell for a few moments on each of these heads:

Our first concern, as lovers of our country, must be to *enlighten* it.—Why are the nations of the world so patient under despotism?—Why do they crouch to tyrants, or submit to be treated as if they were a herd of cattle? Is it not because they are kept in darkness, and want knowledge? Enlighten them and you will elevate them. Shew them they are *men*, and they will act like *men*. Give them just ideas of civil government, and let them know that it is an expedient for gaining protection against injury and defending their rights, and it will be impossible for them to submit to governments which, like most of those now in the world, are usurpations on the rights of men, and little better than contrivances for enabling the *few* to oppress the *many*.... Ignorance is the parent of bigotry, intolerance, persecution and slavery. Inform and instruct mankind; and these evils will be excluded.—Happy is the person who, himself raised above vulgar errors, is conscious of having aimed at giving mankind this instruction. Happy is the Scholar or Philosopher who at the close of life can reflect that he has made this use of his learning and abilities: but happier far must he be, if at the same time he has reason to believe he has been successful, and actually contributed, by his instructions, to disseminate among his fellow-creatures just notions of themselves, of their rights, of religion, and the nature and end of civil government. Such were *Milton, Locke, Sidney, Hoadly,* &c. in this country; such were *Montesquieu, Fenelon, Turgot,* &c. in France. They sowed a seed which has since taken root, and is now growing up to a glorious harvest. To the information they conveyed by their writings we owe those revolutions in which every friend to mankind is now exulting.—What an encouragement is this to us all in our endeavours to enlighten the world? ...

The next great blessing of human nature which I have mentioned is VIRTUE. This ought to follow knowledge, and to be directed by it. Virtue without knowledge makes enthusiasts; and knowledge without virtue makes devils; but both united elevates to the top of human dignity and perfection.—We must, therefore, if we would serve our country, make both these the objects of our zeal....

LIBERTY is the next great blessing which I have mentioned as the object of patriotic zeal. It is inseparable from knowledge and virtue, and together with them completes the glory of a community. An enlightened and virtuous country must be a free country. It cannot suffer invasions of its rights, or bend to tyrants....

Civil government (as I have before observed) is an institution of human prudence for guarding our persons, our property, and our good name, against invasion; and for securing to the members of a community that liberty to which all have an equal right, as far as they do not, by any overt act, use it to injure the liberty of others. Civil laws are regulations agreed upon by the community for gaining these ends; and civil magistrates are officers appointed by the community for executing these laws. Obedience, therefore, to the laws and to magistrates, are necessary expressions of our regard to the community; and without this obedience the ends of government cannot be obtained, or a community avoid falling into a state of anarchy that will destroy those rights and subvert that liberty, which government is instituted to protect.

I wish it was in my power to give you a just account of the importance of this observation. It shews the ground on which the duty of obeying civil governors stands, and that there are two extremes in this case which ought to be avoided.—These extremes are adulation and servility on one hand; and a proud and licentious contempt on the other. The former is the extreme to which mankind in general have been most prone....

Adulation is always odious, and when offered to men in power it corrupts *them*, by giving them improper ideas of their situation; and it debases those who offer it, by manifesting an abjectness founded on improper ideas of *themselves*. I have lately observed in this kingdom too near approaches to this abjectness. In our late addresses to the King, on his recovery from the severe illness with which God has been pleased to afflict him, we have appeared more like a herd crawling at the feet of a master, than like enlightened and manly citizens rejoicing with a beloved sovereign, but at the same time conscious that he derives all his consequence from themselves. But, perhaps, these servilities in the language of our late addresses should be pardoned, as only *forms* of civility and expressions of an overflow of good-nature. They have, however, a dangerous tendency. The potentates of this world are sufficiently apt to consider themselves as possessed of an inherent superiority, which gives them a right to govern, and makes mankind *their own*; and this infatuation is almost every where fostered in them by the creeping sycophants about them, and the language of flattery which they are continually hearing.

Civil governors are properly the servants of the public; and a King is no more than the first servant of the public, created by it, maintained by it, and responsible to it: and all the homage paid him, is due to him on no other account than his relation to the public. His sacredness is the sacredness of the community. His authority is the authority of the community; and the term MAJESTY, which it is usual to apply to him, is by no means *his own* majesty, but the MAJESTY OF THE PEOPLE....

You cannot be too attentive to this observation. The improvement of the world depends on the attention to it: nor will mankind be ever as virtuous and happy as they are capable of being, till the attention to it becomes universal and efficacious. If we forget it, we shall be in danger of an idolatry as gross and stupid as that of the ancient heathens, who, after fabricating blocks of wood and stone, fell down and worshipped them.—The disposition in mankind to this kind of idolatry is indeed a very mortifying subject of reflexion.—In TURKEY, millions of human beings adore a silly mortal, and are ready to throw themselves at his feet, and to submit their lives to his discretion.—In RUSSIA, the common people are only a STOCK on the lands of grandees, or appendages to their estates, which, like the fixtures in a house, are bought and sold with the estates. In SPAIN, in GERMANY, and under most of the governments of the world, mankind are in a similar state of humiliation. Who, that has a just sense of the dignity of his nature, can avoid execrating such a debasement of it?

Had I been to address the King on a late occasion, I should have been inclined to do it in style very different from that of most of the addressers, and to use some such language as the following:—

> I rejoice, Sir, in your recovery. I thank God for his goodness to you. I honour you not only as my King, but as almost the only lawful King in the world, because the only one who owes his crown to the choice of his people. May you enjoy all possible happiness. May God shew you the

folly of those effusions of adulation which you are now receiving, and guard you against their effects. May you be led to such a sense of the nature of your situation, and endowed with such wisdom, as shall render your restoration to the government of these kingdoms a blessing to it, and engage you to consider yourself as more properly the *Servant* than the *Sovereign* of your people.

But I must not forget the opposite extreme to that now taken notice of; that is, a disdainful pride, derived from a consciousness of equality, or, perhaps, superiority, in respect of all that gives true dignity to men in power, and producing a contempt of them, and a disposition to treat them with rudeness and insult....

We are met to thank God for that event in this country to which the name of THE REVOLUTION has been given; and which, for more than a century, it has been usual for the friends of freedom, and more especially Protestant Dissenters, under the title of the REVOLUTION SOCIETY, to celebrate with expressions of joy and exultation.... By a bloodless victory, the fetters which despotism had been long preparing for us were broken; the rights of the people were asserted, a tyrant expelled, and a Sovereign of our own choice appointed in his room....

It is well known that King James was not far from gaining his purpose; and that probably he would have succeeded, had he been less in a hurry. But he was a fool as well as a bigot. He wanted courage as well as prudence; and, therefore, fled, and left us to settle quietly for ourselves that constitution of government which is now our boast.... But let us remember that we ought not to satisfy ourselves with thanksgivings. Our gratitude, if genuine, will be accompanied with endeavours to give stability to the deliverance our country has obtained, and to extend and improve the happiness with which the Revolution has blest us— Let us, in particular, take care not to forget the principles of the Revolution. This Society has, very properly, in its Reports, held out these principles, as an instruction to the public. I will only take notice of the three following:

First; The right to liberty of conscience in religious
matters.
Secondly; The right to resist power when abused. And,
Thirdly; The right to chuse our own governors; to cashier them for misconduct; and to frame a government for ourselves.

On these three principles, and more especially the last, was the Revolution founded.... Cherish in your breasts this conviction, and act under its influence; detesting the odious doctrines of passive obedience, non-resistance, and the divine right of kings—doctrines which, had they been acted upon in this country, would have left us at this time wretched slaves—doctrines which imply, that God made mankind to be oppressed and plundered; and which are no less a blasphemy against him, than an insult on common sense....

You may reasonably expect that I should now close this address to you. But I cannot yet dismiss you. I must not conclude without recalling, particularly, to your recollection, a consideration to which I have more than once alluded, and which, probably, your thoughts have been all along anticipating: A consideration with which my mind is impressed more than I can express. I mean the consideration of the favourableness of the present times to all exertions in the cause of public liberty.

What an eventful period is this! I am thankful that I have lived to it; and I could almost say, *Lord, now lettest thou thy servant depart in peace, for mine eyes have seen thy salvation.* I have lived to see a diffusion of knowledge, which has undermined superstition and error—I have lived to see the rights of men better understood than ever; and nations panting for liberty, which seemed to have lost the idea of it.—I have lived to see THIRTY MILLIONS of people, indignant and resolute, spurning at slavery, and demanding liberty with an irresistible voice; their king led in triumph, and an arbitrary monarch surrendering himself to his subjects.—After sharing in the benefits of one Revolution, I have been spared to be a witness to two other Revolutions, both glorious.—And now, methinks, I see the ardour for liberty catching and spreading; a general amendment beginning in human affairs; the dominion of kings changed for the dominion of laws, and the dominion of priests giving way to the dominion of reason and conscience.

Be encouraged, all ye friends of freedom, and writers in its defence! The times are auspicious. Your labours have not been in vain. Behold kingdoms, admonished by you, starting from sleep, breaking their fetters, and claiming justice from their oppressors! Behold, the light you have struck out, after setting AMERICA free, reflected in FRANCE, and there kindled into a blaze that lays despotism in ashes, and warms and illuminates EUROPE!

Tremble all ye oppressors of the world! Take warning all ye supporters of slavish governments, and slavish hierarchies! Call no more (absurdly and wickedly) REFORMATION, innovation. You cannot now hold the world in darkness. Struggle no longer against increasing light and liberality. Restore to mankind their rights; and consent to the correction of abuses, before they and you are destroyed together.

6. Congratulatory Address from the Revolution Society to the National Assembly of France (4 November 1789), *A Letter from Earl Stanhope to the Right Honourable Edmund Burke: Containing a Short Answer to His Late Speech on the French Revolution* (George Stafford, 1790), 21–22

The Society for commemorating the Revolution in Great Britain, disdaining National Partialities, and rejoicing at every triumph of Liberty and Justice over Arbitrary Power, offer to the National Assembly of France, their congratulations on the Revolution in that Country, and on the prospect it gives to the two first Kingdoms in the World, of a common participation in the blessings of civil and religious Liberty.

They cannot help adding their ardent wishes of an happy Settlement of so important a Revolution, and at the same time expressing the particular satisfaction, with which they reflect on the tendency of the glorious Example given in France to encourage other Nations to assert the unalienable Rights of Mankind, and thereby to introduce a General Reformation in the Governments of Europe, and to make the World free and happy.

STANHOPE, Chairman.

Appendix B: Burke and the American Revolution

The tenor of Burke's thoughts on the American Revolution remained consistent with (and was indeed largely a continuing defence of) the policy toward the colonies adopted by the brief administration of Charles Watson-Wentworth, Marquess of Rockingham (1730–82), who was prime minister in 1765–66 (and again for three months before his death in 1782). Rockingham's repeal of the Stamp Act (a repeal tempered by the new Declaratory Act of 1766, which asserted Parliament's authority "to make Laws and Statutes of sufficient force and validity to bind the Colonies and people of *America*, Subjects of the Crown of *Great Britain*, in all cases whatsoever") quieted the unrest of the colonists, an achievement that Burke described concisely in his *Short Account of a Late Short Administration*: "The passions and animosities of the colonies, by judicious and lenient measures, were allayed and composed, and the foundation laid for a lasting agreement amongst them."[1] The tranquility thereby established was compromised and ultimately destroyed by the imposition in 1767 of the Townshend Duties (taxes on glass, lead, paints, paper and tea). Burke spoke against these in the House of Commons,[2] and in 1769 he continued to write of the taxes imposed on America as the source of colonial unrest: "By this measure was let loose that dangerous spirit of disquisition, not in the coolness of philosophical inquiry, but inflamed with all the passions of a haughty, resentful people, who thought themselves deeply injured, and that they were contending for every thing that was valuable in the world."[3] In 1770 the Townshend duties were in the main repealed—the Tea Duty remaining in place as the (fateful) solitary exception—but Townshend's fiscal innovations had by then already sown discord in the colonies. In a Commons speech, Burke lamented

---

1 Edmund Burke, *A Short Account of a Late Short Administration*, *Works* III, 2.
2 There is controversy over whether this speech was in fact delivered. See O'Brien, *Great Melody* 119–20.
3 Edmund Burke, *Observations on a Late State of the Nation*, *Works* III, 79.

the course of action that had disrupted the colonial serenity: "We began to tire of the Tranquility which we enjoyed.... Thus after we had been in Harbour we had got to Sea again.... We were on a Rotten bottom. The Winds began to blow."[1]

This theme of the avoidable disturbance of a prior tranquility runs through the two most famous of Burke's speeches on America: the *Speech on American Taxation* (19 April 1774) and the *Speech on Conciliation with America* (22 March 1775). These speeches occurred in the aftermath of the Boston Tea Party (16 December 1773) and demonstrate Burke's preference for a conciliatory (rather than coercive) policy toward the rebellious colonies. The speech on taxation constitutes essentially a defence of the policy of the Rockingham Administration (in F.P. Lock's words, the compromise position of "imperial supremacy in theory, virtual colonial independence in practice" [*Edmund Burke*, vol. I, p. 314]) and a plea for restraint, for a return to an ancient situation of tranquility. A representative passage:

> Recover your old ground, and your old tranquillity—try it—I am persuaded the Americans will compromise with you. When confidence is once restored, the odious and suspicious *summum jus* will perish of course. The spirit of practicability, of moderation, and mutual convenience, will never call in geometrical exactness as the arbitrator of an amicable settlement. Consult and follow your experience. Let not the long story, with which I have exercised your patience, prove fruitless to your interests....
>
> Again, and again, revert to your old principles—seek peace and ensue it—leave America, if she has taxable matter in her, to tax herself. I am not here going into the distinctions of rights, not attempting to mark their boundaries. I do not enter into these metaphysical distinctions; I hate the very sound of them. Leave the Americans as they anciently stood, and these distinctions, born of our unhappy contest, will die along with it. They and we, and their and our ancestors, have been happy under that system. Let the memory of all actions, in contradiction to that good old mode, on both sides, be extinguished for ever. Be content to bind America by laws of trade; you have always done

---

1 Edmund Burke, "Speech on American Resolutions," 9 May 1770, in Paul Langford et al., *The Writings and Speeches of Edmund Burke* (Oxford UP, 1981–2015), vol. II, pp. 326–27.

it. Let this be your reason for binding their trade. Do not burden them by taxes; you were not used to do so from the beginning. Let this be your reason for not taxing. These are the arguments of states and kingdoms. Leave the rest to the schools; for there only they may be discussed with safety. But if, intemperately, unwisely, fatally, you sophisticate and poison the very source of government, by urging subtle deductions, and consequences odious to those you govern, from the unlimited and illimitable nature of supreme sovereignty, you will teach them by these means to call that sovereignty itself in question. When you drive him hard, the boar will surely turn upon the hunters. If that sovereignty and their freedom cannot be reconciled, which will they take? They will cast your sovereignty in your face. No body will be argued into slavery. Sir, let the gentlemen on the other side call forth all their ability; let the best of them get up, and tell me, what one character of liberty the Americans have, and what one brand of slavery they are free from, if they are bound in their property and industry, by all the restraints you can imagine on commerce, and at the same time are made pack-horses of every tax you choose to impose, without the least share in granting them. When they bear the burdens of unlimited monopoly, will you bring them to bear the burdens of unlimited revenue too? The Englishman in America will feel that this is slavery—that it is *legal* slavery, will be no compensation, either to his feelings or his understanding.[1]

The speech on conciliation continues these themes, urging the government to "restore order and repose"[2] and to do this by means of magnanimity, kindness, and "prudent management" (*Conciliation* 252). "All government, indeed every human benefit and enjoyment, every virtue, and every prudent act, is founded on compromise and barter. We balance inconveniences; we give and take; we remit some rights, that we may enjoy others; and we choose rather to be happy citizens, than subtle disputants" (284). This magnanimous approach is presented as the alternative to force, which he contends to be wrongheaded and impractical: "I

1 Edmund Burke, *Speech on American Taxation, Works* III, 218–20.
2 Edmund Burke, *Speech on Moving His Resolutions for Conciliation with America, Works* III, 243; hereafter cited as *Conciliation* with page numbers.

do not know the method of drawing up an indictment against an whole people" (263). The speech is notable also for the emphasis Burke places on the circumstances and temper of the American colonists. There is no question that Burke had deeply familiarized himself with the character of the colonists, having penned—with his kinsman William Burke—a two-volume *Account of the European Settlements in America* (1757); he expressed, moreover, unbounded admiration (even yearning) for America, referring to it on one occasion as "the most beautiful object that has ever appeared upon this Globe,"[1] and in a letter to General Charles Lee comparing unfavourably "our dull worn out Hemisphere" with "the infinite Objects of Curiosity, that are so exuberantly spread out before you, in the vast Field of America."[2] In the conciliation speech, Burke emphasizes the colonists' "fierce spirit of liberty" (*Conciliation* 253), a spirit connected with their Protestant religion ("All protestantism," he writes, "is a sort of dissent" [255]) and exacerbated by their education, particularly in the law, an education that leads them to anticipate evils (to "augur misgovernment at a distance, and snuff the approach of tyranny in every tainted breeze" [256]). In addition to the temper of the colonists, distance ("Three thousand miles of ocean" [256]) is also stressed: "The ocean remains. You cannot pump this dry; and as long as it continues in its present bed, so long all the causes which weaken authority by distance will continue" (262). The resolutions contained in Burke's speech—repeal of the Tea Duty and the penal ("Intolerable") acts, dropping of the right to tax the colonies—were substantially the same as Lord North's Conciliatory Propositions to the Americans, offered in February 1778. Three years on, it was all too late.

The deteriorating situation—hostilities commencing in 1775 with the Lexington massacre and the battle of Bunker Hill, and the Declaration of Independence adopted by the Second Continental Congress on 4 July 1776—distressed Burke greatly, as can be seen from a letter written to his old friend Richard Shackleton (1726–92) on 11 August 1776:

We are deeply in blood. We expect now to hear of some sharp affair, every hour. God knows how it will be. I do not know how to wish success to those whose Victory is to

---

1 Burke to the Duke of Richmond (26 September 1775), *Corr.* III, 219.

2 Burke to General Charles Lee (1 February 1774), *Corr.* II, 517.

seperate from us a large and noble part of our Empire. Still less do I wish success to injustice, oppression and absurdity. Things are in a bad train and in more ways than one. No good can come of any Event in this War to any Virtuous Interest. We have forgot or thrown away all our antient principles. This view sometimes sinks my Spirits.[1]

The mention here of the abandonment of "antient principles" is consistent with the contentions of the conciliation speech, Burke there resolving "not to be guilty of tampering: the odious vice of restless and unstable minds. I put my foot in the tracks of our forefathers; where I can neither wander nor stumble" (*Conciliation* 276).

In sympathy with the colonists' cause and disdainful of the authoritarian policy of George III's government, Burke spoke in the House of Commons on 6 November 1776 and placed the responsibility for the Declaration of Independence squarely at the door of the British: "you drove them into the declaration of independency; *not* as a matter of *choice*, but *necessity*."[2] Burke's indictment of British policy is next on display in his "Address to the British Colonists in North America," a further articulation of the Rockinghamite position, written in January 1777. The "Address" is noteworthy also for the characteristic Burkean balance of reverence for the constitution and willingness, where necessary, to reform and improve:

We admit ... that violent addresses have been procured with uncommon pains by wicked and designing men, purporting to be the genuine voice of the whole people of England; that they have been published by authority here; and made known to you by proclamations;[3] in order, by despair and resentment, incurably to poison your minds against the origin of your race, and to render all cordial reconciliation between us utterly impracticable....

We do not call you rebels and traitors. We do not call for the vengeance of the crown against you. We do not know how to qualify millions of our countrymen, contending with

---

1 Burke to Richard Shackleton (11 August 1776), *Corr.* III, 286–87.
2 Edmund Burke, "Speech on Cavendish's Motion on America" (6 November 1776), in Langford et al., vol. III, p. 253.
3 The reference is presumably to "A Proclamation by the King for the Suppressing Rebellion and Sedition," 23 August 1775.

one heart for an admission to privileges which we have ever thought our own happiness and honour, by odious and unworthy names. On the contrary, we highly revere the principles on which you act, though we lament some of their effects. Armed as you are, we embrace you as our friends and as our brethren by the best and dearest ties of relation....

Arguments may be used to weaken your confidence in that public security; because, from some unpleasant appearances, there is a suspicion that parliament itself is somewhat fallen from its independent spirit. How far this supposition may be founded in fact we are unwilling to determine. But we are well assured from experience, that even if all were true that is contended for, and in the extent too in which it is argued, yet as long as the solid and well-disposed forms of this constitution remain, there ever is within parliament itself a power of renovating its principles, and effecting a self-reformation, which no other plan of government has ever contained. This constitution has therefore admitted innumerable improvements, either for the correction of the original scheme, or for removing corruptions, or for bringing its principles better to suit those changes which have successively happened in the circumstances of the nation, or in the manners of the people.

We feel, that the growth of the colonies is such a change of circumstances; and that our present dispute is an exigency as pressing as any which ever demanded a revision of our government. Public troubles have often called upon this country to look into its constitution. It has ever been bettered by such a revision. If our happy and luxuriant increase of dominion, and our diffused population, have outgrown the limits of a constitution made for a contracted object, we ought to bless God, who has furnished us with this noble occasion for displaying our skill and beneficence in enlarging the scale of rational happiness, and of making the politic generosity of this kingdom as extensive as its fortune. If we set about this great work, on both sides, with the same conciliatory turn of mind, we may now, as in former times, owe even to our mutual mistakes, contentions and animosities, the lasting concord, freedom, happiness, and glory of this empire.[1]

---

1 Edmund Burke, "Address to the British Colonists in North America," *Works* V, 539–40, 543, 545–46.

Burke's last major pronouncements on America are found in his *Letter to the Sheriffs of Bristol* (dated 3 April 1777). The letter is significant as a statement of Burke's final position on the American Revolution, and it merits here the inclusion of lengthy selections:

I think I know America. If I do not, my ignorance is incurable, for I have spared no pains to understand it; and I do most solemnly assure those of my constituents who put any sort of confidence in my industry and integrity, that every thing that has been done there has arisen from a total misconception of the object: that our means of originally holding America, that our means of reconciling with it after quarrel, of recovering it after separation, of keeping it after victory, did depend, and must depend in their several stages and periods, upon a total renunciation of that unconditional submission, which has taken such possession of the minds of violent men. The whole of those maxims, upon which we have made and continued this war, must be abandoned. Nothing indeed (for I would not deceive you) can place us in our former situation. That hope must be laid aside. But there is a difference between bad and the worst of all. Terms relative to the cause of the war ought to be offered by the authority of parliament. An arrangement at home promising some security for them ought to be made. By doing this, without the least impairing of our strength, we add to the credit of our moderation, which, in itself, is always strength more or less.

I know many have been taught to think, that moderation, in a case like this, is a sort of treason; and that all arguments for it are sufficiently answered by railing at rebels and rebellion, and by charging all the present, or future miseries, which we may suffer, on the resistance of our brethren. But I would wish them, in this grave matter, and if peace is not wholly removed from their hearts, to consider seriously, first, that to criminate and recriminate never yet was the road to reconciliation, in any difference amongst men. In the next place, it would be right to reflect, that the American English (whom they may abuse, if they think it honourable to revile the absent) can, as things now stand, neither be provoked at our railing, nor bettered by our instruction. All communication is cut off between us, but this we know with certainty, that, though we cannot reclaim them, we may reform ourselves. If measures of peace are necessary, they must begin somewhere; and a conciliatory temper must precede and prepare every plan of reconciliation. Nor do I conceive that we suffer any thing by thus regulating our own minds. We are not disarmed by being disencumbered of our passions. Declaiming on rebellion never added a bayonet, or a charge of powder, to your military force; but I am afraid that it has been the means of taking up many muskets against you.

This outrageous language, which has been encouraged and kept alive by every art, has already done incredible mischief. For a long time, even amidst the desolations of war, and the insults of hostile laws daily accumulated on one another, the American leaders seem to have had the greatest difficulty in bringing up their people to a declaration of total independence. But the court gazette accomplished what the abettors of independence had attempted in vain.[1] When that disingenuous compilation, and strange medley of railing and flattery, was adduced as a proof of the united sentiments of the people of Great Britain, there was a great change throughout all America. The tide of popular affection, which had still set towards the parent country, began immediately to turn, and to flow with great rapidity in a contrary course. Far from concealing these wild declarations of enmity, the author of the celebrated pamphlet, which prepared the minds of the people for independence, insists largely on the multitude and the spirit of these addresses; and he draws an argument from them, which (if the fact were as he supposes) must be irresistible.[2] For I never knew a writer on the theory of government so partial to authority as not to allow, that the hostile mind of the rulers to their people did fully justify a change of government: nor can any reason whatever be given, why one people should voluntarily yield any degree of preeminence to another, but on a supposition of great affection

---

1 The "Proclamation for the Suppressing Rebellion and Sedition" was supported by a large number of addresses, and was printed in the *London Gazette* in the latter half of 1775.

2 Burke is here referring to *Common Sense*, the pamphlet written in 1776 by Thomas Paine (1737–1809). Paine there wrote: "The last cord now is broken; the people of England are presenting addresses against us."

and benevolence towards them, Unfortunately your rulers, trusting to other things, took no notice of this great principle of connexion. From the beginning of this affair, they have done all they could to alienate your minds from your own kindred; and if they could excite hatred enough in one of the parties towards the other, they seemed to be of opinion that they had gone half the way towards reconciling the quarrel....

When any community is subordinately connected with another, the great danger of the connexion is the extreme pride and self-complacency of the superior, which in all matters of controversy will probably decide in its own favour. It is a powerful corrective to such a very rational cause of fear, if the inferior body can be made to believe, that the party inclination, or political views, of several in the principal state, will induce them in some degree to counteract this blind and tyrannical partiality. There is no danger that any one acquiring consideration or power in the presiding state should carry this leaning to the inferior too far. The fault of human nature is not of that sort. Power, in whatever hands, is rarely guilty of too strict limitations on itself. But one great advantage to the support of authority attends such an amicable and protecting connexion, that those who have conferred favours obtain influence; and from the foresight of future events can persuade men, who have received obligations, sometimes to return them. Thus by the mediation of those healing principles (call them good or evil), troublesome discussions are brought to some sort of adjustment; and every hot controversy is not a civil war.

But, if the colonies (to bring the matter home to us) could see, that, in Great Britain, the mass of the people is melted into its government, and that every dispute with the ministry must of necessity be always a quarrel with the nation; they can stand no longer in the equal and friendly relation of fellow-citizens to the subjects of this kingdom. Humble as this relation may appear to some, when it is once broken, a strong tie is dissolved. Other sort of connexions will be sought. For there are very few in the world, who will not prefer an useful ally to an insolent master.

Such discord has been the effect of the unanimity into which so many have of late been seduced or bullied, or into the appearance of which they have sunk through mere despair. They have been told that their dissent from violent measures is an encouragement to rebellion. Men of great presumption and little knowledge will hold a language which is contradicted by the whole course of history. *General* rebellions and revolts of a whole people never were *encouraged*, now or at any time. They are always *provoked*....

Therefore at the first fatal opening of this contest, the wisest course seemed to be to put an end as soon as possible to the immediate causes of the dispute; and to quiet a discussion, not easily settled upon clear principles, and arising from claims, which pride would permit neither party to abandon, by resorting as nearly as possible to the old, successful course. A mere repeal of the obnoxious tax, with a declaration of the legislative authority of this kingdom, was then fully sufficient to procure peace to *both sides*.[1] Man is a creature of habit, and, the first breach being of very short continuance, the colonies fell back exactly into their ancient state. The congress has used an expression with regard to this pacification, which appears to me truly significant. After the repeal of Stamp Act, "the colonies fell," says this assembly, "into their ancient state of *unsuspecting confidence in the mother country*."[2] This unsuspecting confidence is the true centre of gravity amongst mankind, about which all the parts are at rest. It is this *unsuspecting confidence* that removes all difficulties, and reconciles all the contradictions which occur in the complexity of all ancient, puzzled, political establishments. Happy are the rulers which have the secret of preserving it!

The whole empire has reason to remember, with eternal gratitude, the wisdom and temper of that man[3] and his excellent associates, who, to recover this confidence, formed

---

1 This refers to the twin pillars of Rockingham colonial policy: the repeal of the Stamp Act and the passing of the Declaratory Act.

2 The reference is to a passage in the "Memorial to the Inhabitants of the British Colonies," drafted by members of the Continental Congress: "After the repeal of the Stamp Act, having again resigned ourselves to our ancient unsuspicious affections for the parent state, and anxious to avoid any controversy with her, in hopes of a favourable alteration in sentiments and measures towards us, we did not press our objections against the above mentioned Statutes, made subsequent to that repeal."

3 I.e., Rockingham.

a plan of pacification in 1766. That plan, being built upon the nature of man, and the circumstances and habits of the two countries, and not on any visionary speculations, perfectly answered its end, as long as it was thought proper to adhere to it. Without giving a rude shock to the dignity (well or ill understood) of this parliament, they gave perfect content to our dependencies. Had it not been for the mediatorial spirit and talents of that great man, between such clashing pretensions and passions, we should then have rushed headlong (I know what I say) into the calamities of that civil war, in which, by departing from his system, we are at length involved; and we should have been precipitated into that war, at a time when circumstances both at home and abroad were far, very far, more unfavourable to us than they were at the breaking out of the present troubles.

I had the happiness of giving my first votes in parliament for that pacification. I was one of those almost unanimous members, who, in the necessary concessions of parliament, would as much as possible have preserved its authority, and respected its honour. I could not at once tear from my heart prejudices which were dear to me, and which bore a resemblance to virtue. I had then, and I have still my partialities. What parliament gave up, I wished to be given as of grace, and favour, and affection, and not as a restitution of stolen goods. High dignity relented as it was soothed; and a benignity from old acknowledged greatness had its full effect on our dependencies. Our unlimited declaration of legislative authority produced not a single murmur. If this undefined power has become odious since that time, and full of horror to the colonies, it is because the *unsuspicious confidence* is lost, and the parental affection, in the bosom of whose boundless authority they reposed their privileges, is become estranged and hostile.

It will be asked, if such was then my opinion of the mode of pacification, how I came to be the very person who moved, not only for a repeal of all the late coercive statutes, but for mutilating, by a positive law, the entireness of the legislative power of parliament, and cutting off from it the whole right of taxation? I answer, because a different state of things requires a different conduct. When the dispute had gone to these last extremities (which no man laboured more to prevent than I did), the concessions which had satisfied in the beginning, could satisfy no longer; because the violation of tacit faith required explicit security. The same cause which has introduced all formal compacts and covenants among men made it necessary. I mean habits of soreness, jealousy, and distrust. I parted with it, as with a limb; but as a limb to save the body; and I would have parted with more, if more had been necessary; any thing rather than a fruitless, hopeless, unnatural civil war. This mode of yielding, would, it is said, give way to independency, without a war. I am persuaded from the nature of things, and from every information, that it would have had a directly contrary effect. But if it had this effect, I confess that I should prefer independency without war, to independency with it; and I have so much trust in the inclinations and prejudices of mankind, and so little in any thing else, that I should expect ten times more benefit to this kingdom from the affection of America, though under a separate establishment, than from her perfect submission to the crown and parliament, accompanied with her terror, disgust, and abhorrence. Bodies tied together by so unnatural a bond of union, as mutual hatred, are only connected to their ruin.[1]

It is worth noting two final contributions Burke made with regard to American affairs. In his contribution to the debate in the House of Commons on the Repeal of the Declaratory Act on 6 April 1778, Burke—in accordance with his thoughts in the letter to the Sheriffs of Bristol—duly renounced the Act, thinking it "wise to give it up, if thereby the minds of the Americans could be conciliated, and their affections regained."[2] Lastly, in his "Speech on Army Estimates" on 14 December 1778, Burke urges the British to acknowledge the Declaration of Independence as a matter of necessity. The words that follow are as summarized in the *Parliamentary Register*:

With regard to avowing the Independency of America, Gentlemen looked at the position in a wrong point of view,

---

1 Edmund Burke, *A Letter to John Farr and John Harris, Esqrs., Sheriffs of the City of Bristol, on the Affairs of America*, Works III, 310–11, 314–15, 325–27.

2 Edmund Burke, "Speech on Repeal of Declaratory Act" (6 April 1778), in Langford et al., vol. III, p. 374.

and talked of it merely as a matter of choice, when in fact it was now become a matter of necessity. It was in this latter light only that he regarded it, in this latter light only that he maintained that it was incumbent on Great Britain to acknowledge it directly. On the day when he first heard of the American states having claimed Independency, it made him sick at heart; it struck him to the soul, because he saw it was a claim essentially injurious to this country, and a claim which Great Britain could never get rid of. Never! Never! Never! It was not therefore to be thought that he wished for the Independency of America.—Far from it.— He felt it as a circumstance exceedingly detrimental to the fame, and exceedingly detrimental to the interest of his country. But when by a wrong management of the cards a gamester had lost much, it was right for him to make the most of the game as it then stood, and to take care that he did not lose more. This was our case at present, the stake already gone was material, but the very existence of our empire was more, and we were now madly putting that to the risque.[1]

---

1 Edmund Burke, "Speech on Army Estimates" (14 December 1778), in Langford et al., vol. III, p. 394.

Appendix C: Burke's First Responses to the French Revolution

[Initial reactions in Britain to the French Revolution were somewhat enthusiastic, even among the leading politicians of the day. Charles James Fox (1749–1806), the leader of the Whig Party, was wildly enthusiastic, declaring it "the greatest event ... that ever happened in the world! and how much the best!" William Pitt the Younger (1759–1806), the Tory prime minister, while not sharing Fox's zeal, took a calculating view, seeing the confusion in France as beneficial to British national interest. Burke's feelings were, of course, markedly different. His first recorded response is found in a letter of 9 August 1789 to the Earl of Charlemont (James Caulfeild, 1728–99). That letter is marked by caution and ambivalence, but the more critical tone that emerges two months later in his letter to Charles-Jean-François Depont (1767–96), the addressee of the subsequent *Reflections*, erupts with full force in Burke's "Speech on the Army Estimates" in the House of Commons on 9 February 1790. Relevant excerpts from all three of these texts are included here and are vital for an understanding of how Burke came to develop the distinctive position annunciated in *Reflections on the Revolution in France*.]

1. From a Letter to the Earl of Charlemont, 9 August 1789 (*Corr.* VI, 10)

... As to us here our thoughts of every thing at home are suspended, by our astonishment at the wonderful Spectacle which is exhibited in a Neighbouring and rival Country—what Spectators, and what actors! England gazing with astonishment at a French struggle for Liberty and not knowing whether to blame or to applaud! The thing indeed, though I thought I saw something like it in progress for several years, has still something in it paradoxical and Mysterious. The spirit it is impossible not to admire; but the old Parisian ferocity has broken out in a shocking manner.[1] It is true, that this may be no more than a sud-

---

1 Burke's allusion here is to the murder of Foullon and Bertier, hanged from lamp-posts and decapitated, on 22 July.

den explosion: If so no indication can be taken from it. But if it should be character rather than accident, then that people are not fit for Liberty, and must have a Strong hand like that of their former masters to coerce them. Men must have a certain fund of natural moderation to qualifye them for Freedom, else it become noxious to themselves and a perfect Nuisance to every body else. What will be the Event it is hard I think still to say. To form a solid constitution requires Wisdom as well as spirit, and whether the French have wise heads among them, or if they possess such whether they have authority equal to their wisdom, is to be seen; In the mean time the progress of this whole affair is one of the most curious matters of Speculation that ever was exhibited.

2. From a Letter to Charles-Jean-François Depont, November 1789 (*Corr.* VI, 39–50)

You may easily believe, that I have had my Eyes turned with great Curiosity to the astonishing scene now displayed in France. It has certainly given rise in my Mind to many Reflexions, and to some Emotions. These are natural and unavoidable; but it would ill become Me to be too ready in forming a positive opinion upon matters transacted in a Country, with the correct, political Map of which I must be very imperfectly acquainted. Things indeed have already happen'd so much beyond the scope of all speculation, that persons of infinitely more sagacity than I am ought to be ashamed of any thing like confidence in their reasoning upon the operation of any principle or the effect of any measure. It would become me least of all to be so confident, who ought at my time of life, to have well learn'd the important lesson of self distrust; A lesson of no small Value in company with the best information; but which alone can make any sort of amends for our not having learn'd other lessons so well as it was our business to learn them. I beg you, once for all, to apply this corrective of the diffidence I have on my own Judgment to whatever I may happen to say with more positiveness than suits my knowledge and situation. If I should seem any where to express myself in the language of disapprobation, be so good to consider it as no more than the expression of doubt.

You hope, Sir, that I think the French deserving of Liberty? I certainly do. I certainly think that all Men who desire it, deserve it. It is not the Reward of our Merit or the acquisition of our Industry. It is our Inheritance. It is the birthright of our Species.

We cannot forfeit our right to it, but by what forfeits our title to the privileges of our kind; I mean the abuse or oblivion of our rational faculties, and a ferocious indocility, which makes us prompt to wrong and Violence, destroys our social Nature, and transforms us into something little better than the description of Wild beasts. To Men so degraded, a state of strong constraint is a sort of necessary substitute for freedom; since, bad as it is, it may deliver them in some Measure from the worst of all Slavery, that is the despotism of their own blind and brutal passions.

You have kindly said, that You began to love freedom from Your intercourse with Me. This is the more necessary because of all the loose Terms in the world Liberty is the most indefinite. Permit me then to continue our conversation, and to tell You what the freedom is that I love and that to which I think all men intitled. It is not solitary, unconnected, individual, selfish Liberty. As if every Man was to regulate the whole of his Conduct by his own will. The Liberty I mean is *social* freedom. It is that state of things in which Liberty is secured by the equality of Restraint; A Constitution of things in which the liberty of no one Man, and no body of Men and no Number of men can find Means to trespass on the liberty of any Person or any description of Persons in the Society. This kind of liberty is indeed but another name for Justice, ascertained by wise Laws, and secured by well constructed institutions. I am sure, that Liberty, so incorporated, and in a manner, identified, with justice, must be infinitely dear to every one, who is capable of conceiving what it is. But whenever a separation is made between Liberty and Justice, neither is, in my opinion, safe. I do not believe that Men ever did submit, certain I am that they never ought to have submitted, to the arbitrary pleasure of one Man, but under circumstances in which the arbitrary pleasure of many Persons in the Community, pressed with an intolerable hardship upon the just and equal Rights of their fellows. Such a choice might be made as among Evils. The moment *Will* is set above Reason and Justice in any Community, a great Question may arise in sober Minds, in what part or portion of the Community that dangerous dominion of *Will* may be the least Mischievously placed....

I have nothing to check my wishes towards the establishment of a solid and rational scheme of Liberty in France. On the subject of the Relative power of Nations I may have my prejudices; but I envy internal freedom, security, and good order to none. When therefore I shall learn, that in France, the Citizen, by whatever description he is qualified, is in a perfect state of legal security, with regard to his life, to his property, to the uncontrolled disposal of his Person, to the free use of his Industry and his faculties;—When I hear that he is protected in the beneficial Enjoyment of the Estates, to which, by the course of settled Law, he was born, or is provided with a fair compensation for them;—that he is maintain'd in the full fruition of the advantages belonging to the state and condition of life, in which he had lawfully engaged himself, or is supplied with a substantial, equitable Equivalent;—When I am assured, that a simple Citizen may decently express his sentiments upon Publick Affairs, without hazard to his life or safety, even tho' against a predominant and fashionable opinion; When I know all this of France, I shall be as well pleased as every one must be, who has not forgot the general communion of Mankind, nor lost his natural sympathy in local and accidental connexions.

If a Constitution is settled in France upon these principles and calculated for those ends, I believe there is no Man in this Country whose heart and Voice would not go along with You....

But if (for in my present want of information I must only speak hypothetically) neither your great Assemblies, nor your Judicatures nor your Municipalities Act and forbear to Act in the particulars, upon the principles, and in the spirit that I have stated, I must delay my congratulations on your acquisition of Liberty. You may have made a Revolution, but not a Reformation. You may have subverted Monarchy, but not recover'd freedom....

You are now to live in a new order of things; under a plan of Government of which no Man can speak from experience. Your talents, Your publick spirit, and your fortune give you fair pretensions to a considerable share in it. Your settlement may be at hand; But that it is still at some distance is more likely. The French may be yet to go through more transmigrations. They may pass, as one of our Poets says, 'thro' many varieties of untried being'[1] before their State obtains its final form. In that progress thro' Chaos and darkness, you will find it necessary (at all times it is more or less so) to fix Rules to keep your life and Conduct in some steady course. You have theories enough concerning the Rights of Men. It may not be amiss to add a small degree of attention to their Nature and disposition. It is with Man in the concrete, it is with common human life and human Actions you are to be concerned. I have taken so many liberties

---

1 Joseph Addison, *Cato*, 5.1.11, quoted also at the end of the *Reflections*.

with You, that I am almost got the length of venturing to suggest something which may appear in the assuming tone of advice. You will however be so good as to receive my very few hints with your usual indulgence, tho' some of them I confess are not in the taste of this enlighten'd age, and indeed are no better than the late ripe fruit of mere experience.—Never wholly seperate in your Mind the merits of any Political Question from the Men who are concerned in it. You will be told, that if a measure is good, what have you [to] do with the Character and views of those who bring it forward. But designing Men never seperate their Plans from their Interests; and if You assist them in their Schemes, You will find the pretended good in the end thrown aside or perverted, and the interested object alone compassed, and that perhaps thro' Your means. The power of bad Men is no indifferent thing.

At this Moment, you may not perceive the full sense of this Rule, but you will recollect it, when the Cases are before you; You will then see and find its use. It will often keep your Virtue from becoming a tool of the Ambition and ill designs of others. Let me add, what, I think has some connexion with the Rule I mention: That you ought not to be so fond of any Political Object, as not to think the means of compassing it a serious consideration. No Man is less disposed than I am to put You under the Tuition of a petty Pedantick scruple in the management of arduous affairs; All I recommend is, that whenever the sacrifice of any subordinate point of Morality, or of honour, or even of common liberal sentiment and feeling is called for, one ought to be tolerably sure, that the object is worth it. Nothing is good, but in proportion, and with Reference. There are several who give an air of consequence to very petty designs and Actions, by the Crimes thro' which they make their way to their objects. Whatever is obtain'd smoothly and by easy means appears of no value in their Eyes. But when violent Methods are in agitation, one ought to be pretty clear, that there are no others to which we can Resort, and that a predilection from Character to such Methods is not the true cause of their being proposed....

I admit that Evils may be so very great and urgent that other Evils are to be submitted to for the mere hope of their Removal. A War, for instance, may be necessary, and we know what are the Rights of War, But before we use those Rights, We ought to be clearly in the state which alone can justify them; and not, in the very fold of Peace and security, by a bloody sophistry, to act towards any persons, at once as Citizens and as Enemies; and without the necessary formalities and evident distinctive lines of War, to exercise upon our Countrymen the most dreadful of all hostilities. Strong Party contentions, and a very violent opposition to our desires and opinions, are not War, nor can justify any one of its operations.

One form of Government may be better than another; and this difference may be worth a struggle. I think so. I do not mean to treat any of those forms, which are often the contrivances of deep human Wisdom (not the Rights of Men, as some people, in my opinion, not very wisely, talk of them) with slight or disrespect; Nor do I mean to level them.

A positively Vicious and abusive Government ought to be chang'd, and if necessary, by Violence, if it cannot be, (as sometimes it is the case) Reformed: But when the Question is concerning the more or the less *perfection* in the organization of a Government, the allowance to *means* is not of so much latitude. There is, by the essential fundamental Constitution of things a radical infirmity in all human contrivances, and the weakness is often so attached to the very perfection of our political Mechanism, that some defect in it, something that stops short of its principle, something that controls, that mitigates, that moderates it, becomes a necessary corrective to the Evils that the Theoretick Perfection would produce. I am pretty sure it often is so, and this truth may be exemplified abundantly.

It is true, that every defect is not of course, such a corrective as I state; but supposing it is not, an imperfect good is still a good; The defect may be tolerable, and may be Removed at some future time. In that Case, Prudence (in all things a Virtue, in Politicks the first of Virtues) will lead us rather to acquiesce in some qualified plan that does not come up to the full perfection of the abstract Idea, than to push for the more perfect, which cannot be attain'd without tearing to pieces the whole contexture of the Commonwealth, and creating an heart-ache in a thousand worthy bosoms. In that case combining the means and end, the less perfect is the more desirable. The *means* to any end, being first in order, are *immediate* in their good or their Evil, they are always, in a manner, *certainties*; The *End* is doubly problematical; first whether it is to be attain'd; then, whether supposing it obtaind, we obtain the true object we sought for.

But allow it in any degree probable, that theoretick and practical Perfection may differ, that an object pure and absolute may not be so good as one lower'd, mixed, and qualified, then, what we abate in our demand in favour of moderation and Justice and tenderness to Individuals, would be neither more nor less than a real improvement which a wise Legislator would make if he had no collateral Motive whatsoever, and only look'd in the formation of his Scheme, to its own independent Ends and purposes. Would it then be right to make way, thro' Temerity and Crime, to a form of things, which when obtained, evident Reason, perhaps imperious Necessity would compel us to alter, with the disgrace of inconsistency in our Conduct, and of want of foresight in our designs.

Believe me, Sir, in all changes in the State, Moderation is a Virtue not only amiable but powerful. It is a disposing, arranging, conciliating, cementing Virtue. In the formation of New Constitutions it is in its Province: Great Powers reside in those who can make great Changes. Their own Moderation is their only check; and if this Virtue is not paramount in their minds, their Acts will taste more of their Power than of their Wisdom or their benevolence. Whatever they do will be in extremes; it will be crude, harsh, precipitate. It will be submitted to with grudging and Reluctance; Revenge will be smother'd and hoarded; and the duration of schemes made in that temper will be as precarious as their Establishment was odious. The Virtue of Moderation (which times and Situations will clearly distinguish from the counterfeits of pusillanimity and indecision) is the Virtue only of superior Minds. It requires a deep Courage, and full of Reflexion, to be temperate, when the voice of Multitudes (the specious mimick of fame and Reputation) passes Judgment against you; the impetuous desires of an unthinking Publick will endure no course but what conducts to splendid and perilous extremes. Then to dare to be fearful, when all about you are full of presumption and confidence, and when those who are bold at the hazard of others, would punish your caution as disaffection, is to shew a Mind prepared for its trial; it discovers in the midst of general levity, a self possessing and collected Character which sooner or later bids fair to attract every thing to it, as to a Center....

... Pardon the liberty I have taken; though it seems somewhat singular, that I, whose opinions have so little weight in my own Country, where I have some share in a Publick Trust, should write as if it were possible they should affect one Man, with regard to Affairs in which I have no concern. But for the present, my time is my own, and to tire your patience is the only injury I can do You.

3. From "Substance of the Speech on the Army Estimates," 9 February 1790 (*Works* IV, 135–48)

Mr. Burke's speech on the report of the army estimates has not been correctly stated in some of the public papers. It is of consequence to him not to be misunderstood....

Mr. Burke said in substance, ...

That France is, at this time, in a political light, to be considered as expunged out of the system of Europe. Whether she could ever appear in it again, as a leading power, was not easy to determine: but at present he considered France as not politically existing; and most assuredly it would take her much time to restore her to her former active existence....

In a political view, France was low indeed. She had lost every thing, even to her name.... He was astonished at it—he was alarmed at it—he trembled at the uncertainty of all human greatness.

Since the House had been prorogued in the summer much work was done in France. The French had shown themselves the ablest architects of ruin that had hitherto existed in the world. In that very short space of time they had completely pulled down to the ground their monarchy, their church, their nobility, their law, their revenue, their army, their navy, their commerce, their arts, and their manufactures. They had done their business for us as rivals, in a way in which twenty Ramilies or Blenheims[1] could never have done it....

France, by the mere circumstance of its vicinity, had been, and in a degree always must be, an object of our vigilance, either with regard to her actual power, or to her influence and example. As to the former, he had spoken; as to the latter (her example) he should say a few words: for by this example our friendship and our intercourse with that nation had once been, and might again become, more dangerous to us than their worst hostility.

In the last century, Louis XIV. had established a greater and better disciplined military force than ever had been before seen in Europe, and with it a perfect despotism. Though that despotism was proudly arrayed in manners, gallantry, splendour, magnificence, and even covered over with the imposing robes of science, literature, and arts, it was, in government, nothing better than a painted and gilded tyranny; in religion, a hard, stern

---

1   The Battles of Ramilies (1706) and Blenheim (1704) resulted in overwhelming English victories over the French.

intolerance, the fit companion and auxiliary to the despotic tyranny which prevailed in its government. The same character of despotism insinuated itself into every court of Europe—the same spirit of disproportioned magnificence—the same love of standing armies, above the ability of the people. In particular, our then sovereigns, King Charles and King James, fell in love with the government of their neighbour, so flattering to the pride of kings. A similarity of sentiments brought on connexions equally dangerous to the interests and liberties of their country. It were well that the infection had gone no farther than the throne. The admiration of a government flourishing and successful, unchecked in its operations, and seeming therefore to compass its objects more speedily and effectually, gained something upon all ranks of people. The good patriots of that day, however, struggled against it. They sought nothing more anxiously than to break off all communication with France, and to beget a total alienation from its councils and its example; which, by the animosity prevalent between the abettors of their religious system and the assertors of ours, was, in some degree, effected.

This day the evil is totally changed in France: but there is an evil there. The disease is altered; but the vicinity of the two countries remains, and must remain; and the natural mental habits of mankind are such, that the present distemper of France is far more likely to be contagious than the old one; for it is not quite easy to spread a passion for servitude among the people; but in all evils of the opposite kind our natural inclinations are flattered....

In the last age we were in danger of being entangled by the example of France in the net of a relentless despotism. It is not necessary to say any thing upon that example. It exists no longer. Our present danger from the example of a people, whose character knows no medium, is, with regard to government, a danger from anarchy; a danger of being led, through an admiration of successful fraud and violence, to an imitation of the excesses of an irrational, unprincipled, proscribing, confiscating, plundering, ferocious, bloody, and tyrannical democracy. On the side of religion, the danger of their example is no longer from intolerance, but from atheism; a foul, unnatural vice, foe to all the dignity and consolation of mankind; which seems in France, for a long time, to have been embodied into a faction, accredited, and almost avowed....

That the House must perceive ... how anxious he was to keep the distemper of France from the least countenance in England, where he was sure some wicked persons had shown a strong disposition to recommend an imitation of the French spirit of reform. He was so strongly opposed to any the least tendency towards the *means* of introducing a democracy like theirs, as well as to the *end* itself, that much as it would afflict him, if such a thing could be attempted, and that any friend of his could concur in such measures (he was far, very far, from believing they could), he would abandon his best friends, and join with his worst enemies to oppose either the means or the end; and to resist all violent exertions of the spirit of innovation, so distant from all principles of true and safe reformation; a spirit well calculated to overturn states, but perfectly unfit to amend them.

That he was no enemy to reformation. Almost every business in which he was much concerned, from the first day he sat in that House to that hour, was a business of reformation; and when he had not been employed in correcting, he had been employed in resisting abuses. Some traces of this spirit in him now stand on their statute book. In his opinion, any thing which unnecessarily tore to pieces the contexture of the state, not only prevented all real reformation, but introduced evils which would call, but perhaps call in vain, for new reformation.

That he thought the French nation very unwise. What they valued themselves on, was a disgrace to them. They had gloried (and some people in England had thought fit to take share in that glory) in making a revolution; as if revolutions were good things in themselves. All the horrors, and all the crimes of the anarchy which led to their revolution, which attend its progress, and which may virtually attend it in its establishment, pass for nothing with the lovers of revolutions. The French have made their way, through the destruction of their country, to a bad constitution, when they were absolutely in possession of a good one....

Instead of redressing grievances, and improving the fabric of their state, to which they were called by their monarch, and sent by their country, they were made to take a very different course. They first destroyed all the balances and counterpoises which serve to fix the state, and to give it a steady direction; and which furnish sure correctives to any violent spirit which may prevail in any of the orders. These balances existed in their oldest constitution; and in the constitution of this country; and in the constitution of all the countries in Europe. These they rashly destroyed, and then they melted down the whole into one incongruous, ill-connected, mass.

When they had done this, they instantly, and with the most atrocious perfidy and breach of all faith among men, laid the axe to the root of all property, and consequently of all national prosperity, by the principles they established, and the example they set, in confiscating all the possessions of the Church. They made and recorded a sort of *institute* and *digest* of anarchy, called the rights of man, in such a pedantic abuse of elementary principles as would have disgraced boys at school; but this declaration of rights was worse than trifling and pedantic in them; as by their name and authority they systematically destroyed every hold of authority by opinion, religious or civil, on the minds of the people. By this mad declaration they subverted the state; and brought on such calamities as no country, without a long war, has ever been known to suffer; and which may in the end produce such a war, and perhaps, many such....

That if they should perfectly succeed in what they propose, as they are likely enough to do, and establish a democracy, or a mob of democracies, in a country circumstanced like France, they will establish a very bad government—a very bad species of tyranny....

He felt some concern that this strange thing, called a Revolution in France, should be compared with the glorious event commonly called the Revolution in England; and the conduct of the soldiery, on that occasion, compared with the behaviour of some of the troops of France in the present instance. At that period the Prince of Orange, a prince of the blood-royal in England, was called in by the flower of the English aristocracy to defend its ancient constitution, and not to level all distinctions. To this prince, so invited, the aristocratic leaders who commanded the troops went over with their several corps, in bodies, to the deliverer of their country.... The troops were ready for war, but indisposed to mutiny.

But as the conduct of the English armies was different, so was that of the whole English nation at that time. In truth, the circumstances of our Revolution (as it is called) and that of France are just the reverse of each other in almost every particular, and in the whole spirit of the transaction. With us it was the case of a legal monarch attempting arbitrary power—in France it is the case of an arbitrary monarch, beginning, from whatever cause, to legalize his authority. The one was to be resisted, the other was to be managed and directed; but in neither case was the order of the state to be changed, lest government might be ruined, which ought only to be corrected and legalized. With us we got rid of the man, and preserved the constituent parts of the state. There they get rid of the constituent parts of the state, and keep the man. What we did was in truth and substance, and in a constitutional light, a revolution, not made, but prevented. We took solid securities; we settled doubtful questions; we corrected anomalies in our law. In the stable, fundamental parts of our constitution we made no revolution; no, nor any alteration at all. We did not impair the monarchy. Perhaps it might be shown that we strengthened it very considerably. The nation kept the same ranks, the same orders, the same privileges, the same franchises, the same rules for property, the same subordinations, the same order in the law, in the revenue, and in the magistracy; the same lords, the same commons, the same corporations, the same electors.

The Church was not impaired. Her estates, her majesty, her splendour, her orders and gradations continued the same. She was preserved in her full efficiency, and cleared only of a certain intolerance, which was her weakness and disgrace. The Church and the State were the same after the Revolution that they were before, but better secured in every part.

Was little done because a revolution was not made in the constitution? No! Every thing was done; because we commenced with reparation, not with ruin. Accordingly the state flourished. Instead of lying as dead, in a sort of trance, or exposed as some others, in an epileptic fit, to the pity or derision of the world, for her wild, ridiculous, convulsive movements, impotent to every purpose but that of dashing out her brains against the pavement, Great Britain rose above the standard even of her former self. An era of a more improved domestic prosperity then commenced, and still continues, not only unimpaired, but growing, under the wasting hand of time....

Mr. Burke said he should have felt very unpleasantly if he had not delivered these sentiments. He was near the end of his natural, probably still nearer the end of his political, career; that he was weak and weary; and wished for rest. That he was little disposed to controversies, or what is called a detailed opposition. That at his time of life, if he could not do something by some sort of weight of opinion, natural or acquired, it was useless and indecorous to attempt any thing by mere struggle. *Turpe senex miles*.[1]

---

1 "An old man is a bad soldier." Ovid (43 BCE–17 CE), *Amores*, Book I, 9.

Appendix D: Burke's Later Thoughts on the Revolution

[Burke had written a great deal about the evils of the French Revolution (that "most unnatural and perfidious Rebellion"[1]), but by the beginning of 1791 he had concluded that words should surrender to action. He expressed such a sentiment in a letter to the Comtesse de Montrond (d. 1827), written on 25 January 1791. Dreading "the contagious nature of these abominable principles, and vile manners, which threaten the worst and most degrading barbarism to every adjacent Country," Burke laments the "utter inutility" of merely *talking* more about the Jacobin threat. Instead, "Something must be done. You have an armed Tyranny to deal with; and nothing but arms can pull it down."[2] From this point onwards, Burke's writings on French affairs are devoted to making the case for war against France. *Thoughts on French Affairs* was the first in this new line of attack from Burke, and selections from this important text are included below. It was followed by a series of other writings including *Heads for Consideration on the Present State of Affairs* (1792) and *Remarks on the Policy of the Allies with Respect to France* (1793), both of which agitate more aggressively for war. The pro-war stance becomes solidified in Burke's mind following the execution of Louis XVI on 21 January 1793. In the selections from the *Remarks* included below, Burke directs his thoughts to the aftermath of war and specifically to the punishments suitable for the Jacobins. The appendix closes with selections from Burke's late masterpiece, the *Letters on a Regicide Peace* (or *Letters on the Proposals for Peace with the Regicide Directory of France*), composed in 1795–97. Written when Britain was seeking a peace treaty with France, Burke's *Letters* furiously denounce the peace overtures and set out the case for a continuation of the war that Britain had been waging since 1793. The selections from this

---

1 Letter to John Trevor, January 1791, *Corr.* VI, 217.

2 Letter to the Comtesse de Montrond, 25 January 1791, *Corr.* VI, 211–12. Compare with the Fourth Letter on a Regicide Peace: "Their bosom is a rock of granite, on which falsehood has long since built her strong hold. Poor truth has had a hard work of it with her little pickaxe. Nothing but gunpowder will do" (*Works* V, 447).

lengthy text are chosen in order to illustrate a number of Burkean themes. First, we see him making a contribution to the field of philosophy of history, casting doubt here on the idea that nations go through inevitable life-cycles and, accordingly, doubting both that the fall of the monarchy in France was inevitable and that Britain's power to fight was irreversibly enervated. Second, Burke analyzes the character of the revolutionary government, defining clearly its component qualities (it is, by establishment, Regicide, Jacobin, and Atheistic); the low character of the regicides ("a gang of strolling players") is here memorably described, and here also we see Burke's depiction of the important revolution in *manners* that he sees effected in France. Burke recognizes (and this is the third theme covered in these selections) that the war with France is "a war of a *peculiar* nature," a war that goes beyond national and territorial borders, and is more akin to a civil war pitting "the partisans of the ancient civil, moral, and political order of Europe" against a faction of radical fanatics who seek to destroy that old world. As Tocqueville also would later claim, the French Revolution was best to be seen as something akin to a religious revolution, transcending particular nationalities, offering a non-localized, "abstract view of the citizen," and aiming "at the regeneration of the human race."[1] Burke's case for war is centred ultimately on the need to expunge completely that global threat to the old order.]

1. From *Thoughts on French Affairs* (December 1791) (*Works* IV, 553–58, 566, 591)

In all our transactions with France, and at all periods, we have treated with that state on the footing of a monarchy. Monarchy was considered in all the external relations of that kingdom with every power in Europe as its legal and constitutional government, and that in which alone its federal capacity was vested....

If it be our policy to assimilate our government to that of France, we ought to prepare for this change, by encouraging the schemes of authority established there. We ought to wink at the captivity and deposition of a prince, with whom, if not in close alliance, we were in friendship....

The question is, whether this policy be suitable to the interests of the crown and subjects of Great Britain. Let us, therefore,

---

1 Alexis de Tocqueville, *The Ancien Régime and the French Revolution* (1856; Cambridge UP, 2011), 21.

a little consider the true nature and probable effects of the revolution which, in such a very unusual manner, has been twice diplomatically announced to his majesty.

There have been many internal revolutions in the government of countries, both as to persons and forms, in which the neighbouring states have had little or no concern. Whatever the government might be with respect to those persons and those forms, the stationary interests of the nation concerned have most commonly influenced the new governments in the same manner in which they influenced the old; and the revolution, turning on matter of local grievance, or of local accommodation, did not extend beyond its territory.

The present revolution in France seems to me to be quite of another character and description; and to bear little resemblance or analogy to any of those which have been brought about in Europe, upon principles merely political. *It is a revolution of doctrine and theoretic dogma.* It has a much greater resemblance to those changes which have been made upon religious grounds, in which a spirit of proselytism makes an essential part.

The last revolution of doctrine and theory which has happened in Europe, is the Reformation. It is not for my purpose to take any notice here of the merits of that revolution, but to state one only of its effects.

That effect was *to introduce other interests into all countries than those which arose from their locality and natural circumstances.* The principle of the Reformation was such as, by its essence, could not be local or confined to the country in which it had its origin. For instance, the doctrine of "justification by faith or by works," which was the original basis of the Reformation, could not have one of its alternatives true as to Germany, and false as to every other country. Neither are questions of theoretic truth and falsehood governed by circumstances any more than by places. On that occasion, therefore, the spirit of proselytism expanded itself with great elasticity upon all sides: and great divisions were every where the result....

The political dogma, which, upon the new French system, is to unite the factions of different nations, is this, "That the majority, told by the head, of the taxable people in every country, is the perpetual, natural, unceasing, indefeasible sovereign; that this majority is perfectly master of the form, as well as the administration, of the state, and that the magistrates, under whatever names they are called, are only functionaries to obey the orders (general as laws or particular as decrees) which that majority may make; that this is the only natural government; that all others are tyranny and usurpation."

In order to reduce this dogma into practice, the republicans in France, and their associates in other countries, make it always their business, and often their public profession, to destroy all traces of ancient establishments, and to form a new commonwealth in each country, upon the basis of the French *Rights of Men....*

... When I contemplate what they [the new French politicians] have done at home, which is, in effect, little less than an amazing conquest wrought by a change of opinion, in a great part (to be sure far from altogether) very sudden, I cannot help letting my thoughts run along with their designs, and, without attending to geographical order, considering the other states of Europe so far as they may be any way affected by this astonishing revolution. If early steps are not taken in some way or other to prevent the spreading of this influence, I scarcely think any of them perfectly secure....

What is to be done?

It would be a presumption in me to do more than to make a case. Many things occur. But as they, like all political measures, depend on dispositions, tempers, means, and external circumstances, for all their effect, not being well assured of these, I do not know how to let loose any speculations of mine on the subject. The evil is stated, in my opinion, as it exists. The remedy must be where power, wisdom, and information, I hope, are more united with good intentions than they can be with me. I have done with this subject, I believe, for ever. It has given me many anxious moments for the two last years. If a great change is to be made in human affairs, the minds of men will be fitted to it; the general opinions and feelings will draw that way. Every fear, every hope, will forward it; and then they, who persist in opposing this mighty current in human affairs, will appear rather to resist the decrees of Providence itself, than the mere designs of men. They will not be resolute and firm, but perverse and obstinate.

2. From *Remarks on the Policy of the Allies with Respect to France* (October 1793) (*Works* V, 42, 53–57)

In all that we do, whether in the struggle or after it, it is necessary that we should constantly have in our eye the nature and character of the enemy we have to contend with. The Jacobin revolution is carried on by men of no rank, of no consideration, of wild, savage minds, full of levity, arrogance, and presumption, without morals, without probity, without prudence. What have they then to supply their innumerable defects, and to make them terrible even to the firmest minds? *One* thing, and *one* thing only—but that one thing is worth a thousand—they have *energy*. In France, all things being put into an universal ferment, in the decomposition of society, no man comes forward but by his spirit of enterprise and the vigour of his mind. If we meet this dreadful and portentous energy, restrained by no consideration of God or man, that is always vigilant, always on the attack, that allows itself no repose, and suffers none to rest an hour with impunity; if we meet this energy with poor common-place proceeding, with trivial maxims, paltry old saws, with doubts, fears, and suspicions, with a languid, uncertain hesitation, with a formal, official spirit, which is turned aside by every obstacle from its purpose, and which never sees a difficulty but to yield to it, or at best to evade it; down we go to the bottom of the abyss—and nothing short of Omnipotence can save us. We must meet a vicious and distempered energy with a manly and rational vigour....

A valuable friend of mine ... asked me what I thought of acts of general indemnity and oblivion, as a means of settling France, and reconciling it to monarchy....

... I am not for a total indemnity, nor a general punishment. And first, the body and mass of the people never ought to be treated as criminal. They may become an object of more or less constant watchfulness and suspicion, as their preservation may best require, but they can never become an object of punishment. This is one of the few fundamental and unalterable principles of politics.

To punish them capitally would be to make massacres. Massacres only increase the ferocity of men, and teach them to regard their own lives and those of others as of little value; whereas the great policy of government is to teach the people to think both of great importance in the eyes of God and the state, and never to be sacrificed or even hazarded to gratify their passions, or for any thing but the duties prescribed by the rules of morality, and under the direction of public law and public authority. To punish them with lesser penalties would be to debilitate the commonwealth, and make the nation miserable, which it is the business of government to render happy and flourishing.

As to crimes too, I would draw a strong line of limitation. For no one offence, *politically an offence of rebellion*, by council, contrivance, persuasion, or compulsion, for none properly a *military offence of rebellion*, or any thing done by open hostility in the field, should any man at all be called in question; because such seems to be the proper and natural death of civil dissensions. The offences of war are obliterated by peace.

Another class will of course be included in the indemnity, namely, all those who by their activity in restoring lawful government shall obliterate their offences. The offence previously known, the acceptance of service is a pardon for crimes. I fear this class of men will not be very numerous.

So far as to indemnity. But where are the objects of justice, and of example, and of future security to the public peace? They are naturally pointed out, not by their having outraged political and civil laws, nor their having rebelled against the state as a state, but by their having rebelled against the law of nature, and outraged man as man. In this list, all the regicides in general, all those who laid sacrilegious hands on the king, who without any thing in their own rebellious mission to the convention to justify them, brought him to his trial and unanimously voted him guilty; all those who had a share in the cruel murder of the queen, and the detestable proceedings with regard to the young king, and the unhappy princesses; all those who committed cold-blooded murder any where, and particularly in their revolutionary tribunals, where every idea of natural justice and of their own declared rights of man have been trodden under foot with the most insolent mockery; all men concerned in the burning and demolition of houses or churches, with audacious and marked acts of sacrilege and scorn offered to religion; in general, all the leaders of Jacobin clubs;—not one of these should escape a punishment suitable to the nature, quality, and degree of their offence, by a steady but a measured justice.

In the first place, no man ought to be subject to any penalty, from the highest to the lowest, but by a trial according to the course of law, carried on with all that caution and deliberation which has been used in the best times and precedents of the French jurisprudence, the criminal law of which country, faulty to be sure in some particulars, was highly laudable and tender of the lives of men. In restoring order and justice, every thing like retaliation ought to be religiously avoided; and an example ought to be set of a total alienation from the Jacobin proceedings in their accursed revolutionary tribunals. Every thing like lumping men in masses, and of forming tables of proscription, ought to be avoided.

In all these punishments, any thing which can be alleged in mitigation of the offence should be fully considered. Mercy is not a thing opposed to justice. It is an essential part of it: as necessary in criminal cases, as in civil affairs equity is to law. It is only for the Jacobins never to pardon. They have not done it in a single instance. A council of mercy ought therefore to be appointed, with powers to report on each case, to soften the penalty, or entirely to remit it, according to circumstances....

I know it sounds plausible, and is readily adopted by those who have little sympathy with the sufferings of others, to wish to jumble the innocent and guilty into one mass, by a general indemnity. This cruel indifference dignifies itself with the name of humanity.

It is extraordinary that as the wicked arts of this regicide and tyrannous faction increase in number, variety, and atrocity, the desire of punishing them becomes more and more faint, and the talk of an indemnity towards them every day stronger and stronger. Our ideas of justice appear to be fairly conquered and overpowered by guilt, when it is grown gigantic. It is not the point of view in which we are in the habit of viewing guilt. The crimes we every day punish are really below the penalties we inflict. The criminals are obscure and feeble. This is the view in which we see ordinary crimes and criminals. But when guilt is seen, though but for a time, to be furnished with the arms and to be invested with the robes of power, it seems to assume another nature, and to get, as it were, out of our jurisdiction. This I fear is the case with many. But there is another cause full as powerful towards this security to enormous guilt, the desire which possesses people, who have once obtained power, to enjoy it at their ease. It is not humanity, but laziness and inertness of mind, which produces the desire of this kind of indemnities. This description of men love general and short methods. If they punish, they make a promiscuous massacre; if they spare, they make a general act of oblivion. This is a want of disposition to proceed laboriously according to the cases, and according to the rules and principles of justice on each case; a want of disposition to assort criminals, to discriminate the degrees and modes of guilt, to separate accomplices from principals, leaders from followers, seducers from the seduced, and then, by following the same principles in the same detail, to class punishments, and to fit them to the nature and kind of the delinquency. If that were once attempted, we should soon see that the task was neither infinite, nor the execution cruel. There would be deaths, but, for the number of criminals, and the extent of France, not many. There would be cases of transportation; cases of labour to restore what has been wickedly destroyed; cases of imprisonment, and cases of mere exile. But be this as it may, I am sure that if justice is not done there, there can be neither peace nor justice there, nor in any part of Europe.

3. From *Letters on a Regicide Peace* (1795–97) (*Works* V, 253–56, 260–61, 263–64, 296–307, 320–22)

a. From Letter I: "On the Overtures of Peace" (1796)

I shall not live to behold the unravelling of the intricate plot, which saddens and perplexes the awful drama of Providence, now acting on the moral theatre of the world. Whether for thought or for action, I am at the end of my career.... In what part of its orbit the nation, with which we are carried along, moves at this instant, it is not easy to conjecture. It may, perhaps, be far advanced in its aphelion[1]—but when to return?

Not to lose ourselves in the infinite void of the conjectural world, our business is with what is likely to be affected, for the better or the worse, by the wisdom or weakness of our plans. In all speculations upon men and human affairs, it is of no small moment to distinguish things of accident from permanent causes, and from effects that cannot be altered. It is not every irregularity in our movement that is a total deviation from our course. I am not quite of the mind of those speculators, who seem assured, that necessarily, and by the constitution of things, all states have the same periods of infancy, manhood, and decrepitude, that are found in the individuals who compose them. Parallels of this sort rather furnish similitudes to illustrate or to adorn, than supply analogies from whence to reason. The objects which are attempted to be forced into an analogy are not found in the same classes of existence. Individuals are physical beings subject to laws universal and invariable. The immediate cause acting in these laws may be obscure: the general results are subjects of certain calculation. But commonwealths are not physical but moral essences. They are artificial combinations, and, in their proximate efficient cause, the arbitrary productions of the human mind. We are not yet acquainted with the laws which necessarily influence the stability of that kind of work made by that kind of agent. There is not in the physical order

---

1 The point in the orbit of a planetary body at which it is farthest from the sun.

(with which they do not appear to hold any assignable connexion) a distinct cause by which any of those fabrics must necessarily grow, flourish, or decay; nor, in my opinion, does the moral world produce any thing more determinate on that subject, than what may serve as an amusement (liberal indeed, and ingenious, but still only an amusement) for speculative men. I doubt whether the history of mankind is yet complete enough, if ever it can be so, to furnish grounds for a sure theory on the internal causes which necessarily affect the fortune of a state. I am far from denying the operation of such causes: but they are infinitely uncertain, and much more obscure, and much more difficult to trace, than the foreign causes that tend to raise, to depress, and sometimes to overwhelm a community.

It is often impossible, in these political inquiries, to find any proportion between the apparent force of any moral causes we may assign and their known operation. We are therefore obliged to deliver up that operation to mere chance, or, more piously, (perhaps more rationally,) to the occasional interposition and irresistible hand of the Great Disposer. We have seen states of considerable duration, which for ages have remained nearly as they have begun, and could hardly be said to ebb or flow. Some appear to have spent their vigour at their commencement. Some have blazed out in their glory a little before their extinction. The meridian of some has been the most splendid. Others, and they the greatest number, have fluctuated, and experienced at different periods of their existence a great variety of fortune. At the very moment when some of them seemed plunged in unfathomable abysses of disgrace and disaster, they have suddenly emerged. They have begun a new course and opened a new reckoning; and, even in the depths of their calamity, and on the very ruins of their country, have laid the foundations of a towering and durable greatness. All this has happened without any apparent previous change in the general circumstances which had brought on their distress. The death of a man at a critical juncture, his disgust, his retreat, his disgrace, have brought innumerable calamities on a whole nation. A common soldier, a child, a girl at the door of an inn, have changed the face of fortune, and almost of nature.

Such, and often influenced by such causes, has commonly been the fate of monarchies of long duration. They have their ebbs and their flows. This has been eminently the fate of the monarchy of France. There have been times in which no power has ever been brought so low. Few have ever flourished in greater glory. By turns elevated and depressed, that power had been, on the whole, rather on the increase; and it continued not only powerful but formidable to the hour of the total ruin of the monarchy. This fall of the monarchy was far from being preceded by any exterior symptoms of decline. The interior were not visible to every eye; and a thousand accidents might have prevented the operation of what the most clear-sighted were not able to discern, nor the most provident to divine. A very little time before its dreadful catastrophe, there was a kind of exterior splendour in the situation of the crown, which usually adds to government strength and authority at home.... In that its acmé of human prosperity and greatness, in the high and palmy state of the monarchy of France, it fell to the ground without a struggle. It fell without any of those vices in the monarch, which have sometimes been the causes of the fall of kingdoms, but which existed, without any visible effect on the state, in the highest degree in many other princes; and, far from destroying their power, had only left some slight stains on their character. The financial difficulties were only pretexts and instruments of those who accomplished the ruin of that monarchy. They were not the causes of it.

Deprived of the old government, deprived in a manner of all government, France fallen as a monarchy, to common speculators might have appeared more likely to be an object of pity or insult, according to the disposition of the circumjacent powers, than to be the scourge and terror of them all: but out of the tomb of the murdered monarchy in France has arisen a vast, tremendous, unformed spectre, in a far more terrific guise than any which ever yet have overpowered the imagination, and subdued the fortitude of man. Going straight forward to its end, unappalled by peril, unchecked by remorse, despising all common maxims and all common means, that hideous phantom overpowered those who could not believe it was possible she could at all exist, except on the principles, which habit rather than nature had persuaded them were necessary to their own particular welfare, and to their own ordinary modes of action....

The allies, and Great Britain amongst the rest (and perhaps amongst the foremost), have been miserably deluded by this great fundamental error: that it was in our power to make peace with this monster of a state, whenever we chose to forget the crimes that made it great, and the designs that made it formidable. People imagined that their ceasing to resist was the sure way to be secure. This "pale cast of thought"[1] sicklied over all their enterprises, and turned all their politics awry. They could not, or rather they would not, read, in the most unequivocal declarations of the enemy, and in his uniform conduct, that more safety was to be found in the most arduous war, than in the friendship of that kind of being....

Is it that the people are changed, that the commonwealth cannot be protected by its laws? I hardly think it. On the contrary, I conceive, that these things happen because men are not changed, but remain always what they always were; they remain what the bulk of us ever must be, when abandoned to our vulgar propensities, without guide, leader, or control: that is, made to be full of a blind elevation in prosperity; to despise untried dangers; to be overpowered with unexpected reverses; to find no clue in a labyrinth of difficulties; to get out of a present inconvenience with any risk of future ruin; to follow and to bow to fortune; to admire successful though wicked enterprise, and to imitate what we admire; to contemn the government which announces danger from sacrilege and regicide, whilst they are only in their infancy and their struggle, but which finds nothing that can alarm in their adult state, and in the power and triumph of those destructive principles. In a mass we cannot be left to ourselves. We must have leaders. If none will undertake to lead us right, we shall find guides who will contrive to conduct us to shame and ruin.

We are in a war of a *peculiar* nature. It is not with an ordinary community, which is hostile or friendly as passion or as interest may veer about: not with a state which makes war through wantonness, and abandons it through lassitude. We are at war with a system, which, by its essence, is inimical to all other governments, and which makes peace or war, as peace and war may best contribute to their subversion. It is with an *armed doctrine* that we are at war. It has, by its essence, a faction of opinion, and of interest, and of enthusiasm, in every country. To us it is a Colossus which bestrides our channel. It has one foot on a foreign shore, the other upon the British soil. Thus advantaged, if it can at all exist, it must finally prevail. Nothing can so completely ruin any of the old governments, ours in particular, as the acknowledgment, directly or by implication, of any kind of superiority in this new power. This acknowledgment we make, if, in a bad or doubtful situation of our affairs, we solicit peace;

---

1 Shakespeare, *Hamlet* 3.1.86.

or if we yield to the modes of new humiliation, in which alone she is content to give us a hearing. By that means the terms cannot be of our choosing; no, not in any part....

In that great war carried on against Louis XIV. for near eighteen years, government spared no pains to satisfy the nation, that though they were to be animated by a desire of glory, glory was not their ultimate object; but that every thing dear to them, in religion, in law, in liberty, every thing which as freemen, as Englishmen, and as citizens of the great commonwealth of Christendom, they had at heart, was then at stake. This was to know the true art of gaining the affections and confidence of a high-minded people; this was to understand human nature. A danger to avert a danger—a present inconvenience and suffering to prevent a foreseen future, and a worse calamity—these are the motives that belong to an animal, who, in his constitution, is at once adventurous and provident; circumspect and daring; whom his Creator has made, as the poet says, "of large discourse, looking before and after."[1] ...

If a war to prevent Louis XIV. from imposing his religion was just, a war to prevent the murderers of Louis XVI. from imposing their irreligion upon us is just; a war to prevent the operation of a system, which makes life without dignity, and death without hope, is a just war....

A government of the nature of that set up at our very door has never been hitherto seen, or even imagined, in Europe. What our relation to it will be cannot be judged by other relations. It is a serious thing to have connexion with a people, who live only under positive, arbitrary, and changeable institutions; and those not perfected nor supplied, nor explained, by any common acknowledged rule of moral science....

Instead of the religion and the law by which they were in a great politic communion with the Christian world, they have constructed their republic on three bases, all fundamentally opposite to those on which the communities of Europe are built. Its foundation is laid in regicide, in Jacobinism, and in atheism; and it has joined to those principles a body of systematic manners, which secures their operation.

If I am asked, how I would be understood in the use of these terms, regicide, Jacobinism, atheism, and a system of correspondent manners, and their establishment? I will tell you:

I call a commonwealth *regicide*, which lays it down as a fixed

---

1 Shakespeare, *Hamlet* 4.4.36–37.

law of nature, and a fundamental right of man, that all government, not being a democracy, is an usurpation. That all kings, as such, are usurpers; and for being kings may and ought to be put to death, with their wives, families, and adherents. The commonwealth which acts uniformly upon those principles, and which, after abolishing every festival of religion, chooses the most flagrant act of a murderous regicide treason for a feast of eternal commemoration, and which forces all her people to observe it—this I call *regicide by establishment*.

Jacobinism is the revolt of the enterprising talents of a country against its property. When private men form themselves into associations for the purpose of destroying the pre-existing laws and institutions of their country; when they secure to themselves an army, by dividing amongst the people of no property the estates of the ancient and lawful proprietors; when a state recognizes those acts; when it does not make confiscations for crimes, but makes crimes for confiscations; when it has its principal strength, and all its resources in such a violation of property; when it stands chiefly upon such a violation; massacring by judgments, or otherwise, those who make any struggle for their old legal government, and their legal, hereditary, or acquired possessions—I call this *Jacobinism by establishment*.

I call it *atheism by establishment*, when any state, as such, shall not acknowledge the existence of God as a moral governor of the world; when it shall offer to Him no religious or moral worship;—when it shall abolish the Christian religion by a regular decree;—when it shall persecute with a cold, unrelenting, steady cruelty, by every mode of confiscation, imprisonment, exile, and death, all its ministers;—when it shall generally shut up, or pull down churches; when the few buildings which remain of this kind shall be opened only for the purpose of making a profane apotheosis of monsters, whose vices and crimes have no parallel amongst men, and whom all other men consider as objects of general detestation, and the severest animadversion of law. When, in the place of that religion of social benevolence, and of individual self-denial, in mockery of all religion, they institute impious, blasphemous, indecent theatric rites, in honour of their vitiated, perverted reason, and erect altars to the personification of their own corrupted and bloody republic;—when schools and seminaries are founded at the public expense to poison mankind, from generation to generation, with the horrible maxims of this impiety;—when wearied out with incessant martyrdom, and the cries of a people hungering and thirsting for religion, they permit it, only as a tolerated evil—I call this *atheism by establishment.*

When to these establishments of regicide, of Jacobinism, and of atheism, you add the *correspondent system of manners,* no doubt can be left on the mind of a thinking man concerning their determined hostility to the human race. Manners are of more importance than laws. Upon them, in a great measure, the laws depend. The law touches us but here and there, and now and then. Manners are what vex or soothe, corrupt or purify, exalt or debase, barbarize or refine us, by a constant, steady, uniform, insensible operation, like that of the air we breathe in. They give their whole form and colour to our lives. According to their quality, they aid morals, they supply them, or they totally destroy them. Of this the new French legislators were aware; therefore, with the same method, and under the same authority, they settled a system of manners, the most licentious, prostitute, and abandoned, that ever has been known, and at the same time the most coarse, rude, savage, and ferocious. Nothing in the revolution, no, not to a phrase or a gesture, not to the fashion of a hat or a shoe, was left to accident. All has been the result of design; all has been matter of institution. No mechanical means could be devised in favour of this incredible system of wickedness and vice, that has not been employed. The noblest passions, the love of glory, the love of country, have been debauched into means of its preservation and its propagation. All sorts of shows and exhibitions, calculated to inflame and vitiate the imagination, and pervert the moral sense, have been contrived....

To all this let us join the practice of *cannibalism,* with which, in the proper terms, and with the greatest truth, their several factions accuse each other. By cannibalism, I mean their devouring as a nutriment of their ferocity, some part of the bodies of those they have murdered; their drinking the blood of their victims, and forcing the victims themselves to drink the blood of their kindred slaughtered before their faces. By cannibalism, I mean also to signify all their nameless, unmanly, and abominable insults on the bodies of those they slaughter.

As to those whom they suffer to die a natural death, they do not permit them to enjoy the last consolations of mankind, or those rights of sepulture, which indicate hope, and which mere nature has taught to mankind, in all countries, to soothe the afflictions, and to cover the infirmity of mortal condition. They disgrace men in the entry into life, they vitiate and enslave them through the whole course of it, and they deprive them of all comfort at the conclusion of their dishonoured and depraved existence. Endeavouring to persuade the people that they are no better than beasts, the whole body of their institution tends to make them beasts of prey, furious and savage....

... It struck us that the habits of Paris had no resemblance to the finished virtues, or to the polished vice, and elegant, though not blameless luxury, of the capital of a great empire. Their society was more like that of a den of outlaws upon a doubtful frontier; of a lewd tavern for the revels and debauches of banditti, assassins, bravos, smugglers, and their more desperate paramours, mixed with bombastic players, the refuse and rejected offal of strolling theatres, puffing out ill-sorted verses about virtue, mixed with the licentious and blasphemous songs, proper to the brutal and hardened course of life belonging to that sort of wretches.[1] This system of manners in itself is at war with all orderly and moral society, and is in its neighbourhood unsafe. If great bodies of that kind were any where established in a bordering territory, we should have a right to demand of their governments the suppression of such a nuisance. What are we to do if the government and the whole community is of the same description? Yet that government has thought proper to invite ours to lay by its unjust hatred, and to listen to the voice of humanity as taught by their example.

The operation of dangerous and delusive first principles obliges us to have recourse to the true ones. In the intercourse between nations, we are apt to rely too much on the instrumental part. We lay too much weight upon the formality of treaties and compacts. We do not act much more wisely when we trust

---

1 A first sketch of this passage is to be found in the earlier-written letter to Earl Fitzwilliam, later published as the "Fourth Letter on a Regicide Peace": "All elegance of mind and manners is banished. A theatrical, bombastic, windy phraseology of heroic virtue, blended and mingled up with a worse dissoluteness, and joined to a murderous and savage ferocity, forms the tone and idiom of their language and their manners. Any one, who attends to all their own descriptions, narratives, and dissertations, will find in that whole place more of the air of a body of assassins, banditti, house-breakers, and outlawed smugglers, joined to that of a gang of strolling players, expelled from and exploded in orderly theatres, with their prostitutes in a brothel, at their debauches and bacchanals, than any thing of the refined and perfected virtues, or the polished, mitigated vices of a great capital" (*Works* V, 485).

to the interests of men as guarantees of their engagements. The interests frequently tear to pieces the engagements; and the passions trample upon both. Entirely to trust to either, is to disregard our own safety, or not to know mankind. Men are not tied to one another by papers and seals. They are led to associate by resemblances, by conformities, by sympathies. It is with nations as with individuals. Nothing is so strong a tie of amity between nation and nation as correspondence in laws, customs, manners, and habits of life. They have more than the force of treaties in themselves. They are obligations written in the heart. They approximate men to men, without their knowledge, and sometimes against their intentions. The secret, unseen, but irrefragable bond of habitual intercourse holds them together, even when their perverse and litigious nature sets them to equivocate, scuffle, and fight, about the terms of their written obligations....

The whole body of this new scheme of manners, in support of the new scheme of politics, I consider as a strong and decisive proof of determined ambition and systematic hostility. I defy the most refining ingenuity to invent any other cause for the total departure of the Jacobin republic from every one of the ideas and usages, religious, legal, moral, or social, of this civilized world, and for her tearing herself from its communion with such studied violence, but from a formed resolution of keeping no terms with that world. It has not been, as has been falsely and insidiously represented, that these miscreants had only broke with their old government. They made a schism with the whole universe, and that schism extended to almost every thing great and small. For one, I wish, since it is gone thus far, that the breach had been so complete, as to make all intercourse impracticable: but partly by accident, partly by design, partly from the resistance of the matter, enough is left to preserve intercourse, whilst amity is destroyed or corrupted in its principle.

This violent breach of the community of Europe we must conclude to have been made (even if they had not expressly declared it over and over again) either to force mankind into an adoption of their system, or to live in perpetual enmity with a community the most potent we have ever known.

b. From Letter II: "On the Genius and Character of the French Revolution as It Regards Other Nations" (1796)

My ideas and my principles led me, in this contest, to encounter France, not as a state, but as a faction. The vast territorial extent of that country, its immense population, its riches of production, its riches of commerce and convention—the whole aggregate mass of what, in ordinary cases, constitutes the force of a state, to me were but objects of secondary consideration. They might be balanced; and they have been often more than balanced. Great as these things are, they are not what make the faction formidable. It is the faction that makes them truly dreadful. That faction is the evil spirit that possesses the spirit of France; that informs it as a soul; that stamps upon its ambition, and upon all its pursuits, a characteristic mark, which strongly distinguishes them from the same general passions, and the same general views, in other men and in other communities. It is that spirit which inspires into them a new, a pernicious, a desolating activity. Constituted as France was ten years ago, it was not in that France to shake, to shatter, and to overwhelm Europe in the manner that we behold. A sure destruction impends over those infatuated princes, who, in the conflict with this new and unheard-of power, proceed as if they were engaged in a war that bore a resemblance to their former contests; or that they can make peace in the spirit of their former arrangements of pacification. Here the beaten path is the very reverse of the safe road.

As to me, I was always steadily of opinion, that this disorder was not in its nature intermittent. I conceived that the contest, once begun, could not be laid down again, to be resumed at our discretion; but that our first struggle with this evil would also be our last. I never thought we could make peace with the system; because it was not for the sake of an object we pursued in rivalry with each other, but with the system itself that we were at war. As I understood the matter, we were at war not with its conduct, but with its existence; convinced that its existence and its hostility were the same.

The faction is not local or territorial. It is a general evil. Where it least appears in action, it is still full of life. In its sleep it recruits its strength, and prepares its exertion. Its spirit lies deep in the corruption of our common nature. The social order which restrains it, feeds it. It exists in every country in Europe; and among all orders of men in every country, who look up to France as to a common head. The centre is there. The circumference is the world of Europe wherever the race of Europe may be settled. Every where else the faction is militant; in France it is triumphant. In France is the bank of deposit, and the bank of circulation, of all the pernicious principles that are forming in every state. It will be a folly scarcely deserving of pity, and too mischievous for contempt, to think of restraining it in any other country whilst it is predominant there. War, instead of being the cause of its force, has suspended its operation. It has given a reprieve, at least, to the Christian world ...

... It is a dreadful truth, but it is a truth that cannot be concealed; in ability, in dexterity, in the distinctness of their views, the Jacobins are our superiors. They saw the thing right from the very beginning. Whatever were the first motives to the war among politicians, they saw that in its spirit, and for its objects, it was a *civil war*; and as such they pursued it. It is a war between the partisans of the ancient, civil, moral, and political order of Europe against a sect of fanatical and ambitious atheists which means to change them all. It is not France extending a foreign empire over other nations: it is a sect aiming at universal empire, and beginning with the conquest of France.

Appendix E: Burke on Reform and Innovation

[Although often depicted as a reactionary defender of the status quo, Burke's reputation, before the advent of his writings on the French Revolution, was as a reformer of abuses. This attitude, indeed, is not expunged in the *Reflections* ("A disposition to preserve, and an ability to improve, taken together, would be my standard of a statesman" [p. 138]). The selections that follow, drawn from 1769–96, illustrate the continuity of Burke's thinking, the idea of timely, prudent, and moderate reform consistently contrasted by him with that of rash and theory-driven innovation.]

1. From "Speech on St. George's Fields Massacre" (8 March 1769), *The Writings and Speeches of Edmund Burke* (Oxford UP, 1981–2015), vol. II, pp. 225–26

I would have it observed too that I do not mean to recommend a Lax and effeminate execution of Justice; or to weaken the Springs of Government. In the next place I do not wish to deprive Government of the possession, or the use of any one power it enjoys at present judicial or executive, civil or even Military. Order I know must be preserved at any rate or at any price—if the Voice of the Magistrate will not do it; The Staff of the Constable must do it; If the Staff fails we must have recourse to the Sword of the Soldier. If nothing but blood can purchase peace, it must be purchased with blood. Peace is the great End in *all* Governments; Liberty is an End only in the Best. I am far I have ever been far from entertaining any extreme or immoderate thoughts upon that subject. My Ideas of Liberty have been always very much temperd and chastened; they have been pitched a key lower than I think is common, because I am afraid of myself; I wish that they may stick by me, and that I may stick by them to the End of my Life at all Events; and in all Circumstances I am by opinion, principle, Constitution, an hater of violence and *innovation*.

2. From *Thoughts on the Cause of the Present Discontents*, 1770 (*Works* III, 163–64)

... It is no inconsiderable part of wisdom, to know how much of an evil ought to be tolerated; lest, by attempting a degree of purity impracticable in degenerate times and manners, instead of cutting off the subsisting ill-practices, new corruptions might be produced for the concealment and security of the old.... Our constitution stands on a nice equipoise, with steep precipices and deep waters upon all sides of it. In removing it from a dangerous leaning towards one side, there may be a risk of oversetting it on the other. Every project of a material change in a government so complicated as ours, combined at the same time with external circumstances still more complicated, is a matter full of difficulties: in which a considerate man will not be too ready to decide; a prudent man too ready to undertake; or an honest man too ready to promise....

3. From "Speech on the Bill for Explaining the Powers of Juries in Prosecutions for Libels," 7 March 1771 (*Works* VI, 146)

I am not of the opinion of those gentlemen who are against disturbing the public repose; I like a clamour whenever there is an abuse. The fire-bell at midnight disturbs your sleep, but it keeps you from being burned in your bed. The hue and cry alarms the county, but it preserves all the property of the province. All these clamours aim at *redress*. But a clamour made merely for the purpose of rendering the people discontented with their situation, without an endeavour to give them a practical remedy, is indeed one of the worst acts of sedition.

4. From "Speech on Presenting to the House of Commons (on the 11th February, 1780) a Plan for the Better Security of the Independence of Parliament, and the Economical Reformation of the Civil and Other Establishments," 1780 (*Works* III, 345–46, 352–53, 368–69, 400–01)

MR. SPEAKER,
I rise, in acquittal of my engagement to the House, in obedience to the strong and just requisition of my constituents, and, I am persuaded, in conformity to the unanimous wishes of the

whole nation, to submit to the wisdom of parliament, "A Plan of Reform in the Constitution of several Parts of the Public Economy." ...

Sir, I assure you, very solemnly, and with a very clear conscience, that nothing in the world has led me to such an undertaking, but my zeal for the honour of this House, and the settled, habitual, systematic affection I bear to the cause, and to the principles of government.

I enter perfectly into the nature and consequences of my attempt; and I advance to it with a tremor that shakes me to the inmost fibre of my frame. I feel that I engage in a business, in itself most ungracious, totally wide of the course of prudent conduct; and, I really think, the most completely adverse that can be imagined to the natural turn and temper of my own mind. I know, that all parsimony is of a quality approaching to unkindness; and that (on some person or other) every reform must operate as a sort of punishment....

If there is any one eminent criterion, which above all the rest, distinguishes a wise government from an administration weak and improvident, it is this;—"well to know the best time and manner of yielding what it is impossible to keep." ...

... I do most seriously put it to the administration, to consider the wisdom of a timely reform. Early reformations are amicable arrangements with a friend in power; late reformations are terms imposed upon a conquered enemy: early reformations are made in cool blood; late reformations are made under a state of inflammation....

But when the reason of old establishments is gone, it is absurd to preserve nothing but the burden of them. This is superstitiously to embalm a carcass not worth an ounce of the gums that are used to preserve it. It is to burn precious oils in the tomb; it is to offer meat and drink to the dead,—not so much an honour to the deceased, as a disgrace to the survivors. Our palaces are vast inhospitable halls. There the bleak winds, there "Boreas, and Eurus, and Caurus, and Argestes loud,"[1] howling through the vacant lobbies, and clattering the doors of deserted guardrooms, appal the imagination, and conjure up the grim spectres of departed tyrants—the Saxon, the Norman, and the Dane;

---

1   John Milton, *Paradise Lost*, Book X, 699. "Boreas, and Caecias and Argestes loud / And Thrascias rend the woods and seas upturn." All these are names of the various winds. The fourth wind mentioned by Burke ("Eurus") appears a few lines later (X, 705).

the stern Edwards and fierce Henries—who stalk from desolation to desolation, through the dreary vacuity, and melancholy succession of chill and comfortless chambers. When this tumult subsides, a dead, and still more frightful silence would reign in this desert, if every now and then the tacking of hammers did not announce, that those constant attendants upon all courts in all ages, jobs, were still alive; for whose sake alone it is, that any trace of ancient grandeur is suffered to remain. These palaces are a true emblem of some governments; the inhabitants are decayed, but the governors and magistrates still flourish. They put me in mind of *Old Sarum*,[1] where the representatives, more in number than the constituents, only serve to inform us, that this was once a place of trade, and sounding with "the busy hum of men,"[2] though now you can only trace the streets by the colour of the corn; and its sole manufacture is in members of parliament....

This plan, I really flatter myself, is laid, not in official formality, nor in airy speculation, but in real life, and in human nature, in what "comes home" (as Bacon says) "to the business and bosoms of men."[3] ...

... I know it is common for men to say, that such and such things are perfectly right—very desirable; but that unfortunately, they are not practicable. Oh! no, sir, no. Those things, which are not practicable, are not desirable. There is nothing in the world really beneficial, that does not lie within the reach of an informed understanding, and a well-directed pursuit. There is nothing that God has judged good for us, that he has not given us the means to accomplish, both in the natural and the moral world. If we cry, like children, for the moon, like children, we must cry on.

We must follow the nature of our affairs, and conform ourselves to our situation. If we do, our objects are plain and compassable....

---

1 Until its abolition as a parliamentary constituency under the 1832 Reform Act, Old Sarum was a so-called rotten borough with an extremely small electorate.

2 John Milton, *L'Allegro*, 118.

3 See "The Epistle Dedicatorie" of Francis Bacon's *Essayes* (1625).

5. From "Speech on a Motion Made in the House of Commons, the 7th of May, 1782, for a Committee to Inquire into the State of the Representation of the Commons in Parliament," 1782/84[1] (*Works* VI, 128–36)

MR. SPEAKER,

We have now discovered, at the close of the eighteenth century, that the constitution of England, which for a series of ages had been the proud distinction of this country, always the admiration, and sometimes the envy of the wise and learned in every other nation, we have discovered that this boasted constitution, in the most boasted part of it, is a gross imposition upon the understanding of mankind, an insult to their feelings, and acting by contrivances destructive to the best and most valuable interests of the people. Our political architects have taken a survey of the fabric of the British constitution. It is singular that they report nothing against the crown, nothing against the lords; but in the House of Commons every thing is unsound; it is ruinous in every part. It is infested by the dry rot, and ready to tumble about our ears without their immediate help. You know by the faults they find what are their ideas of the alteration. As all government stands upon opinion, they know that the way utterly to destroy it is to remove that opinion, to take away all reverence, all confidence from it; and then, at the first blast of public discontent and popular tumult, it tumbles to the ground.

In considering this question they who oppose it oppose it on different grounds: one is, in the nature of a previous question; that some alterations may be expedient, but that this is not the time for making them. The other is, that no essential alterations are at all wanting: and that neither *now*, nor at *any* time, is it prudent or safe to be meddling with the fundamental principles, and ancient tried usages of our constitution—that our representation is as nearly perfect as the necessary imperfection of human affairs and of human creatures will suffer it to be; and that it is a subject of prudent and honest use and thankful enjoyment, and not of captious criticism and rash experiment.

On the other side there are two parties, who proceed on two grounds, in my opinion, as they state them, utterly irreconcilable. The one is juridical, the other political. The one is in the

---

1 Though listed in the *Works* as a speech from 1782, it seems more likely to be a contribution to a parliamentary debate on 16 June 1784.

nature of a claim of right, on the supposed rights of man as man; this party desire the decision of a suit. The other ground, as far as I can divine what it directly means, is, that the representation is not so politically framed as to answer the theory of its institution. As to the claim of *right*, the meanest petitioner, the most gross and ignorant, is as good as the best; in some respects his claim is more favourable on account of his ignorance; his weakness, his poverty and distress, only add to his titles; he sues in *formá pauperis*;[1] he ought to be a favourite of the court. But when the *other* ground is taken, when the question is political, when a new constitution is to be made on a sound theory of government, then the presumptuous pride of didactic ignorance is to be excluded from the counsel in this high and arduous matter, which often bids defiance to the experience of the wisest. The first claims a personal representation, the latter rejects it with scorn and fervour. The language of the first party is plain and intelligible; they who plead an absolute right cannot be satisfied with any thing short of personal representation, because all *natural* rights must be the rights of individuals; as by *nature* there is no such thing as politic or corporate personality; all these ideas are mere fictions of law, they are creatures of voluntary institution; men as men are individuals, and nothing else. They, therefore, who reject the principle of natural and personal representation, are essentially and eternally at variance with those who claim it. As to the first sort of reformers, it is ridiculous to talk to them of the British constitution upon any or upon all of its bases; for they lay it down that every man ought to govern himself, and that where he cannot go himself, he must send his representative; that all other government is usurpation, and is so far from having a claim to our obedience, it is not only our right but our duty to resist it. Nine-tenths of the reformers argue thus, that is, on the natural right. It is impossible not to make some reflection on the nature of this claim, or avoid a comparison between the extent of the principle and the present object of the demand. If this claim be founded, it is clear to what it goes. The House of Commons, in that light, undoubtedly is no representative of the people, as a collection of individuals. Nobody pretends it, nobody can justify such an assertion. When you come to examine into this claim of right, founded on the right of self-government in each individual, you find the thing demanded infinitely

---

1 In the form or character of a pauper, referring to a poor person's ability to sue without liability for costs.

short of the principle of the demand. What! one-*third* only of the legislature, and of the government no share at all? What sort of treaty of partition is this for those who have an inherent right to the whole? Give them all they ask, and your grant is still a cheat; for how comes only a third to be their younger children's fortune in this settlement? How came they neither to have the choice of kings, or lords, or judges, or generals, or admirals, or bishops, or priests, or ministers, or justices of peace? Why, what have you to answer in favour of the prior rights of the crown and peerage but this—our constitution is a prescriptive constitution; it is a constitution whose sole authority is, that it has existed time out of mind. It is settled in these *two* portions against one, legislatively; and in the whole of the judicature, the whole of the federal capacity, of the executive, the prudential and the financial administration, in one alone. Nor was your House of Lords and the prerogatives of the crown settled on any adjudication in favour of natural rights, for they could never be so partitioned. Your king, your lords, your judges, your juries, grand and little, are all prescriptive; and what proves it, is, the disputes not yet concluded, and never near becoming so, when any of them first originated. Prescription is the most solid of all titles, not only to property, but, which is to secure that property, to government. They harmonize with each other, and give mutual aid to one another. It is accompanied with another ground of authority in the constitution of the human mind, presumption. It is a presumption in favour of any settled scheme of government against any untried project, that a nation has long existed and flourished under it. It is a better presumption even of the *choice* of a nation, far better than any sudden and temporary arrangement by actual election. Because a nation is not an idea only of local extent and individual momentary aggregation, but it is an idea of continuity which extends in time as well as in numbers and in space. And this is a choice not of one day, or one set of people, not a tumultuary and giddy choice; it is a deliberate election of ages and of generations; it is a constitution made by what is ten thousand times better than choice, it is made by the peculiar circumstances, occasions, tempers, dispositions, and moral, civil, and social habitudes of the people, which disclose themselves only in a long space of time. It is a vestment which accommodates itself to the body. Nor is prescription of government formed upon blind unmeaning prejudices—for man is a most unwise and a most wise being. The individual is foolish. The multitude, for the moment, is foolish when they act without deliberation; but the species is wise, and when time is given to it, as a species, it almost always acts right.

The reason for the crown as it is, for the lords as they are, is my reason for the commons as they are, the electors as they are. Now if the crown, and the lords, and the judicatures, are all prescriptive, so is the House of Commons of the very same origin, and of no other. We and our electors have their powers and privileges both made and circumscribed by prescription, as much to the full as the other parts; and as such we have always claimed them, and on no other title. The House of Commons is a legislative body corporate by prescription, not made upon any given theory, but existing prescriptively—just like the rest. This prescription has made it essentially what it is, an aggregate collection of three parts, knights, citizens, burgesses. The question is, whether this has been always so, since the House of Commons has taken its present shape and circumstances, and has been an essential operative part of the constitution; which, I take it, it has been for at least five hundred years.

This I resolve to myself in the affirmative: and then another question arises, whether this House stands firm upon its ancient foundations, and is not, by time and accidents, so declined from its perpendicular, as to want the hand of the wise and experienced architects of the day to set it upright again, and to prop and buttress it up for duration;—whether it continues true to the principles upon which it has hitherto stood;—whether this be *de facto* the constitution of the House of Commons, as it has been since the time that the House of Commons has, without dispute, become a necessary and an efficient part of the British constitution? To ask whether a thing which has always been the same stands to its usual principle, seems to me to be perfectly absurd; for how do you know the principles but from the construction? and if that remains the same, the principles remain the same. It is true that to say your constitution is what it has been, is no sufficient defence for those who say it is a bad constitution. It is an answer to those who say that it is a degenerate constitution. To those who say it is a bad one, I answer, look to its effects. In all moral machinery, the moral results are its test.

On what grounds do we go to restore our constitution to what it has been at some given period, or to reform and re-construct it upon principles more conformable to a sound theory of government? A prescriptive government, such as ours, never was the work of any legislator, never was made upon any foregone theory. It seems to me a preposterous way of reasoning, and a perfect confusion of ideas, to take the theories which learned and speculative men have made from that government, and then supposing it made on those theories which were made from it, to accuse the government as not corresponding with them. I do not vilify theory and speculation—no, because that would be to vilify reason itself. *Neque decipitur ratio, neque decipit unquam.*[1] No; whenever I speak against theory, I mean always a weak, erroneous, fallacious, unfounded, or imperfect theory; and one of the ways of discovering that it is a false theory, is by comparing it with practice. This is the true touchstone of all theories which regard man and the affairs of men—does it suit his nature in general;—does it suit his nature as modified by his habits?

The more frequently this affair is discussed, the stronger the case appears to the sense and the feelings of mankind. I have no more doubt than I entertain of my existence that this very thing, which is stated as a horrible thing, is the means of the preservation of our constitution whilst it lasts; of curing it of many of the disorders which, attending every species of institution, would attend the principle of an exact local representation, or a representation on the principle of numbers. If you reject personal representation, you are pushed upon expedience; and then what they wish us to do is, to prefer their speculations on that subject to the happy experience of this country of a growing liberty and a growing prosperity for five hundred years. Whatever respect I have for their talents, this, for one, I will not do. Then what is the standard of expedience? Expedience is that which is good for the community, and good for every individual in it. Now this expedience is the *desideratum*, to be sought either without the experience of means, or with that experience. If without, as in case of the fabrication of a new commonwealth, I will hear the learned arguing what promises to be expedient: but if we are to judge of a commonwealth actually existing, the first thing I inquire is, what has been *found* expedient or inexpedient? And I will not take their *promise* rather than the *performance* of the constitution ...

In every political proposal we must not leave out of the question the political views and object of the proposer; and these we discover, not by what he says, but by the principles he lays down. I mean, says he, a moderate and temperate reform; that is, I mean to do as little good as possible. If the constitution be what you represent it, and there be no danger in the change, you do wrong not

1 "Reason neither deceives nor is deceived ever." Manilius (1st century CE), *Astronomicon*, Book II, 132.

to make the reform commensurate to the abuse. Fine reformer indeed! generous donor! What is the cause of this parsimony of the liberty which you dole out to the people? Why all this limitation in giving blessings and benefits to mankind? You admit that there is an extreme in liberty, which may be infinitely noxious to those who are to receive it, and which in the end will leave them no liberty at all. I think so too; they know it, and they feel it. The question is then what is the standard of that extreme? What that gentleman, and the associations, or some parts of their phalanxes, think proper? Then our liberties are in their pleasure; it depends on their arbitrary will how far I shall be free. I will have none of that freedom. If, therefore, the standard of moderation be sought for, I will seek for it. Where? Not in their fancies, nor in my own: I will seek for it where I know it is to be found, in the constitution I actually enjoy. Here it says to an encroaching prerogative,—your sceptre has its length, you cannot add a hair to your head, or a gem to your crown, but what an eternal law has given to it. Here it says to an overweening peerage,—your pride finds banks that it cannot overflow: here to a tumultuous and giddy people,—there is a bound to the raging of the sea. Our constitution is like our island, which uses and restrains its subject sea; in vain the waves roar. In that constitution I know, and exultingly I feel, both that I am free, and that I am not free dangerously to myself or to others. I know that no power on earth, acting as I ought to do, can touch my life, my liberty, or my property. I have that inward and dignified consciousness of my own security and independence, which constitutes, and is the only thing which does constitute, the proud and comfortable sentiment of freedom in the human breast. I know too, and I bless God for, my safe mediocrity.... I know there is an order, that keeps things fast in their place; it is made to us, and we are made to it....

It suggests melancholy reflections, in consequence of the strange course we have long held, that we are now no longer quarrelling about the character, or about the conduct of men, or the tenor of measures; but we are grown out of humour with the English constitution itself; this is become the object of the animosity of Englishmen. This constitution in former days used to be the admiration and the envy of the world; it was the pattern for politicians; the theme of the eloquent; the meditation of the philosopher in every part of the world. As to Englishmen, it was their pride, their consolation. By it they lived, for it they were ready to die. Its defects, if it had any, were partly covered by partiality, and partly borne by prudence. Now all its excellencies are forgot, its faults are now forcibly dragged into day, exaggerated by every artifice of representation. It is despised and rejected of men;[1] and every device and invention of ingenuity, or idleness, set up in opposition or in preference to it. It is to this humour, and it is to the measures growing out of it, that I set myself (I hope not alone) in the most determined opposition. Never before did we at any time in this country meet upon the theory of our frame of government, to sit in judgment on the constitution of our country, to call it as a delinquent before us, and to accuse it of every defect and every vice; to see whether it, an object of our veneration, even our adoration, did or did not accord with a pre-conceived scheme in the minds of certain gentlemen. Cast your eyes on the journals of parliament. It is for fear of losing the ines-timable treasure we have, that I do not venture to game it out of my hands for the vain hope of improving it. I look with filial rev-erence on the constitution of my country, and never will cut it in pieces, and put it into the kettle of any magician, in order to boil it, with the puddle of their compounds, into youth and vigour. On the contrary, I will drive away such pretenders; I will nurse its venerable age, and with lenient arts extend a parent's breath.

6. From *An Appeal from the New to the Old Whigs*, 1791 (*Works* IV, 404–07)

The excellencies of the British constitution had already exer-cised and exhausted the talents of the best thinkers, and the most eloquent writers and speakers, that the world ever saw. But in the present case, a system declared to be far better, and which certainly is much newer (to restless and unstable minds no small recommendation), was held out to the admiration of the good people of England. In that case, it was surely proper for those, who had far other thoughts of the French constitution, to scruti-nize that plan which has been recommended to our imitation by active and zealous factions, at home and abroad. Our complexion is such, that we are palled with enjoyment, and stimulated with hope; that we become less sensible to a long-possessed benefit, from the very circumstance that it is become habitual. Specious, untried, ambiguous prospects of new advantage, recommend themselves to the spirit of adventure, which more or less prevails in every mind. From this temper, men and factions, and nations

---

1 Isaiah 53:3: "He is despised and rejected of men, a man of sorrows, and acquainted with grief: and we hid as it were our faces from him; he was despised, and we esteemed him not."

too, have sacrificed the good, of which they had been in assured possession, in favour of wild and irrational expectations....

... When that nameless thing, which has been lately set up in France, was described[1] as "the most stupendous and glorious edifice of liberty, which had been erected on the foundation of human integrity in any time or country," it might at first have led the hearer into an opinion, that the construction of the new fabric was an object of admiration, as well as the demolition of the old.... Far from meriting the praises of a great genius like Mr. Fox, it cannot be approved by any man of common sense, or common information. He cannot admire the change of one piece of barbarism for another, and a worse. He cannot rejoice at the destruction of a monarchy, mitigated by manners, respectful to laws and usages, and attentive, perhaps but too attentive to public opinion, in favour of the tyranny of a licentious, ferocious, and savage multitude, without laws, manners, or morals, and which, so far from respecting the general sense of mankind, insolently endeavours to alter all the principles and opinions, which have hitherto guided and contained the world, and to force them into a conformity to their views and actions. His mind is made to better things....

The subversion of a government, to deserve any praise, must be considered but as a step preparatory to the formation of something better, either in the scheme of the government itself, or in the persons who administer it, or in both. These events cannot in reason be separated. For instance, when we praise our Revolution of 1688, though the nation in that act was on the defensive, and was justified in incurring all the evils of a defensive war, we do not rest there. We always combine with the subversion of the old government, the happy settlement which followed. When we estimate that revolution, we mean to comprehend in our calculation both the value of the thing parted with, and the value of the thing received in exchange.

The burden of proof lies heavily on those who tear to pieces the whole frame and contexture of their country, that they could find no other way of settling a government fit to obtain its rational ends, except that which they have pursued by means unfavourable to all the present happiness of millions of people, and to the utter ruin of several hundreds of thousands. In their political arrangements, men have no right to put the well-being of the present generation wholly out of the question. Perhaps the only moral trust with any certainty in our hands, is the care of our

---

1 By Charles James Fox (1749–1806), on 15 April 1791.

own time. With regard to futurity, we are to treat it like a ward. We are not so to attempt an improvement of his fortune, as to put the capital of his estate to any hazard.

It is not worth our while to discuss, like sophisters, whether, in no case, some evil, for the sake of some benefit, is to be tolerated. Nothing universal can be rationally affirmed on any moral, or any political subject. Pure metaphysical abstraction does not belong to these matters. The lines of morality are not like ideal lines of mathematics. They are broad and deep as well as long. They admit of exceptions; they demand modifications. These exceptions and modifications are not made by the process of logic, but by the rules of prudence. Prudence is not only the first in rank of the virtues political and moral, but she is the director, the regulator, the standard of them all. Metaphysics cannot live without definition; but prudence is cautious how she defines. Our courts cannot be more fearful in suffering fictitious cases to be brought before them for eliciting their determination on a point of law, than prudent moralists are in putting extreme and hazardous cases of conscience upon emergencies not existing. Without attempting therefore to define, what never can be defined, the case of a revolution in government, this, I think, may be safely affirmed, that a sore and pressing evil is to be removed, and that a good, great in its amount, and unequivocal in its nature, must be probable almost to certainty, before the inestimable price of our own morals, and the well-being of a number of our fellow-citizens, is paid for a revolution. If ever we ought to be economists even to parsimony, it is in the voluntary production of evil. Every revolution contains in it something of evil.

7. From *A Letter to Sir Hercules Langrishe on the Subject of the Roman Catholics of Ireland*, 1792 (*Works* IV, 510–11, 514, 544–45)

[Sir Hercules Langrishe (1729–1811) was a member of the Irish House of Commons and a supporter of Catholic emancipation. Langrishe had sought Burke's views on a petition by the Irish Catholic Committee for a relaxation of the Penal Laws against Catholics, some elements of which had already been repealed in 1778 and 1782.]

MY DEAR SIR,
... The case, upon which your letter of the 10th of December turns, is hardly before me with precision enough to enable me to form any very certain judgment upon it. It seems to be some

plan of further indulgence proposed for the Catholics of Ireland. You observe, that your "general principles are not changed, but that *times and circumstances are altered.*" I perfectly agree with you, that times and circumstances, considered with reference to the public, ought very much to govern our conduct; though I am far from slighting, when applied with discretion to those circumstances, general principles, and maxims of policy....

In my present state of imperfect information, you will pardon the errors into which I may easily fall. The principles you lay down are, "that the Roman Catholics should enjoy every thing *under* the state, but should not be *the state itself.*" ...

... You, who have looked deeply into the spirit of the popery laws, must be perfectly sensible, that a great part of the present mischief, which we abhor in common (if it at all exists) has arisen from them. Their declared object was to reduce the Catholics of Ireland to a miserable populace, without property, without estimation, without education. The professed object was to deprive the few men who, in spite of those laws, might hold or obtain any property amongst them, of all sort of influence or authority over the rest. They divided the nation into two distinct bodies, without common interest, sympathy, or connexion. One of these bodies was to possess *all* the franchises, *all* the property, *all* the education: the other was to be composed of drawers of water and cutters of turf for them.[1] Are we to be astonished, when, by the efforts of so much violence in conquest, and so much policy in regulation, continued without intermission for near a hundred years, we had reduced them to a mob; that, whenever they came to act at all, many of them would act exactly like a mob, without temper, measure, or foresight? Surely it might be just now a matter of temperate discussion, whether you ought not to apply a remedy to the real cause of the evil....

Between the extreme of *a total exclusion*, to which your maxim goes, and *an universal unmodified capacity*, to which the fanatics pretend, there are many different degrees and stages, and a great variety of temperaments, upon which prudence may give full scope to its exertions. For you know that the decisions of prudence (contrary to the system of the insane reasoners) differ from those of judicature: and that almost all the former are determined

---

1 Joshua 9:21: "And the princes said unto them, 'Let them live; but let them be hewers of wood and drawers of water unto all the congregation'; as the princes had promised them." The words are proverbially used to indicate the lowest social class.

on the more or the less, the earlier or the later, and on a balance of advantage and inconvenience, of good and evil....

It is a consideration of great moment, that you make the desired admission without altering the system of your representation in the smallest degree, or in any part. You may leave that deliberation of a parliamentary change or reform, if ever you should think fit to engage in it, uncomplicated and unembarrassed with the other question. Whereas, if they are mixed and confounded, as some people attempt to mix and confound them, no one can answer for the effects on the constitution itself.

There is another advantage in taking up this business, singly and by an arrangement for the single object. It is that you may proceed by *degrees*. We must all obey the great law of change. It is the most powerful law of nature, and the means perhaps of its conservation. All we can do, and that human wisdom can do, is to provide that the change shall proceed by insensible degrees. This has all the benefits which may be in change, without any of the inconveniences of mutation. Every thing is provided for as it arrives. This mode will, on the one hand, prevent the *unfixing old interests at once*: a thing which is apt to breed a black and sullen discontent in those who are at once dispossessed of all their influence and consideration. This gradual course, on the other side, will prevent men, long under depression, from being intoxicated with a large draught of new power, which they always abuse with a licentious insolence. But wishing, as I do, the change to be gradual and cautious, I would, in my first steps, lean rather to the side of enlargement than restriction.

8. *From A Letter to a Noble Lord*, 1796 (*Works* V, 223–25, 241–42)

[The "Noble Lord" of this work's title, though unidentified in the text, is William Wyndham Grenville (1759–1834). Since Burke's stated purpose in this letter is to defend himself against the attacks made upon him and his pension by Francis Russell, Duke of Bedford (1765–1802), the "noble lord" becomes, as F.P. Lock writes, "a representative figure of true nobility, a foil to the renegade Duke of Bedford" (*Edmund Burke*, vol. II, p. 523).]

MY LORD,

... [T]here is a manifest, marked distinction, which ill men, with ill designs, or weak men incapable of any design, will constantly be confounding, that is, a marked distinction between change and reformation. The former alters the substance of the objects themselves; and gets rid of all their essential good, as well as of all the accidental evil annexed to them. Change is novelty; and whether it is to operate any one of the effects of reformation at all, or whether it may not contradict the very principle upon which reformation is desired, cannot be certainly known beforehand. Reform is, not a change in the substance, or in the primary modification of the object, but a direct application of a remedy to the grievance complained of. So far as that is removed, all is sure. It stops there; and, if it fails, the substance which underwent the operation, at the very worst, is but where it was.

All this, in effect, I think, but am not sure, I have said elsewhere. It cannot at this time be too often repeated; line upon line; precept upon precept; until it comes into the currency of a proverb, *to innovate is not to reform.* The French revolutionists complained of every thing; they refused to reform any thing; and they left nothing, no, nothing at all *unchanged.* The consequences are *before* us,—not in remote history; not in future prognostication: they are about us; they are upon us. They shake the public security; they menace private enjoyment. They dwarf the growth of the young; they break the quiet of the old. If we travel, they stop our way. They infest us in town; they pursue us to the country. Our business is interrupted; our repose is troubled; our pleasures are saddened; our very studies are poisoned and perverted, and knowledge is rendered worse than ignorance, by the enormous evils of this dreadful innovation. The revolution harpies of France, sprung from night and hell, or from that chaotic anarchy, which generates equivocally "all monstrous, all prodigious things,"[1] cuckoo-like, adulterously lay their eggs, and brood over, and hatch them in the nest of every neighbouring state. These obscene harpies, who deck themselves in I know not what divine attributes, but who in reality are foul and ravenous birds of prey, (both mothers and daughters,) flutter over our heads, and souse down upon our tables, and leave nothing unrent, unrifled, unravaged, or unpolluted with the slime of their filthy offal.[2] ...

---

1   Milton, *Paradise Lost,* Book II, 625.
2   [Burke's note:]
    Tristius haud illis monstrum, nec sævior ulla
    Pestis, et ira Deûm Stygiis sese extulit undis.
    Virginei volucrum vultus; fœdissima ventris
    Proluvies; uncæque manus; et pallida semper
    Ora fame.*

It was then not my love, but my hatred, to innovation, that produced my plan of reform. Without troubling myself with the exactness of the logical diagram, I considered them as things substantially opposite. It was to prevent that evil, that I proposed the measures, which his grace is pleased, and I am not sorry he is pleased, to recall to my recollection. I had (what I hope that noble duke will remember in all his operations) a state to preserve, as well as a state to reform. I had a people to gratify, but not to inflame, or to mislead. I do not claim half the credit for what I did, as for what I prevented from being done. In that situation of the public mind, I did not undertake, as was then proposed, to new-model the House of Commons or the House of Lords; or to change the authority under which any officer of the crown acted, who was suffered at all to exist. Crown, lords, commons, judicial system, system of administration, existed as they had existed before; and in the mode and manner in which they had always existed. My measures were, what I then truly stated them to the House to be, in their intent, healing and mediatorial....

... I have lived long and variously in the world. Without any considerable pretensions to literature in myself, I have aspired to the love of letters. I have lived for a great many years in habitudes with those who professed them. I can form a tolerable estimate of what is likely to happen from a character, chiefly dependent for fame and fortune on knowledge and talent, as well in its morbid and perverted state, as in that which is sound and natural. Naturally men so formed and finished are the first gifts of Providence to the world. But when they have thrown off the fear of God, which was in all ages too often the case, and the fear of men, which is now the case, and when in that state they come

---

Here the poet breaks the line, because he (and that he is Virgil) had not verse or language to describe that monster even as he had conceived her. Had he lived in our time, he would have been more overpowered with the reality than he was with the imagination. Virgil only knew the horror of the times before him. Had he lived to see the revolutionists and constitutionalists of France, he would have had more horrid and disgusting features of his harpies to describe, and more frequent failures in the attempt to describe them. [*"No monster more baneful than these, no fiercer plague or wrath of the gods ever rose from the Stygian waves. Maiden faces have these birds, foulest filth they drop, clawed hands are theirs, and faces ever gaunt with hunger." (Virgil, *Aeneid*, Book III, 214–18.)]

to understand one another, and to act in corps, a more dreadful calamity cannot arise out of hell to scourge mankind. Nothing can be conceived more hard than the heart of a thorough-bred metaphysician. It comes nearer to the cold malignity of a wicked spirit than to the frailty and passion of a man. It is like that of the principle of evil himself, incorporeal, pure, unmixed, dephlegmated, defecated evil. It is no easy operation to eradicate humanity from the human breast. What Shakespeare calls the "compunctious visitings of nature"[1] will sometimes knock at their hearts, and protest against their murderous speculations. But they have a means of compounding with their nature. Their humanity is not dissolved. They only give it a long prorogation. They are ready to declare, that they do not think two thousand years too long a period for the good that they pursue. It is remarkable, that they never see any way to their projected good but by the road of some evil. Their imagination is not fatigued with the contemplation of human suffering through the wild waste of centuries added to centuries of misery and desolation. Their humanity is at their horizon—and, like the horizon, it always flies before them. The geometricians, and the chemists, bring, the one from the dry bones of their diagrams, and the other from the soot of their furnaces, dispositions that make them worse than indifferent about those feelings and habitudes, which are the supports of the moral world. Ambition is come upon them suddenly; they are intoxicated with it, and it has rendered them fearless of the danger, which may from thence arise to others or to themselves. These philosophers consider men in their experiments no more than they do mice in an air-pump, or in a recipient of mephitic gas....

---

1 Shakespeare, *Macbeth* 1.5.35.

Appendix F: Burke on Rousseau and "The Philosophy of Vanity"

1. From *A Letter to a Member of the National Assembly in Answer to Some Objections to His Book on French Affairs* (1791) (*Works* IV, 372–78, 389–92)

[In *Reflections on the Revolution in France*, Burke makes passing reference to Jean-Jacques Rousseau (1712–78) as an "acute, though eccentric, observer" (p. 145). That rather measured judgment was consistent with the line he had taken at least since 1759, when, in his review in the *Annual Register* of Rousseau's *Letter to d'Alembert*, Burke had noted how Rousseau's rare talents and learning were compromised by a range of intellectual vices: "A tendency to paradox, which is always the bane of solid learning, and threatens now to destroy it, a splenetic disposition carried to misanthropy, and an austere virtue pursued to an unsociable fierceness, have prevented a great deal of the good effects which might be expected from such a genius."[1] In the following passages from *A Letter to a Member of the National Assembly*,[2] this tempered position has hardened into outright censure: Rousseau is seen now as the architect of a philosophy that is entirely corrosive of manners and morals. These selections also reveal a telling difference between the views held by Rousseau and Burke on the chains restricting human liberty: whereas Rousseau in *The Social Contract* famously bewailed that, though born free, man is "every where in chains," Burke sees the need for "fetters" wherever human beings are incapable of controlling their appetites.]

SIR,
... Those who have made the exhibition of the 14th of July are capable of every evil. They do not commit crimes for their designs; but they form designs that they may commit crimes. It is not their necessity, but their nature, that impels them. They

---

1 *The Annual Register, or a View of the History, Politicks, and Literature, for the Year 1759* (J. Dodsley, 1765), 479.
2 The Member of the Assembly was François-Louis-Thibault de Menonville (1740–1816).

are modern philosophers; which when you say of them you express every thing that is ignoble, savage, and hard-hearted.

Besides the sure tokens which are given by the spirit of their particular arrangements, there are some characteristic lineaments in the general policy of your tumultuous despotism, which, in my opinion, indicate, beyond a doubt, that no revolution whatsoever *in their disposition* is to be expected. I mean their scheme of educating the rising generation, the principles which they intend to instil, and the sympathies which they wish to form in the mind at the season in which it is the most susceptible. Instead of forming their young minds to that docility, to that modesty, which are the grace and charm of youth, to an admiration of famous examples, and to an averseness to any thing which approaches to pride, petulance, and self-conceit, (distempers to which that time of life is of itself sufficiently liable,) they artificially foment these evil dispositions, and even form them into springs of action. Nothing ought to be more weighed than the nature of books recommended by public authority. So recommended, they soon form the character of the age. Uncertain indeed is the efficacy, limited indeed is the extent, of a virtuous institution. But if education takes in *vice* as any part of its system, there is no doubt but that it will operate with abundant energy, and to an extent indefinite. The magistrate, who in favour of freedom thinks himself obliged to suffer all sorts of publications, is under a stricter duty than any other well to consider what sort of writers he shall authorize; and shall recommend by the strongest of all sanctions, that is, by public honours and rewards. He ought to be cautious how he recommends authors of mixed or ambiguous morality. He ought to be fearful of putting into the hands of youth writers indulgent to the peculiarities of their own complexion, lest they should teach the humours of the professor, rather than the principles of the science. He ought, above all, to be cautious in recommending any writer who has carried marks of a deranged understanding; for where there is no sound reason there can be no real virtue; and madness is ever vicious and malignant.

The assembly proceeds on maxims the very reverse of these. The assembly recommends to its youth a study of the bold experimenters in morality. Every body knows that there is a great dispute amongst their leaders, which of them is the best resemblance of Rousseau. In truth, they all resemble him. His blood they transfuse into their minds and into their manners. Him they study; him they meditate; him they turn over in all the time they can spare from the laborious mischief of the day, or the debauches of the night. Rousseau is their canon of holy writ; in his life he is their canon of *Polycletus*;[1] he is their standard figure of perfection. To this man and this writer, as a pattern to authors and to Frenchmen, the foundries of Paris are now running for statues, with the kettles of their poor and the bells of their churches. If an author had written like a great genius on geometry, though his practical and speculative morals were vicious in the extreme, it might appear, that in voting the statue, they honoured only the geometrician. But Rousseau is a moralist, or he is nothing. It is impossible, therefore, putting the circumstances together, to mistake their design in choosing the author, with whom they have begun to recommend a course of studies.

Their great problem is to find a substitute for all the principles which hitherto have been employed to regulate the human will and action. They find dispositions in the mind of such force and quality as may fit men, far better than the old morality, for the purposes of such a state as theirs, and may go much further in supporting their power, and destroying their enemies. They have therefore chosen a selfish, flattering, seductive, ostentatious vice, in the place of plain duty. True humility, the basis of the Christian system, is the low, but deep and firm foundation of all real virtue. But this, as very painful in the practice, and little imposing in the appearance, they have totally discarded. Their object is to merge all natural and all social sentiment in inordinate vanity. In a small degree, and conversant in little things, vanity is of little moment. When full grown, it is the worst of vices, and the occasional mimic of them all. It makes the whole man false. It leaves nothing sincere or trustworthy about him. His best qualities are poisoned and perverted by it, and operate exactly as the worst. When your lords had many writers as immoral as the object of their statue (such as Voltaire and others) they chose Rousseau; because in him that peculiar vice, which they wished to erect into ruling virtue, was by far the most conspicuous.

We have had the great professor and founder of *the philosophy of vanity* in England. As I had good opportunities of knowing his proceedings almost from day to day, he left no doubt on my mind that he entertained no principle either to influence his heart, or to guide his understanding, but *vanity*. With this

---

1 Greek sculptor of the fifth century BCE.

vice he was possessed to a degree little short of madness. It is from the same deranged, eccentric vanity, that this, the insane *Socrates*[1] of the National Assembly, was impelled to publish a mad confession of his mad faults,[2] and to attempt a new sort of glory from bringing hardily to light the obscure and vulgar vices, which we know may sometimes be blended with eminent talents. He has not observed on the nature of vanity who does not know that it is omnivorous; that it has no choice in its food; that it is fond to talk even of its own faults and vices, as what will excite surprise and draw attention, and what will pass at worst for openness and candour.

It was this abuse and perversion, which vanity makes even of hypocrisy, that has driven Rousseau to record a life not so much as chequered, or spotted here and there, with virtues, or even distinguished by a single good action. It is such a life he chooses to offer to the attention of mankind. It is such a life that, with a wild defiance, he flings in the face of his Creator, whom he acknowledges only to brave. Your assembly, knowing how much more powerful example is found than precept, has chosen this man (by his own account without a single virtue) for a model. To him they erect their first statue. From him they commence their series of honours and distinctions.

It is that new-invented virtue, which your masters canonize, that led their moral hero constantly to exhaust the stores of his powerful rhetoric in the expression of universal benevolence; whilst his heart was incapable of harbouring one spark of common parental affection. Benevolence to the whole species, and want of feeling for every individual with whom the professors come in contact, form the character of the new philosophy. Setting up for an unsocial independence, this their hero of vanity refuses the just price of common labour, as well as the tribute which opulence owes to genius, and which, when paid, honours the giver and the receiver; and then he pleads his beggary as an excuse for his crimes. He melts with tenderness for those only who touch him by the remotest relation, and then, without one natural pang, casts away, as a sort of offal and excrement, the spawn of his disgustful amours, and sends his children to the hospital of foundlings. The bear loves, licks, and forms her young; but bears are not philosophers. Vanity, however, finds its

---

1 Athenian philosopher (469–399 BCE) condemned to death for impiety and for corrupting the young.

2 Rousseau's *Confessions*, published in 1782.

account in reversing the train of our natural feelings. Thousands admire the sentimental writer; the affectionate father is hardly known in his parish.

Under this philosophic instructor in the *ethics of vanity*, they have attempted in France a regeneration of the moral constitution of man. Statesmen, like your present rulers, exist by every thing which is spurious, fictitious, and false; by every thing which takes the man from his house, and sets him on a stage; which makes him up an artificial creature, with painted, theatric sentiments, fit to be seen by the glare of candle-light, and formed to be contemplated at a due distance. Vanity is too apt to prevail in all of us, and in all countries. To the improvement of Frenchmen it seems not absolutely necessary that it should be taught upon system. But it is plain that the present rebellion was its legitimate offspring, and it is piously fed by that rebellion with a daily dole.

If the system of institution recommended by the assembly be false and theatric, it is because their system of government is of the same character. To that, and to that alone, it is strictly conformable. To understand either, we must connect the morals with the politics of the legislators. Your practical philosophers, systematic in every thing, have wisely begun at the source. As the relation between parents and children is the first amongst the elements of vulgar, natural morality, they erect statues to a wild, ferocious, low-minded, hard-hearted father, of fine general feelings; a lover of his kind, but a hater of his kindred. Your masters reject the duties of this vulgar relation, as contrary to liberty; as not founded in the social compact; and not binding according to the rights of men; because the relation is not, of course, the result of *free election*; never so on the side of the children, not always on the part of the parents.

The next relation which they regenerate by their statues to Rousseau is that which is next in sanctity to that of a father. They differ from those old-fashioned thinkers, who considered pedagogues as sober and venerable characters, and allied to the parental. The moralists of the dark times, *preceptorem sancti voluere parentis esse loco.*[1] In this age of light, they teach the people that preceptors ought to be in the place of gallants. They systematically corrupt a very corruptible race (for some time a growing nuisance amongst you), a set of pert, petulant literators, to whom instead of their proper, but severe

---

1 "Who wanted the teacher to stand in a revered parent's place."
Juvenal, *Satires*, VII, 209–10.

unostentatious duties, they assign the brilliant part of men of wit and pleasure, of gay, young, military sparks, and danglers at toilets. They call on the rising generation in France to take a sympathy in the adventures and fortunes, and they endeavour to engage their sensibility on the side of pedagogues, who betray the most awful family trusts, and vitiate their female pupils. They teach the people that the debauchers of virgins, almost in the arms of their parents, may be safe inmates in their houses, and even fit guardians of the honour of those husbands who succeed legally to the office which the young literators had pre-occupied, without asking leave of law or conscience.

Thus they dispose of all the family relations of parents and children, husbands and wives. Through this same instructor, by whom they corrupt the morals, they corrupt the taste. Taste and elegance, though they are reckoned only among the smaller and secondary morals, yet are of no mean importance in the regulation of life. A moral taste is not of force to turn vice into virtue; but it recommends virtue with something like the blandishments of pleasure; and it infinitely abates the evils of vice. Rousseau, a writer of great force and vivacity, is totally destitute of taste in any sense of the word. Your masters, who are his scholars, conceive that all refinement has an aristocratic character. The last age had exhausted all its powers in giving a grace and nobleness to our natural appetites, and in raising them into a higher class and order than seemed justly to belong to them. Through Rousseau, your masters are resolved to destroy these aristocratic prejudices. The passion called love has so general and powerful an influence; it makes so much of the entertainment, and indeed so much the occupation of that part of life which decides the character for ever, that the mode and the principles on which it engages the sympathy, and strikes the imagination, become of the utmost importance to the morals and manners of every society. Your rulers were well aware of this; and in their system of changing your manners to accommodate them to their politics, they found nothing so convenient as Rousseau. Through him they teach men to love after the fashion of philosophers; that is, they teach to men, to Frenchmen, a love without gallantry; a love without any thing of that fine flower of youthfulness and gentility, which places it, if not among the virtues, among the ornaments of life. Instead of this passion, naturally allied to grace and manners, they infuse into their youth an unfashioned, indelicate, sour, gloomy, ferocious medley of pedantry and lewdness; of metaphysical speculations blended with the coarsest sensuality. Such is the general morality of the passions to be found in their famous philosopher, in his famous work of philosophic gallantry, the *Nouvelle Éloise*.[1]

When the fence from the gallantry of preceptors is broken down, and your families are no longer protected by decent pride, and salutary domestic prejudice, there is but one step to a frightful corruption. The rulers in the National Assembly are in good hopes that the females of the first families in France may become an easy prey to dancing-masters, fiddlers, pattern-drawers, friseurs, and valets de chambre, and other active citizens of that description, who having the entry into your houses, and being half domesticated by their situation, may be blended with you by regular and irregular relations. By a law they have made these people their equals. By adopting the sentiments of Rousseau they have made them your rivals. In this manner these great legislators complete their plan of levelling, and establish their rights of men on a sure foundation.

I am certain that the writings of Rousseau lead directly to this kind of shameful evil. I have often wondered how he comes to be so much more admired and followed on the Continent than he is here. Perhaps a secret charm in the language may have its share in this extraordinary difference. We certainly perceive, and to a degree we feel, in this writer, a style glowing, animated, enthusiastic; at the same time that we find it lax, diffuse, and not in the best taste of composition; all the members of the piece being pretty equally laboured and expanded, without any due selection or subordination of parts. He is generally too much on the stretch, and his manner has little variety. We cannot rest upon any of his works, though they contain observations which occasionally discover a considerable insight into human nature. But his doctrines, on the whole, are so inapplicable to real life and manners, that we never dream of drawing from them any rule for laws or conduct, or for fortifying or illustrating any thing by a reference to his opinions. They have with us the fate of older paradoxes,

Cum ventum ad *verum* est *sensus moresque* repugnant,

---

1 Rousseau's epistolary novel *Julie, ou La Nouvelle Héloïse*, published in 1761.

Atque ipsa utilitas, justi prope mater et æqui.[1]

Perhaps bold speculations are more acceptable because more new to you than to us, who have been long since satiated with them. We continue, as in the two last ages, to read, more generally than I believe is now done on the Continent, the authors of sound antiquity. These occupy our minds. They give us another taste and turn; and will not suffer us to be more than transiently amused with paradoxical morality. It is not that I consider this writer as wholly destitute of just notions. Amongst his irregularities, it must be reckoned that he is sometimes moral, and moral in a very sublime strain. But the *general spirit and tendency* of his works is mischievous; and the more mischievous for this mixture: for perfect depravity of sentiment is not reconcilable with eloquence; and the mind (though corruptible, not complexionally vicious) would reject, and throw off with disgust, a lesson of pure and unmixed evil. These writers make even virtue a pander to vice....

... Your despots govern by terror. They know that he who fears God fears nothing else: and therefore they eradicate from the mind, through their Voltaire, their Helvetius, and the rest of that infamous gang, that only sort of fear which generates true courage. Their object is, that their fellow-citizens may be under the dominion of no awe, but that of their committee of research,[2] and of their lanterne....

... Why speculate on the measure and standard of liberty? I doubt much, very much indeed, whether France is at all ripe for liberty on any standard. Men are qualified for civil liberty in exact proportion to their disposition to put moral chains upon their own appetites; in proportion as their love to justice is above their rapacity; in proportion as their soundness and sobriety of understanding is above their vanity and presumption; in proportion as they are more disposed to listen to the counsels of the wise and good, in preference to the flattery of knaves. Society cannot exist unless a controlling power upon will and appetite be placed somewhere, and the less of it there is within, the more

---

1 "When it comes to the truth of the matter, one's instincts revolt, and expediency itself is virtually the mother of justice and equity." Horace, *Satires*, Book I, iii, 97–98.

2 The Committee of Research (*Comité des recherches*) was created in October 1789 as an agency to investigate counterrevolutionary conspiracies.

there must be without. It is ordained in the eternal constitution of things, that men of intemperate minds cannot be free. Their passions forge their fetters.

This sentence the prevalent part of your countrymen execute on themselves....

Excuse my length. I have been somewhat occupied since I was honoured with your letter; and I should not have been able to answer it at all, but for the holidays, which have given me means of enjoying the leisure of the country. I am called to duties which I am neither able nor willing to evade. I must soon return to my old conflict with the corruptions and oppressions which have prevailed in our eastern dominions.[1] I must turn myself wholly from those of France.

In England we *cannot* work so hard as Frenchmen. Frequent relaxation is necessary to us. You are naturally more intense in your application. I did not know this part of your national character, until I went into France in 1773. At present, this your disposition to labour is rather increased than lessened. In your assembly you do not allow yourselves a recess even on Sundays. We[2] have two days in the week, besides the festivals; and besides five or six months of the summer and autumn. This continued, unremitted effort of the members of your assembly, I take to be one among the causes of the mischief they have done. They who always labour can have no true judgment. You never give yourselves time to cool. You can never survey, from its proper point of sight, the work you have finished, before you decree its final execution. You can never plan the future by the past. You never go into the country, soberly and dispassionately to observe the effect of your measures on their objects. You cannot feel distinctly how far the people are rendered better and improved, or more miserable and depraved, by what you have done. You cannot see with your own eyes the sufferings and afflictions you cause. You know them but at a distance, on the statements of those who always flatter the reigning power, and who, amidst their representations of the grievances, inflame your minds against those who are oppressed. These are amongst the effects of unremitted labour, when men exhaust their attention, burn out their candles, and are left in the dark.

---

1 Burke is here referring to his role in the trial of Warren Hastings (1732–1818).

2 By "We" Burke means the members of the British Parliament.

Appendix G: Contemporary Responses to Burke's Censure of the French Revolution

[The following selections indicate the range of reactions produced in the immediate aftermath of the publication of the *Reflections*. All of these (with the exception of the Burke-Mackintosh correspondence in 1796) were written in 1790 and 1791. They range from the exuberantly positive (Fanny Burney, for example, and King George III, as reported in a letter by Burke's wife, Jane) to the appalled and critical (notably Wollstonecraft and Paine). It is worth noting that Burke did not publish rejoinders to any of his critics, most of whom he nonchalantly dismissed. When asked, for example, by French Laurence about James Mackintosh's *Vindiciae Gallicae*, Burke wrote: "I have not read, or even seen Mackintosh;—But Richard tells me, that it is Paine at bottom,—and that indeed all the writers against me are, either Paine with some difference in the way of stating, or even myself" (*Corr.* VI, 312); Paine was described by Burke as simply being "utterly incapable of comprehending his subject" (*Corr.* VI, 303). One notable engagement with a critic happened in 1796, when Mackintosh, by that stage no longer a defender of the French Revolution, wrote to Burke; they subsequently, and with great warmth, met.]

1. The Mercer-Burke Correspondence (February 1790), in James Prior, *Memoir of the Life and Character of the Right Hon. Edmund Burke* (Ticknor, Reed, and Fields, 1854), vol. II, pp. 73–83

[Captain Thomas Mercer (c. 1733–1801) was an Irish acquaintance of Burke's. In February 1790 he wrote to Burke in response to newspaper reports of the latter's "Speech on the Army Estimates" (for which see Appendix C3). James Prior's remark on Mercer's letter is to be noted for its deeply Burkean sensibility: "the reader will be amused if he can repress his astonishment, at the coolness with which the writer talks of subverting a government,—as if it were an affair of little more consequence than pulling down a cow-shed, and rebuilding it in the newest fashion at the pleasure of the owner."]

a. Thomas Mercer to Edmund Burke (19 February 1790)

Dear Sir,

My veneration for your character was great before I had the honor of your personal acquaintance, and it was not diminished when I had the pleasure of seeing and conversing with you. I had long considered you the determined enemy of tyranny and oppression of every kind—the friend of man—and of every thing which might promote his felicity.

It was therefore with extreme surprise that I read in my English newspaper of last post, the imputation to you of sentiments exceedingly inimical to what is thought by many a most glorious revolution in France.

The newspaper represents you as complaining, that the National Assembly had totally subverted their ancient form of government, and that they had also subverted their church.

To complain of the subversion of a government implies a belief of its having been a good one. But I cannot persuade myself to think that such was your opinion of the defunct government of France. Every body has read, more or less, of the late French government; but every one has not been in France as I have been, to see how it operated to the distress and vexation of the people. I saw so much of this, that the word *government* never had a place in my mind when I considered the condition of the French people. In a word, I saw nothing but the most despotic tyranny, the subversion of which would, as I thought, give the greatest pleasure to every sincere lover of civil liberty, of whatever nation he might be.

With respect to the subversion of the church, it does not appear that any change in its doctrine has been attempted. In its discipline there may be some alterations, as it is probable the National Assembly will enlarge those exemptions from the jurisdiction of the Court of Rome which it formerly enjoyed, and which were called the privileges of the Gallican church. For the rest—if to take from pampered and luxurious prelates a part of those sumptuous livings which were accumulated in the times of ignorance and superstition, and to provide for the more comfortable subsistence of parish priests, be the subversion of a church, millions of good men and good Christians will heartily wish (for the honor of true religion distinct from pageantry and hypocrisy) that all such may in this manner be speedily subverted.

Suffer a plain independent man to make some further observations.

Power over our fellow-men, by whatever means it has been acquired—whether by fraud, or force, or thoughtless acquiescence—seems to be considered by its possessor as his dearest birthright. He would lose his right hand, or even his life, rather than part with a jot or tittle of it. He extends it from object to object until the yoke becomes too heavy and too galling to be longer borne. And by what means are the aggrieved to get rid of it? Not by the most reasonable and eloquent representations—not by the most humble and abject intercessions; for both would be equally scouted and laughed to scorn—not by an appeal to the laws of the country, for the laws were made under the influence of the power complained of, and with a view to its perpetuation. There is, therefore, no remedy to be found but in what is called a revolution; the intention of which being either to curtail, or annul, or place in other hands, the powers which be, it cannot be effected without some convulsion; nor is it possible so to order the matter, but in some cases many individuals may suffer injury and outrage; and this, as far as it goes, is to be lamented. But if it ends in freedom, in the deliverance of a nation from the despotism of one man, *no price can be thought too dear to pay for it.*

I flatter myself, my dear Sir, that you do not differ essentially from the sentiments expressed in this letter. I am persuaded you feel, and will always acknowledge that there cannot be a government fit for rational beings to live under and submit to, but where the legislative part of it is chiefly composed of the representatives of the bulk of the people, freely and unbiassedly elected. The new French government promises to be such a one; and notwithstanding what newspapers report to the contrary, I will not take to myself the mortification of supposing that my judgment of points of high and essential importance to the happiness of mankind, differs exceedingly from the opinions of a man celebrated for the clearness of his head, and the philanthropy of his heart.

Perhaps you will cheer me with an assurance that we do not differ widely; than which nothing would be a more exhilarating cordial to one, who has the honor to be, with every possible respect, your most faithful and humble servant, .

THOMAS MERCER

b. Edmund Burke to Thomas Mercer (26 February 1790)

Dear Sir,

The speedy answer I return to your letter, I hope will convince you of the high value I set upon the regard you are so good to express for me, and the obliging trouble which you take to inform my judgment upon matters in which we are all very deeply concerned....

If you are mistaken, it is perhaps owing to the impression almost inevitably made by the various careless conversations which we are engaged in through life; conversations in which those who propagate their doctrines have not been called upon for much reflection concerning their end and tendency; and in which those who imperceptibly imbibe the doctrines taught, are not required, by any particular duty, very closely to examine them, to act from the impressions they receive. I am obliged to *act*, and am therefore bound to call my principles and sentiments to a strict account. As far as my share of a public trust goes, I am in *trust* religiously to maintain the rights and properties of all descriptions of people in the possession which legally they hold; and in the *rule* by which alone they can be legally secure in any possession. I do not find myself at liberty either as a man, or as a trustee for men, to take a *vested* property from one man and to give it to another, because *I* think that the portion of one is too great, and that of another too small. From my first juvenile rudiments of speculative study to the grey hairs of my present experience, I have never learned any thing else. I can never be taught any thing else by *reason*; and when *force* comes, I shall consider whether I am to submit to it, or how I am to resist it. This I am sure of, that an early guard against the manifest tendency of a contrary doctrine, is the only way by which those who love order can be prepared to resist such force.

The calling men by the names of "pampered and luxurious prelates," &c. is in you no more than a mark of your dislike to intemperance and idle expense; but in others it is used for other purposes. It is often used to extinguish the sense of justice in our minds, and the natural feelings of humanity in our bosoms. Such language does not mitigate the cruel effects of reducing men of opulent condition, and their innumerable dependents, to the last distress. If I were to adopt a plan of spoliatory reformation, I should probably employ such language; but it would aggravate instead of extenuating my guilt in overturning the sacred principles of property.

Sir, I say that church and state, and human society too, for which church and state were made, are subverted by such doctrines, joined to such practices as leave no foundation for property in *long possessions*. My dear Captain Mercer, it is not my calling the use you make of your plate in your house, either of dwelling or of prayer, "pageantry and hypocrisy," that can justify me in taking from you your own property and your own liberty, to use your own property according to your own ideas of ornament. When you find me attempting to break into your house to take your plate, under any pretence whatsoever, but most of all under pretence of purity of religion and Christian charity, shoot me for a robber and an hypocrite, as in that case I shall certainly be. The "true Christian religion" never taught me any such practices; nor did the religion of my nature, nor any religion, nor any law....

It is not by calling the landed estates, possessed of old *prescriptive rights*, the "accumulations of ignorance and superstition," that can support me in shaking that grand title, which supersedes all other title, and which all my studies of general jurisprudence have taught me to consider as one principal cause of the formation of states; I mean the ascertaining and securing *prescription*. But these are donations made in "ages of ignorance and superstition." Be it so. It proves that these donations were made long ago; and this is *prescription*; and this gives right and title.

It is possible that many estates about you were originally obtained by arms, that is, by violence, a thing almost as a bad as superstition, and not much short of ignorance; but it is *old violence*; and that which might be wrong in the beginning, is consecrated by time, and becomes lawful. This may be superstition in me, and ignorance; but I had rather remain in ignorance and superstition, than be enlightened and purified out of the first principles of law and natural justice....

You pay me the compliment to suppose me a foe to tyranny and oppression, and you are, therefore, surprised at the sentiments I have lately delivered in Parliament. I am that determined foe to tyranny, or I greatly deceive myself in my character; and I am sure I am not an idiot in my conduct. It is because I am, and mean to continue so, that I abominate the example of France for this country. I know that tyranny seldom attacks the poor, never in the first instance. They are not its proper prey. It falls on the wealthy and the great, whom by rendering objects of envy, and otherwise obnoxious to the multitude, they may more easily destroy; and when they are destroyed, that multitude which was led to that ill-work by the arts of bad men, is itself undone for ever.

I hate tyranny, at least I think so; but I hate it most of all where most are concerned in it. The tyranny of a multitude is a multiplied tyranny. If, as society is constituted in these large countries of France and England, full of unequal property, I must make my choice, (which God avert!) between the despotism of a single person or of the many, my election is made. As much injustice and tyranny has been practised in a few months by a French democracy, as in all the arbitrary monarchies in Europe in the forty years of my observation....

This democracy begins very ill; and I feel no security, that what has been rapacious and bloody at its commencement, will be mild and protecting in its final settlement. They cannot, indeed, in future rob so much, because they have little that can be taken. I go to the full length of my principle. I should think the government of the deposed King of France, or of the late King of Prussia, or the present Emperor, or the present Czarina, none of them perhaps perfectly good people, to be far better than the government of twenty-four millions of men, *all as good as you*, and I do not know any body better; supposing that those twenty-four millions would be subject, as infallibly they would, to the same unrestrained, though virtuous impulses; because it is plain that their majority would think every thing justified by their warm good intentions—they would heat one another by their common zeal—counsel and advice would be lost upon them—they would not listen to temperate individuals, and they would be less capable, infinitely, of moderation than the most heady of those princes....

To discuss the affairs of France and its Revolution would require a volume, perhaps many volumes....

... I have not written this to discuss these matters in a prolonged controversy (I wish we may never say more about them), but to comply with your commands, which ever shall have due weight with me.

I am most respectfully,
And most affectionately yours,
EDMUND BURKE

2. Philip Francis, from a Letter to Edmund Burke, 3 November 1790 (*Corr.* VI, 151–54)

[Philip Francis (1740–1818) was a Member of Parliament and a friend of Burke's. In this letter, Francis describes his immediate impressions of *Reflections on the Revolution in France*, which had been published just two days previously.]

My dear Mr Burke, ...

It has not yet been in my power to read more than one third of your book. I must taste it deliberately; the flavour is too high; the Wine is too rich; I cannot take a draught of it. All that you say of the Revolution in England is excellent in its Substance, and in its illustration incomparable. I wait to see how you will apply that example, with strict justice, to the Reproach of the proceedings in France. For my own part, I am not sufficiently versed in the History of that Country to be able to point out a period, in which the French possessed an effective Constitution, or even such an acknowledged system of tolerable Government, as it would have at all availed them to recur to in their late Situation.... From the plain unlaboured Narrative of history I can produce you pictures of the constant miseries of the people of France, that would surpass every thing that you, with all the efforts of your eloquence, have painted of the Sufferings, great, I own, and much to be regretted, of a few individuals in a single day.... If this state of the case be generally true, it follows that the French of this day could not act as we did in 1688. They had no constitution, as we had, to recur to. They had no foundation to build upon. They had no walls to repair. Much less had they *the Elements of a Constitution very nearly as good as could be wished*.... If they had no model in their own Country, they must, of necessity, begin a new. They could not, in this respect, be guided by the example of England; because in our case there was a Constitution to resort to, in theirs there was none. Allowance should be made for men, whose duty it is to act in such a Situation. They may commit many errours; but neither will I charge them with the fury of the populace, nor with the Crimes of individuals. Many things have been done, which greatly deserve to be lamented; and the more, because they weaken and disgrace a cause, essentially just and honourable. The loss of a single life, in a popular tumult, excites individual tenderness and pity. No tears are shed for Nations.... You will not believe it possible that it can be my wish or intention to justify any atrocious acts of Violence committed by the populace. I do not even undertake to defend the most deliberate acts of the Assembly. With all manner of reason and justice in the assumption of their power, they may possibly have exhibited a total want of wisdom in the exercise of it. These questions are perfectly distinct. In some places, you talk of the National Assembly, as if they were the direct Authors of every thing done by the Mob of Paris; in others, you describe them as the passive instruments of that mob, and acting under the immediate terrours of personal danger. But you dread and detest commotion of every kind. And so should I; and who would not act, if a healthy Repose could be obtained without a tempest or stagnation. But, tell me, has not God himself commanded or permitted the Storm to purify the elements?

3. From Frances Burney (Madame D'Arblay), *The Diary and Letters of Madame D'Arblay (1778–1840)*, edited by Charlotte Barrett (Macmillan and Co., 1905), vol. IV, pp. 435–36

[Frances ("Fanny") Burney (1752–1840), later known as Madame d'Arblay (following her marriage to the French exile General Alexandre d'Arblay), was an English novelist and diarist. In this extract from a letter written on 23 November 1790 to Georgina Waddington, Burney expresses her enthusiasm for Burke's *Reflections*.]

... I own myself entirely of Mrs. Montagu's opinion about Mr. Burke's book; it is the noblest, deepest, most animated, and exalted work that I think I have ever read. I am charmed to hear its *éloge* from Mrs. Montagu; it is a tribute to its excellence which reflects high honour on her own candour, as she was one of those the most vehemently irritated against its author but a short time since. How can man, with all his inequalities, be so little resembling to himself at different periods as this man? He is all ways a prodigy,—in fascinating talents and incomprehensible inconsistencies.

When I read, however, such a book as this, I am apt to imagine the whole of such a being must be right, as well as the parts, and that the time may come when the mists which obscure the motives or incentives to those actions and proceedings which seem incongruous may be chased away, and we may find the internal intention had never been faulty, however ill appearances had supported any claim to right. Have you yet read it? You will

find it to require so deep and so entire an attention, that perhaps
you may delay it till in more established health; but read it you
will, and with an admiration you cannot often feel excited.

4. From Richard Price, Preface to *A Discourse on the Love of Our Country*, 4th ed. (T. Cadell, 1790), iii–vi

[Dr. Richard Price (1723–91) was a dissenting minister and philosopher and the subject of much of Burke's ire in *Reflections on
the Revolution in France*. In the following extract, Price defends
himself against one of Burke's most violent charges, namely that
he (Price) had exulted in the slaughter at Versailles on 6 October
1789.]

Since the former Editions of the following Discourse, many ani-
madversions upon it have been published....

    In p. 49 [of the *Discourse*], I have adopted the words of Scrip-
ture, *Now lettest thou thy servant depart in peace* and expressed
my gratitude to God for having spared my life to see a "diffusion of knowledge that has undermined superstition and error,
a vast kingdom spurning at slavery, and an arbitrary Monarch
led in triumph and surrendering himself to his subjects." These
words have occasioned a comparison of me (by Mr. BURKE in
his Reflections on the Revolution in France) to HUGH PETERS,
attended with an intimation that, like him, *I may not die in peace*;
and he has described me ... as a barbarian delighted with blood,
profaning Scripture, and exulting in the riot and slaughter at
Versailles on the 6th of October last year. I hope I shall be credited
when, in answer to this horrid misrepresentation and menace,
I assure the Public that the events to which I referred in these
words were not those of the 6th of October, but those only of the
14th of July and the subsequent days; when, after the conquest
of the BASTILE, the King of FRANCE sought the protection of
the National Assembly, and, by his own desire, was conducted,
amidst acclamations never before heard in FRANCE to PARIS,
there to shew himself to his people as the restorer of their liberty.

    I am indeed surprised that Mr. BURKE could want candour
so much as to suppose that I had any other events in view. The
letters quoted by him ... were dated in *July* 1789, and might have
shewn him that he was injuring both me and the writer of those
letters. But what candour or what moderation can be expected
in a person so frantic with zeal for hereditary claims and aristocratical distinctions as to be capable of decrying popular rights

and the aid of philosophy in forming governments; of lamenting that the age of Chivalry is gone; and of believing that the insults offered by a mob to the Queen of France have extinguished for ever the glory of EUROPE?

5. From Mary Wollstonecraft, *A Vindication of the Rights of Men, in a Letter to the Right Honourable Edmund Burke Occasioned by His Reflections on the Revolution in France* (J. Johnson, 1790), 9–10, 22–23, 25–26, 102–03, 121, 143–45

[Mary Wollstonecraft (1759–97) was an English philosopher and writer, and her *Vindication of the Rights of Woman* (1792) is one of the founding texts of the feminist movement. *A Vindication of the Rights of Men* was the first of the major critical responses to *Reflections on the Revolution in France* to be published.]

SIR,
... I know that you have a mortal antipathy to reason; but, if there is any thing like argument, or first principles, in your wild declamation, behold the result:—that we are to reverence the rust of antiquity, and term the unnatural customs, which ignorance and mistaken self-interest have consolidated, the sage fruit of experience: and that, if we do discover some errors, our *feelings* should lead us to excuse, with blind love, or unprincipled filial affection, the venerable vestiges of ancient days. These are gothic notions of beauty—the ivy is beautiful though it insidiously destroys the trunk from which it receives support.

Further, that we ought cautiously to remain for ever in frozen inactivity, because a thaw that nourishes the soil spreads a temporary inundation; and that the fear of risking any thing should prevent a struggle for the most estimable advantages. This is sound reasoning, I grant, in the mouth of the rich and short-sighted....

But on what principle Mr. Burke could defend American independence, I cannot conceive; for the whole tenor of his plausible arguments settles slavery on an everlasting foundation. Allowing his servile reverence for antiquity, and prudent attention to self-interest, to have the force which he insists on, it [slavery] ought never to be abolished; and, because our ignorant forefathers, not understanding the native dignity of man, sanctioned a traffic that outrages every suggestion of reason and religion, we are to submit to the inhuman custom, and term an atrocious insult to humanity the love of our country, and a proper submission to those laws which secure our property....

... Misery, to reach your heart, I perceive, must have its cap and bells; your tears are reserved, very *naturally* considering your character, for the declamation of the theatre, or for the downfall of queens, whose rank throws a graceful veil over vices that degrade humanity; but the distress of many industrious mothers, whose *helpmates* have been torn from them, and the hungry cry of helpless babes, were vulgar sorrows that could not move your commiseration, though they might extort an alms. "The tears that are shed for fictitious sorrow are admirably adapted," says Rousseau, "to make us proud of all the virtues which we do not possess." ...

There appears to be such a mixture of real sensibility and fondly cherished romance in your composition, that the present crisis carries you out of yourself; and since you could not be one of the grand movers, the next *best* thing that dazzled your imagination was to be a conspicuous opposer. Full of yourself, you make as much noise to convince the world that you despise the revolution, as Rousseau did to persuade his contemporaries to let him live in obscurity.

Reading your Reflections warily over, it has continually and forcibly struck me, that had you been a Frenchman, you would have been, in spite of your respect for rank and antiquity, a violent revolutionist; and deceived, as you now probably are, by the passions that cloud your reason, have termed your romantic enthusiasm an enlightened love of your country, a respect for the rights of men. Your imagination would have taken fire, and have found arguments, full as ingenious as those you now offer, to prove that the constitution, of which so few pillars remained, that constitution which time had almost obliterated, was not a model sufficiently noble to deserve close adherence. And, for the English constitution, you might not have had such a profound veneration as you have lately acquired; nay, it is not impossible that you might have entertained the same opinion of the English Parliament, that you professed to have during the American war....

... A desperate disease required a powerful remedy. Injustice had no right to rest on prescription....

Surveying civilized life, and seeing, with undazzled eye, the polished vices of the rich, their insincerity, want of natural affections, with all the specious train that luxury introduces, I have turned impatiently to the poor, to look for man undebauched by riches or power—but, alas! what did I see? a being scarcely above the brutes, over which it tyrannized; a broken spirit, worn-out body, and all those gross vices which the example of the rich, rudely copied, could produce. Envy built a wall of separation, that made the poor hate, whilst they bent to their superiors; who, on their part, stepped aside to avoid the loathsome sight of human misery.

What were the outrages of a day[1] to these continual miseries? Let those sorrows hide their diminished head before the tremendous mountain of woe that thus defaces our globe! Man preys on man; and you mourn for the idle tapestry that decorated a gothic pile, and the dronish bell that summoned the fat priest to prayer. You mourn for the empty pageant of a name, when slavery flaps her wing, and the sick heart retires to die in lonely wilds, far from the abodes of men. Did the pangs you felt for insulted nobility, the anguish that rent your heart when the gorgeous robes were torn off the idol human weakness had set up, deserve to be compared with the long-drawn sigh of melancholy reflection, when misery and vice thus seem to haunt our steps, and swim on the top of every cheering prospect? Why is our fancy to be appalled by terrific perspectives of a hell beyond the grave?—Hell stalks abroad;—the lash resounds on the slave's naked sides; and the sick wretch, who can no longer earn the sour bread of unremitting labour, steals to a ditch to bid the world a long good night—or, neglected in some ostentatious hospital, breathes its last amidst the laugh of mercenary attendants.

Such misery demands more than tears—I pause to recollect myself; and smother the contempt I feel rising for your rhetorical flourishes and infantine sensibility.

6. From Catherine Macaulay, *Observations on the Reflections of the Right Hon. Edmund Burke on the Revolution in France* (C. Dilly, 1790), 16, 19–20, 23–26, 46–47

[Catherine Macaulay (1731–91) was an English Whig historian and a vehement critic of Burke's view of the French Revolution. Of note in these selections are Macaulay's objections to Burke's denunciations of the violent excesses of the revolution: these excesses, she contends, have been exaggerated, but where they have occurred they are best seen as the inevitable product of the

---

1 [Wollstonecraft's note:] The 6th of October.

cruelty of the pre-revolutionary state, are eclipsed by previous monarchical and despotic violence, and are the sad though inevitable cost of a beneficial and necessary revolution.]

Mr. Burke seems to adopt *prejudice, opinion*, and the powers of the *imagination*, as the *safest grounds* on which *wise* and *good* statesmen can establish or continue the happiness of societies. These have always been imputed by philosophers (a tribe of men whom indeed Mr. Burke affects much to despise) as causes which have produced all that is *vicious* and *foolish* in man, and consequently have been the fruitful source of human misery.

Mr. Burke has certainly a *fine* imagination; but I would not advise either *him*, or any of *his admirers*, to give *too much* way to such direction; for if from the virtue of our nature it does not lead us into *crimes*, it always involves us in *error*....

... [W]e must take notice of a very heavy charge laid against [Dr. Price] by Mr. Burke—no less than that of *prophaning* the beautiful and prophetic ejaculation, commonly called, *Nunc dimittis*! made on the first proclamation of our Saviour in the Temple, and applying it, "*with an inhuman and unnatural rapture, to the most horrid, atrocious, and afflicting spectacle*, that perhaps was ever exhibited to the *pity* and *indignation* of mankind." That Mr. Burke's imagination was greatly affected by a scene, which he describes in the highest glow of colouring, I can well believe; but Dr. Price, who classes with that description of men stiled by Mr. Burke *abstract philosophers*, has been used to carry his mind, in a long series of ideas, to the consequences of actions which arise in the passing scene. Dr. Price then, with *full as much sympathy* in him *as even Mr. Burke* can have, might not be greatly moved with the mortifications and sufferings of a *very few persons*, however highly distinguished for the splendour of their rank, when those mortifications led the way, or secured the *present and future happiness of twenty-four millions of people, with their posterity*, emancipated by their *manly* exertions, from all that is *degrading* and *afflicting* to the sensible mind; and let into the immediate blessings of *personal security*, and to the enjoyment of those advantages which above *all others* must be delightful to the feelings of an high-spirited people....

Men who have suffered in their personal interests by the new order of things in France, must naturally be inclined to *exaggerate* every blemish which appears in the conduct of a multitude, by whose spirit they have been deprived of many fond privileges. Their *petulant* observations, whilst their minds are *heated* by imaginary wrongs and injuries, is *excusable*; because it is a *weakness* almost inseparable from *human frailty*. It would, however, have become *Englishmen*, from whom might have been expected a *more sympathising* indulgence towards the *friends* and *promoters* of liberty, to have been more candid in their censures; but in no part of Europe perhaps, have the evils which must *necessarily* attend all Revolutions, and especially a Revolution so *complete* and *comprehensive* as that which has taken place in France, been *more exaggerated*, and *more affectedly* lamented.

Had this *great work* been effected without the shedding one drop of *innocent* or even *guilty* blood, without doubt it would have better pleased the *generous* and *benevolent* mind. But, was it *possible* that such a pleasing circumstance could ever have had an existence? ... I do not indeed exactly know how much blood has been spilled in France, or how many individuals have fallen a sacrifice in the public commotions; but by all the general accounts which have been transmitted to us, the history of monarchies will point out as many sufferers who have fallen in *one hour* to the *rage* and *outrageous pride* of kingly despots.

The punishment of the lamp-post, it must be owned, strikes terror to the mind, and calls forth an immediate effusion of *sympathy* to the sufferer. But when *candid reflection* supersedes the *first emotions* of human tenderness, this truth will force itself on our consideration, that a people who had been used to such *barbarous* spectacles as that of beholding wretches, whose *destitute poverty* had in a manner *compelled* to the forlorn course of highway robbery, broken on a wheel, and *lingering* out the last hours of life under the *agonising* strokes of a stern executioner, would naturally regard hanging as a *mild* punishment on men whom they considered as the worst of criminals. Let us rejoice, then, that such *dreadful legal executions*, which must from their nature tend to *barbarize* men, are happily put an end to by the Revolution....

"... Government [says Mr. Burke] is a contrivance of human wisdom, to provide for human wants. Men have a right that these wants should be provided for by this wisdom. Among these wants is to be reckoned the want out of a civil society, of a sufficient restraint upon their passions. Society requires not only that the passions of individuals should be subjected, but even in the mass and body, as well as in the individuals; the inclinations of men should frequently be thwarted, their will controuled, and their passions brought into subjection. This can only be done by a power out of themselves, and not in the exercise of its functions, subject to that will, and to those passions, which it is in its office to bridle and subdue. In this sense, the restraints of men, as well as their liberties, are to be reckoned among their rights."

To this very *ingenious* reasoning, and these *refined* distinctions between natural and social rights, the people may possibly object, that in delivering themselves *passively* over to the *unrestrained rule of others*, on the plea of controuling *their inordinate inclinations* and *passions*, they deliver themselves over to *men*, who, as *men*, and partaking of the *same* nature as themselves, are as liable to be governed by the same *principles* and *errors*; and to men who, by the great superiority of their station, having no *common* interest with themselves which might lead them to preserve a salutary check over their vices, must be inclined to *abuse* in the *grossest manner* their trust....

7. From Joseph Priestley, *Letters to the Right Honourable Edmund Burke Occasioned by His Reflections on the Revolution in France* (Thomas Pearson, 1791), Letter I, pp. 1–4, 7–8

[Joseph Priestley (1733–1804) was an English scientist, theologian, and political theorist. In the Preface to the *Letters*, Priestley laments that he and Burke were on opposite sides of the revolution controversy and that he "must no longer class him [Burke] among the friends of what I deem to be *the cause of liberty*."]

Dear Sir,

I do not wonder that the late revolution in the French government has excited *your* attention, and that of a great part of the nation. "It is," as you justly say, "all circumstances taken together, the most astonishing that has hitherto happened in the world." It is, therefore, a most interesting object both to philosophical and practical politicians. It behoves them particularly to consider the principles on which it has been made, that if the conduct of the leaders in the business has been right, and if the scheme promises to be beneficial to the country, it may, as far as their situations are similar, be imitated in other countries; and that, if their conduct has been wrong, and the result of it unpromising, the example may serve to deter others from any attempt of the like kind.

But though there is nothing extraordinary in this revolution having excited so much of your *attention*, I am surprised that you should be so much *alarmed* and *disturbed* at it. You appear to me not to be sufficiently cool to enter into this serious discussion. Your imagination is evidently heated, and your ideas confused. The objects before you do not appear in their proper shapes and colours; and, without denying them, you lose sight of the great and leading principles, on which all just governments are founded, principles which I imagined had been long settled, and universally assented to, at least by all who are denominated *whigs*, the friends of our own revolution, and of that which has lately taken place in America. To this class of politicians, you, Sir, have hitherto professed to belong, and traces of these principles may be perceived in this work of yours.

Notwithstanding "the sacredness," as you call it, "of an hereditary principle of succession," in our government, you allow of "a power of change in its application in cases of extreme emergency;" adding, however, that "the change should be confined to the *peccant part* only." Nor do you deny that the great end and object of all government, that which makes it preferable to a state of anarchy, is *the good of the people.* It is *better* for them, and they are *happier* in a state of society and government. For the same reason, you must allow that that particular form of government, which is best adapted to promote the happiness of any people, is the best for that people.

If you admit thus much, you must also allow that, since every private person is justified in bettering his condition, and indeed commended for it; a nation is not to be condemned for endeavouring to better theirs. Consequently, if they find their form of government to be a bad one, whether it was so originally, or become so through abuse or accident, they will do very well to change it for a better. A partial change, no doubt, will be preferable to a total one, if a partial change will be sufficient for the purpose. But if it appear that all attempts to mend an old constitution would be in vain, and the people prefer a new one, their neighbours have no more business to find fault with them, than with any individual, who should think it more adviseable to pull down an old and inconvenient house, and build another from the foundation, rather than lay out his money in repairs. Nations, no doubt, as well as individuals, may judge wrong. They may act precipitately, and they may suffer in consequence of it: but this is only a reason for caution, and does not preclude a right of judging and acting for themselves, in the best manner that they can.

"The very idea," you say, "of the fabrication of a new government is enough to fill us with disgust and horror." It is, no doubt, far from being a thing desirable in itself, but it may nevertheless be necessary; and for all the evils arising from the change, you should blame not the framers of the new government, but the wretched state of the old one, and those who brought it into that state....

Without examining into the former system of government, or the administration of it, we may take for granted, that it must have become extremely odious to the country in general, from the almost universal, and the very hearty, concurrence with which the revolution was brought about. A whole people is not apt to revolt, till oppression has become extreme, and been long continued, so that they despair of any other remedy than that desperate one. The strength of an established government, especially when it is in few hands, and has a large standing army at its command, is almost infinite; so that many nations quietly suffer every evil, and the country becomes in a manner desolate, without their making any effort to relieve themselves.... Whenever, therefore, we see a whole nation, or a great majority of it, rising as one man against an old government, and overturning it, we may safely conclude that their provocation was great, and their cause good.

8. From Thomas Paine, *Rights of Man: Being an Answer to Mr. Burke's Attack on the French Revolution* (J.S. Jordan, 1791), 4–12, 16–20, 23–27, 46–49, 124–26, 159–60

[Thomas Paine (1737–1809) was an English-born American philosopher and revolutionary. In his book's preface, Paine—like Priestley—laments that Burke, a supporter of the earlier American struggle, should have changed so much and was no longer to be considered "a friend to mankind." Paine's *Rights of Man* became the most famous, and the most influential, of all the critical responses to Burke.]

Among the incivilities by which nations or individuals provoke and irritate each other, Mr. Burke's pamphlet on the French Revolution is an extraordinary instance. Neither the People of France, nor the National Assembly, were troubling themselves about the affairs of England, or the English Parliament; and why Mr. Burke should commence an unprovoked attack upon them, both in parliament and in public, is a conduct that cannot be pardoned on the score of manners, nor justified on that of policy....

Not sufficiently content with abusing the National Assembly, a great part of his work is taken up with abusing Dr. Price (one of the best-hearted men that lives)....

Dr. Price had preached a sermon on the 4th of November 1789, being the anniversary of what is called in England, the Revolution which took place 1688. Mr. Burke, speaking of this sermon, says, "The Political Divine proceeds dogmatically to assert, that, by the principles of the Revolution, the people of England have acquired three fundamental rights:

1. To choose our own governors.
2. To cashier them for misconduct.
3. To frame a government for ourselves." ...

... Mr. Burke, on the contrary, denies that such a right exists in the nation, either in whole or in part, or that it exists any where; and, what is still more strange and marvellous, he says, "that the people of England utterly disclaim such a right, and that they will resist the practical assertion of it with their lives and fortunes." That men should take up arms, and spend their lives and fortunes, *not* to maintain their rights, but to maintain they have *not* rights, is an entirely new species of discovery, and suited to the paradoxical genius of Mr. Burke.

The method which Mr. Burke takes to prove that the people of England have no such rights, and that such rights do not now exist in the nation, either in whole or in part, or any where at all, is of the same marvellous and monstrous kind with what he has already said; for his arguments are, that the persons, or the generation of persons, in whom they did exist, are dead, and with them the right is dead also. To prove this, he quotes a declaration made by parliament about a hundred years ago, to William and Mary, in these words:

"The Lords Spiritual and Temporal, and Commons, do, in the name of the people aforesaid,"—(meaning the people of England then living)—"most humbly and faithfully *submit* themselves, their *heirs* and *posterities*, for EVER." ...

... I shall, *sans ceremonie*, place another system of principles in opposition to his....

There never did, there never will, and there never can exist a parliament, or any description of men, or any generation of men, in any country, possessed of the right or the power of binding and controuling posterity to the "*end of time*," or of commanding for ever how the world shall be governed, or who shall govern it;

and therefore, all such clauses, acts or declarations, by which the makers of them attempt to do what they have neither the right nor the power to do, nor the power to execute, are in themselves null and void.—Every age and generation must be as free to act for itself, *in all cases*, as the ages and generations which preceded it. The vanity and presumption of governing beyond the grave, is the most ridiculous and insolent of all tyrannies. Man has no property in man; neither has any generation a property in the generations which are to follow. The parliament or the people of 1688, or of any other period, had no more right to dispose of the people of the present day, or to bind or to controul them *in any shape whatever*, than the parliament or the people of the present day have to dispose of, bind or controul those who are to live a hundred or a thousand years hence. Every generation is, and must be, competent to all the purposes which its occasions require. It is the living, and not the dead, that are to be accommodated. When man ceases to be, his power and his wants cease with him; and having no longer any participation in the concerns of this world, he has no longer any authority in directing who shall be its governors, or how its government shall be organized, or how administered.

I am not contending for nor against any form of government, nor for nor against any party here or elsewhere. That which a whole nation chooses to do, it has a right to do. Mr. Burke says, No. Where then *does* the right exist? I am contending for the rights of the *living*, and against their being willed away, and controuled and contracted for, by the manuscript assumed authority of the dead; and Mr. Burke is contending for the authority of the dead over the rights and freedom of the living....

The circumstances of the world are continually changing, and the opinions of men change also; and as government is for the living, and not for the dead, it is the living only that has any right in it. That which may be thought right and found convenient in one age, may be thought wrong and found inconvenient in another. In such cases, Who is to decide, the living, or the dead? ...

We now come more particularly to the affairs of France....

It was not against Louis the XVIth, but against the despotic principles of the government, that the nation revolted. These principles had not their origin in him, but in the original establishment, many centuries back; and they were become too deeply rooted to be removed, and the augean stable of parasites and plunderers too abominably filthy to be cleansed, by any thing short of a complete and universal revolution.... The Monarch and the Monarchy were distinct and separate things; and it was against the established despotism of the latter, and not against the person or principles of the former, that the revolt commenced, and the revolution has been carried.

Mr. Burke does not attend to the distinction between *men* and *principles*; and therefore, he does not see that a revolt may take place against the despotism of the latter, while there lies no charge of despotism against the former....

But Mr. Burke appears to have no idea of principles, when he is contemplating governments. "Ten years ago (says he) I could have felicitated France on her having a government, without enquiring what the nature of that government was, or how it was administered." Is this the language of a rational man? Is it the language of a heart feeling as it ought to feel for the rights and happiness of the human race? On this ground, Mr. Burke must compliment all the governments in the world, while the victims who suffer under them, whether sold into slavery, or tortured out of existence, are wholly forgotten. It is power, and not principles, that Mr. Burke venerates; and under this abominable depravity, he is disqualified to judge between them.—Thus much for his opinion as to the occasions of the French Revolution. I now proceed to other considerations.

I know a place in America called Point-no-Point; because as you proceed along the shore, gay and flowery as Mr. Burke's language, it continually recedes and presents itself at a distance before you; but when you have got as far as you can go, there is no point at all. Just thus it is with Mr. Burke's three hundred and fifty-six pages. It is therefore difficult to reply to him. But as the points he wishes to establish, may be inferred from what he abuses, it is in his paradoxes that we must look for his arguments.

As to the tragic paintings by which Mr. Burke has outraged his own imagination, and seeks to work upon that of his readers, they are very well calculated for theatrical representation, where facts are manufactured for the sake of show, and accommodated to produce, through the weakness of sympathy, a weeping effect. But Mr. Burke should recollect that he is writing History, and not *Plays*; and that his readers will expect truth, and not the spouting rant of high-toned exclamation.

When we see a man dramatically lamenting in a publication intended to be believed, that, "*The age of chivalry is gone!*" that "*The glory of Europe is extinguished for ever!*" that "*The unbought grace of life*" (if anyone knows what it is), "*the cheap defence of*

nations, the nurse of manly sentiment and heroic enterprize, is gone!"
and all this because the Quixot age of chivalry nonsense is gone,
What opinion can we form of his judgment, or what regard can
we pay to his facts? In the rhapsody of his imagination, he has
discovered a world of wind-mills, and his sorrows are, that there
are no Quixots to attack them. But if the age of aristocracy, like
that of chivalry, should fall, (and they had originally some connexion), Mr. Burke, the trumpeter of the Order, may continue his
parody to the end, and finish with exclaiming, *"Othello's occupation's gone!"*[1]

Notwithstanding Mr. Burke's horrid paintings, when the
French Revolution is compared with the revolutions of other
countries, the astonishment will be, that it is marked with so few
sacrifices; but this astonishment will cease when we reflect that
principles, and not *persons*, were the meditated objects of destruction. The mind of the nation was acted upon by a higher stim-
ulus than what the consideration of persons could inspire, and
sought a higher conquest than could be produced by the down-
fal of an enemy. Among the few who fell, there do not appear to
be any that were intentionally singled out. They all of them had
their fate in the circumstances of the moment....

Not one glance of compassion, not one commiserating reflection, that I can find throughout his book, has he bestowed on
those who lingered out the most wretched of lives, a life without
hope, in the most miserable of prisons. It is painful to behold a
man employing his talents to corrupt himself. Nature has been
kinder to Mr. Burke than he is to her. He is not affected by the
reality of distress touching his heart, but by the showy resemblance of it striking his imagination. He pities the plumage, but
forgets the dying bird. Accustomed to kiss the aristocratical
hand that hath purloined him from himself, he degenerates into
a composition of art, and the genuine soul of nature forsakes
him. His hero or his heroine must be a tragedy-victim expiring
in show, and not the real prisoner of misery, sliding into death in
the silence of a dungeon....

I have now to follow Mr. Burke through a pathless wilderness
of rhapsodies, and a sort of descant upon governments, in which
he asserts whatever he pleases, on the presumption of its being
believed, without offering either evidence or reasons for so doing.

Before any thing can be reasoned upon to a conclusion,
certain facts, principles, or data, to reason from, must be

---

1 Shakespeare, *Othello* 3.3.367.

established, admitted, or denied. Mr. Burke, with his usual outrage, abuses the *Declaration of the Rights of Man*, published by the
National Assembly of France as the basis on which the constitution of France is built. This he calls "paltry and blurred sheets
of paper about the rights of man."—Does Mr. Burke mean to
deny that *man* has any rights? If he does, then he must mean
that there are no such things as rights any where, and that he
has none himself; for who is there in the world but man? But
if Mr. Burke means to admit that man has rights, the question
then will be, What are those rights, and how came man by them
originally?

The error of those who reason by precedents drawn from
antiquity, respecting the rights of man, is, that they do not go far
enough into antiquity. They do not go the whole way. They stop
in some of the intermediate stages of an hundred or a thousand
years, and produce what was then done, as a rule for the present day. This is no authority at all. If we travel still farther into
antiquity, we shall find a direct contrary opinion and practice
prevailing; and if antiquity is to be authority, a thousand such
authorities may be produced, successively contradicting each
other: But if we proceed on, we shall at last come out right; we
shall come to the time when man came from the hand of his
Maker. What was he then? Man. Man was the high and only
title, and a higher cannot be given him....

If any generation of men ever possessed the right of dictating
the mode by which the world should be governed for ever, it was
the first generation that existed; and if that generation did it not,
no succeeding generation can shew any authority for doing it,
nor can set any up....

MISCELLANEOUS CHAPTER

To prevent interrupting the argument in the preceding part of
this work, or the narrative that follows it, I reserved some observations to be thrown together into a Miscellaneous Chapter; by
which variety might not be censured for confusion. Mr. Burke's
Book is *all* Miscellany. His intention was to make an attack on
the French Revolution; but instead of proceeding with an orderly
arrangement, he has stormed it with a mob of ideas tumbling
over and destroying one another.

But this confusion and contradiction in Mr. Burke's Book
is easily accounted for.—When a man in a long cause attempts
to steer his course by any thing else than some polar truth or

principle, he is sure to be lost. It is beyond the compass of his capacity to keep all the parts of an argument together, and make them unite in one issue, by any other means than having this guide always in view. Neither memory nor invention will supply the want of it. The former fails him, and the latter betrays him.

Notwithstanding the nonsense, for it deserves no better name, that Mr. Burke has asserted about hereditary rights, and hereditary succession, and that a Nation has not a right to form a Government for itself; it happened to fall in his way to give some account of what Government is. "*Government*," says he, "*is a contrivance of human wisdom.*"

Admitting that Government is a contrivance of human *wisdom*, it must necessarily follow, that hereditary succession, and hereditary rights, (as they are called), can make no part of it, because it is impossible to make wisdom hereditary; and on the other hand, *that* cannot be a wise contrivance, which in its operation may commit the government of a nation to the wisdom of an idiot. The ground which Mr. Burke now takes, is fatal to every part of his cause. The argument changes from hereditary rights to hereditary wisdom; and the question is, Who is the wisest man? He must now shew that every one in the line of hereditary succession was a Solomon, or his title is not good to be a king.—What a stroke has Mr. Burke now made! To use a sailor's phrase, he has *swabbed the deck*, and scarcely left a name legible in the list of Kings; and he has mowed down and thinned the House of Peers, with a scythe as formidable as Death and Time.

But Mr. Burke appears to have been aware of this retort; and he has taken care to guard against it, by making government to be not only a *contrivance* of human wisdom, but a *monopoly* of wisdom. He puts the nation as fools on one side, and places his government of wisdom, all wise men of Gotham, on the other side; and he then proclaims, and says, that "*Men have a* RIGHT *that their* WANTS *should be provided for by this wisdom.*" Having thus made proclamation, he next proceeds to explain to them what their *wants* are, and also what their *rights* are. In this he has succeeded dextrously, for he makes their wants to be a *want* of wisdom; but as this is but cold comfort, he then informs them, that they have a *right* (not to any of the wisdom) but to be governed by it: and in order to impress them with a solemn reverence for this monopoly-government of wisdom, and of its vast capacity for all purposes, possible or impossible, right or wrong, he proceeds with astrological mysterious importance, to tell to them its powers, in these words—"The Rights of men in government are their advantages; and these are often in balances between differences of good; and in compromises sometimes between *good* and *evil*, and sometimes between *evil* and *evil*. Political reason is a *computing principle*; adding—subtracting— multiplying—and dividing, morally, and not metaphysically or mathematically, true moral demonstrations."

As the wondering audience, whom Mr. Burke supposes himself talking to, may not understand all this learned jargon, I will undertake to be its interpreter. The meaning then, good people, of all this, is, *That government is governed by no principle whatever; that it can make evil good, or good evil, just as it pleases. In short, that government is arbitrary power....*

There is a general enigma running through the whole of Mr. Burke's Book. He writes in a rage against the National Assembly; but what is he enraged about? If his assertions were as true as they are groundless, and that France, by her Revolution, had annihilated her power, and become what he calls a *chasm*, it might excite the grief of a Frenchman, (considering himself as a national man), and provoke his rage against the National Assembly; but why should it excite the rage of Mr. Burke?—Alas! it is not the Nation of France that Mr. Burke means, but the COURT; and every Court in Europe, dreading the same fate, is in mourning. He writes neither in the character of a Frenchman nor an Englishman, but in the fawning character of that creature known in all countries, and a friend to none, a COURTIER. Whether it be the Court of Versailles, or the Court of St. James or Carlton-House, or the Court in expectation, signifies not; for the caterpillar principle of all Courts and Courtiers are alike. They form a common policy throughout Europe, detached and separate from the interest of Nations: and while they appear to quarrel, they agree to plunder. Nothing can be more terrible to a Court or a Courtier, than the Revolution of France. That which is a blessing to Nations, is bitterness to them; and as their existence depends on the duplicity of a country, they tremble at the approach of principles, and dread the precedent that threatens their overthrow.

9. Jane Burke, from a Letter to William Burke, 21 March 1791 (*Corr.* VI, 238–39)

[Jane Burke (1734–1812) was Burke's wife. The following extract from a letter to Burke's kinsman William Burke (1728–98) details an encounter between "Ned" and King George III, who expressed gratitude to Burke for his exertions in support of "the cause of the Gentlemen."]

The respect and veneration he [Ned, i.e., Edmund Burke] is in on both sides of the *House* is not to be told, and can scarcely be believed—I do not know whether he told you of his reception when he went to Court, however, as Johnson used to say when he thought he had told a story before and which he thought to be a good one, I will tell it again—On his coming to Town for the Winter, as he generally does, he went to the Levee with the Duke of *Portland*, who went with Lord William to kiss hands on his going into the Guards—while Lord William was kissing hands, The King was talking to The Duke, but his Eyes were fixed on *Ned* who was standing in the Crowd, and when He said His say to The Duke, without waiting for Ned's coming up in his turn, The King went up to him, and, after the usual questions of how long have you been in Town and the weather, He said you have been very much employed of late, and very much confined. Ned said, no, Sir, not more than usual—You have and very well employed too, but there are none so deaf as those that w'ont hear, and none so blind as those that w'ont see—Ned made a low bow, Sir, I certainly now understand you, but was afraid my vanity or presumption might have led me to imagine what Your Majesty has said referred to what I have done—You cannot be vain—You have been of *use to us all*, it is a general opinion, is it not so Lord Stair? who was standing near. It is said Lord Stair;—Your Majesty's adopting it, Sir, will make the opinion general, said Ned—I know it is the general opinion, and I know that there is no Man who calls himself a Gentleman that must not think himself obliged to you, for you have supported the cause of the Gentlemen—You know the tone at Court is a whisper, but The King said all this loud, so as to be heard by every one at Court— ...

10. Thomas Jefferson, from a Letter to Benjamin Vaughan (11 May 1791), in *The Papers of Thomas Jefferson*, vol. XX, edited by Julian P. Boyd (Princeton UP, 1982), 391

[Thomas Jefferson (1743–1826), one of the American founding fathers, was a writer, statesman, and third president of the United States (1801–09).]

The Revolution of France does not astonish me so much as the Revolution of Mr. Burke. I wish I could believe the latter proceeded from as pure motives as the former. But what demonstration could scarcely have established before, less than the hints of Dr. Priestley and Mr. Paine establish firmly now. How mortifying that this evidence of the rottenness of his mind must oblige us now to ascribe to wicked motives those actions of his life which wore the mask of virtue and patriotism....

11. From James Mackintosh, *Vindiciae Gallicae: Defence of the French Revolution and Its English Admirers, against the Accusations of the Right Hon. Edmund Burke* (G.G.J. and J. Robinson, 1791), i-vii, 104–17, 162–66, 202

[Sir James Mackintosh (1765–1832) was a Scottish Whig politician and historian. *Vindiciae Gallicae* was the most measured, systematic, and compelling of the immediate critical responses to *Reflections on the Revolution in France*, though Mackintosh later came to align himself with Burke's own position. The change in Mackintosh's view, and his subsequent meeting with Burke, is the subject of Appendix G12, below.]

Introduction

The late opinions of Mr. Burke furnished more matter of astonishment to those who had distantly observed, than to those who had correctly examined the system of his former political life. An abhorrence for abstract politics, a predilection for aristocracy, and a dread of innovation, have ever been among the most sacred articles of his public creed. It was not likely that at his age he should abandon to the invasion of audacious novelties, opinions which he had received so early, and maintained so long, which had been fortified by the applause of the great, and the assent of the wise, which he had dictated to so many illustrious pupils, and supported against so many distinguished opponents. Men who early attain eminence, repose in their first creed. They neglect the progress of the human mind subsequent to its adoption, and when, as in the present case, it has burst forth into action, they regard it as a transient madness, worthy only of pity or derision. They mistake it for a mountain torrent that will pass away with the storm that gave it birth. They know not that it is the stream of human opinion *in omne volubilis ævum*,[1] which the accession of every day will swell, which is destined to sweep into the same oblivion the resistance of learned sophistry, and of powerful oppression.

But there still remained ample matter of astonishment in the Philippic of Mr. Burke. He might deplore the sanguinary excesses—he might deride the visionary policy that seemed to him to tarnish the lustre of the Revolution, but it was hard to have supposed that he should have exhausted against it every epithet of contumely and opprobrium that language can furnish to indignation; that the rage of his declamation should not for one moment have been suspended; that his heart should not betray one faint glow of triumph, at the splendid and glorious delivery of so great a people. All was invective—the authors, and admirers of the Revolution—every man who did not execrate it, even his own most enlightened and accomplished friends, were devoted to odium and ignominy.

This speech did not stoop to argument—the whole was dogmatical and authoritative; the cause seemed decided without discussion; the anathema fulminated before trial....

The arrangement of his work is as singular as the matter. Availing himself of all the privileges of epistolary effusion, in their utmost latitude and laxity, he interrupts, dismisses, and resumes argument at pleasure. His subject is as extensive as political science—his allusions and excursions reach almost every region of human knowledge. It must be confessed that in this miscellaneous and desultory warfare, the superiority of a man of genius over common men is infinite. He can cover the most ignominious retreat by a brilliant allusion. He can parade his arguments with masterly generalship, where they are strong. He can escape from an untenable position into a splendid declamation. He can sap the most impregnable conviction by pathos, and put to flight a host of syllogisms with a sneer. Absolved from the laws of vulgar method, he can advance a group of magnificent horrors to make a breach in our hearts, through which the most undisciplined rabble of arguments may enter in triumph....

---

1 "Rolling its flood forever." Horace, *Epistles*, Book I, ii, 43.

Section I: The General Expediency and Necessity of a Revolution in France

... The three Aristocracies, Military, Sacerdotal, and Judicial, may be considered as having formed the French Government. They have appeared, so far as we have considered them, incorrigible. All attempts to improve them would have been little better than (to use the words of Mr. Burke) "mean reparations on mighty ruins." They were not perverted by the accidental depravity of their members. They were not infected by any transient passion, which new circumstances would extirpate. The fault was in the essence of the institutions themselves, which were irreconcileable with a free Government. But it is objected, these institutions might have been *gradually* reformed. The spirit of Freedom would have silently entered. The progressive wisdom of an enlightened nation would have remedied, in process of time, their defects, without convulsion.

To this argument I confidently answer, *that these institutions would have destroyed* LIBERTY, *before Liberty had corrected their* SPIRIT. Power vegetates with more vigour after these gentle prunings. A slender reform amuses and lulls the people; the popular enthusiasm subsides, and the moment of effectual reform is irretrievably lost. No important political improvement was ever obtained in a period of tranquillity. The corrupt interest of the Governors is so strong, and the cry of the people so feeble, that it were vain to expect it. If the effervescence of the popular mind is suffered to pass away without effect, it would be absurd to expect from languor what enthusiasm has not obtained. If radical reform is not, at such a moment, procured, all partial changes are evaded and defeated in the tranquility which succeeds. The gradual reform that arises from the presiding principle exhibited in the specious theory of Mr. Burke, is belied by the experience of all ages. Whatever excellence, whatever freedom is discoverable in Governments, has been infused into them by the shock of a revolution, and their subsequent progress has been only the accumulation of abuse. It is hence that the most enlightened politicians have recognized the necessity of *frequently recalling Governments to their first principles*; a truth equally suggested to the penetrating intellect of Machiavel, by his experience of the Florentine democracy, and by his research into the history of ancient Commonwealths.—Whatever is good ought to be pursued at the moment it is attainable. The public voice, irresistible in a period of convulsion, is contemned with impunity, when dictated by that lethargy into which nations are lulled by the tranquil course of their ordinary affairs. The ardor of reform languishes in unsupported tediousness. It perishes in an impotent struggle with adversaries, who receive new strength from the progress of the day. No hope of great political improvement (let us repeat it) is to be entertained from tranquility, for its natural operation is to strengthen all those who are interested in perpetuating abuse. The National Assembly seized the moment of eradicating the corruptions and abuses which afflicted their country. Their reform was total, that it might be commensurate with the evil, and *no part of it was delayed*, because to spare an abuse at such a period was to consecrate it; because the enthusiasm which carries nations to such enterprizes is short-lived, and the opportunity of reform, if once neglected, might be irrevocably fled.

But let us ascend to more general principles, and hazard bolder opinions. Let us grant that the state of France was not so desperately incorrigible. Let us suppose that changes far more gentle, innovations far less extensive, would have remedied the grosser evils of her Government, and placed it almost on a level with free and celebrated Constitutions. These concessions, though too large for truth, will not convict the Assembly. By what principle of reason, or of justice, were they precluded from aspiring to give France a Government less imperfect, than *accident* had formed in other States?—Who will be hardy enough to assert, that a better Constitution is not attainable than any which has hitherto appeared? Is the limit of human wisdom to be estimated in the science of politics alone, by the extent of its present attainments? Is the most sublime and difficult of all arts, the improvement of the social order, the alleviation of the miseries of the civil condition of man, to be alone stationary, amid the rapid progress of every other art, liberal and vulgar, to perfection? Where would be the atrocious guilt of a grand experiment, to ascertain the portion of freedom and happiness, that can be created by political institutions?

That guilt (if it be guilt) is imputable to the National Assembly of France. They are accused of having rejected the guidance of experience, of having abandoned themselves to the illusion of theory, and of having sacrificed great and attainable good to the magnificent chimeras of ideal excellence. If this accusation be just, if they have indeed abandoned *experience*, the basis of human knowledge, as well as the guide of human action, their conduct deserves no longer any serious argument; and if (as Mr. Burke more than once insinuates) their contempt of it is avowed and ostentatious, it was surely unworthy of him to have expended so much genius against so preposterous an insanity. But the explanation of *terms* will diminish our wonder—Experience may, both in the arts and in the conduct of human life, be regarded in a double view, either as furnishing *models*, or *principles*. An artist who frames his machine in exact imitation of his predecessor, is in the *first sense* said to be guided by experience. In this sense all improvements of human life, have been *deviations* from experience. The first visionary innovator was the savage who built a cabin, or covered himself with a rug. If this be experience, man is degraded to the unimproveable level of the instinctive animals—But in the second acceptation, an artist is said to be guided by experience, when the inspection of a machine discovers to him principles, which teach him to improve it, or when the comparison of many both with respect to their excellencies and defects, enables him to frame another more perfect machine, different from any he had examined. In this latter sense, the National Assembly have perpetually availed themselves of experience. History is an immense collection of experiments on the nature and effect of the various parts of various Governments. Some institutions are *experimentally* ascertained to be beneficial; some to be most indubitably destructive. A third class, which produces partial good, obviously possess the capacity of improvement. What, on such a survey, was the dictate of enlightened experience?—Not surely to follow the model of any of those Governments, in which these institutions lay indiscriminately mingled; but, like the mechanic, to compare and generalize; and, guided equally by experience, to imitate and reject. The process is in both cases the same. The rights and the nature of man are to the Legislator what the general properties of matter are to the Mechanic, the first guide, because they are founded on the widest experience. In the second class are to be ranked observations on the excellencies and defects of those Governments which have existed, that teach the construction of a more perfect machine. BUT EXPERIENCE IS THE BASIS OF ALL. Not the puny and trammelled experience of a *Statesman by trade*, who trembles at any change in the *tricks* which he has been taught, or the *routine* in which he has been accustomed to move, but an experience liberal and enlightened, which hears the testimony of ages and nations, and collects from it the general principles which regulate the mechanism of society.

Legislators are under no obligation to retain a constitution, because it has been found "*tolerably* to answer the common purposes of Government." It is absurd to *expect*, but it is not absurd to *pursue* perfection. It is absurd to acquiesce in evils, of which the remedy is obvious, because they are less grievous than those which are endured by others. To suppose the social order is not capable of improvement from the progress of the human understanding, is to betray the inconsistent absurdity of an arrogant confidence in our attainments, and an abject distrust of our powers. If indeed the sum of evil produced by political institutions, even in the least imperfect Governments, were small, there might be some pretence for this dread of innovation, this horror at remedy, which has raised such a clamour over Europe: But, on the contrary, in an estimate of the sources of human misery, after granting that one portion is to be attributed to disease, and another to private vices, it might perhaps be found that a *third equal* part arose from the oppressions and corruptions of Government, disguised under various forms. All the Governments that now exist in the world (except the United States of America) have been fortuitously formed. They are the produce of chance, not the work of art. They have been altered, impaired, improved and destroyed by accidental circumstances, beyond the foresight or controul of wisdom. Their parts thrown up against present emergencies formed no systematic whole. It was certainly not to have been presumed, that these *fortuitous Governments* should have surpassed the works of intellect, and precluded all nearer approaches to perfection. Their origin without doubt furnishes a strong presumption of an opposite nature. It might teach us to expect in them many discordant principles, many jarring forms, much unmixed evil, and much imperfect good, many institutions which had long survived their motive, and many of which reason had never been the author, nor utility the object. Experience, *even in the best of these Governments*, accords with such expectations.

A Government of *art*, the work of legislative intellect, reared on the immutable basis of natural right and general happiness, which should combine the excellencies, and exclude the defects of the various constitutions which chance had scattered over the world, instead of being precluded by the perfection of any of those forms, was loudly demanded by the injustice and absurdity of them all. It was time that men should learn to tolerate nothing ancient that reason does not respect, and to shrink from no novelty to which reason may conduct. It was time that the human powers, so long occupied by subordinate objects, and inferior arts, should mark the commencement of a new æra in history, by giving birth to the art of improving government, and increasing the civil happiness of man. It was time, as it has been wisely and eloquently said, that Legislators, instead of that narrow and dastardly *coasting* which never ventures to lose sight of usage and precedent, should, guided by the *polarity* of reason, hazard a bolder navigation, and discover, in unexplored regions, the treasure of public felicity....

Section III: Popular Excesses which Attended the Revolution

That no great Revolutions can be accomplished without excesses and miseries at which humanity revolts, is a truth which cannot be denied. This unfortunately is true, in a peculiar manner, of those Revolutions, which, like that of France, are strictly *popular*. Where the people are led by a faction, its leaders find no difficulty in the re-establishment of that order, which must be the object of their wishes, because it is the sole security of their power. But when a general movement of the popular mind levels a despotism with the ground, it is far less easy to restrain excess. There is more resentment to satiate and less authority to controul. The passion which produced an effect so tremendous, is too violent to subside in a moment into serenity and submission. The spirit of revolt breaks out with fatal violence after its object is destroyed, and turns against the order of freedom those arms by which it had subdued the strength of tyranny. The attempt to *punish* the spirit that actuates a *people*, if it were just, would be in vain, and if it were possible, would be cruel. They are too *many* to be punished in a view of justice, and too *strong* to be punished in a view of policy. The ostentation of vigor would in such a case prove the display of impotence, and the rigor of justice conduct to the cruelty of extirpation. No remedy is therefore left but the progress of instruction, the force of persuasion, the mild authority of opinion. These remedies, though infallible, are of slow operation; and in the interval which elapses before a calm succeeds the boisterous moments of a Revolution, it is vain to expect that a people, inured to barbarism by their oppressors, and which has ages of oppression to avenge, will be punctiliously generous in their triumph, nicely discriminative in their vengeance, or cautiously mild in their mode of retaliation. "They will break their chains on the heads of their oppressors."[1]

Such was the state of France, and such were the obvious causes that gave birth to scenes which the friends of freedom deplore as tarnishing her triumphs. They *feel* these evils as men

---

1 [Mackintosh's note:] The eloquent expression of Mr. CURRAN in the Parliament of Ireland, respecting the Revolution.

of humanity. But they will not bestow the name on that womanish and complexional sensibility, towards which, even in the still intercourse of private life, *indulgence* is mingled with love. The only humanity which, in the great affairs of men, claims their respect, is that manly and expanded humanity, which fixes its steady eye on the object of general happiness. The sensibility which shrinks at a present evil, without extending its views to future good, is not a virtue, for it is not a quality beneficial to mankind: It would arrest the arm of a Surgeon in amputating a gangrened limb, or the hand of a Judge in signing the sentence of a parricide. I do not say, (God forbid!) that a crime may be committed for the prospect of good. Such a doctrine would shake morals to their center. But the case of the French Revolutionists is totally different. Has any moralist ever pretended, *that we are to decline the pursuit of a good which our duty prescribed to us, because we foresaw that some partial and incidental evil would arise from it?* This is the true view of the question, and it is only by this principle that we are to estimate the responsibility of the leaders of the Revolution for the excesses which attended it....

... To the eye of Mr. Burke, it [the Revolution] exhibits nothing but a scene of horror. In his mind it inspires no emotion but abhorrence of its leaders, commiseration of their victims, and alarms at the influence of an event which menaces the subversion of the policy, the arts, and the manners of the civilized world. Minds who view it through another medium are filled by it with every sentiment of admiration and triumph—of admiration due to splendid exertions of virtue, and of triumph inspired by widening prospects of happiness.

12. The Mackintosh–Burke Correspondence, December 1796 (*Corr.* IX, 192–95)

a. James Mackintosh to Edmund Burke (22 December 1796)

Sir,

The liberty which I take in addressing you is so great and the nature of the address so peculiar that I certainly should not have hazarded such an address to a mind of a different Cast from yours....

From the earliest moments of reflexion your writings were my chief study and delight. The instruction which they contain is endeared to me by being entwined and interwoven in my mind with the recollection of those fresh and lively feelings of youth which are too pure and exquisite a pleasure to be twice tasted by the human heart.

The enthusiasm with which I then embraced them is now ripened into solid Conviction by the experience and meditation of more mature age. For a time indeed seduced by the love of what I thought liberty I ventured to oppose your Opinions without ever ceasing to venerate your character. I speak to state facts—not to flatter—You are above flattery. I am too proud to flatter even you.—Since that time a melancholy experience has undeceived me on many subjects on which I was the dupe of my enthusiasm.—I cannot say (and you would despise me if I dissembled) that I can even now assent to all your opinions on the present politics of Europe. But I can with truth affirm that I subscribe to your general Principles; that I consider them as the only solid foundation both of political Science and of political prudence; that I differ solely as to some applications of them which appear to my poor understanding not entirely accordant to the scheme and Spirit of your System; and that above all if the fatal necessity should arise (which God forbid) there is no Man in England more resolutely determined to Spill the last drop of his blood in defense of the Laws and Constitution of our Forefathers....

I have the honour to be

Sir

with the most unfeigned and (suffer me to add)
the most affectionate veneration
Your faithful humble Servant,
JAMES MACKINTOSH

b. Edmund Burke to James Mackintosh (23 December 1796)

Sir,

The very obliging Letter with which you have honoured me, is well calculated to stir up those remains of vanity, that I hoped had been nearly extinguished in a frame approaching to the dissolution of every thing that can feed that passion. But, in truth, it afforded me a more solid and a more sensible consolation. The view of a vigorous mind subduing by its own constitutional force the maladies which that very force of constitution had produced, is, in itself, a Spectacle very pleasing and very instructive. It is not proper to say any more about myself, who have been, but rather to turn to you who *are*, and who probably *will* be, and from whom the world is yet to expect a great deal of instruction and a great deal of service. You have begun your Opposition by obtaining a great victory over yourself, and it shews how much your own Sagacity operating on your own experience is capable of adding to your very extraordinary natural Talents, and to your early errudition. It was the shew of virtue and the semblance of publick happiness that could alone mislead a mind like yours; and it is a better knowledge of their substance which alone has put you again in the way that leads the most securely and most certainly to your End. As it is on all hands allowed that you were the most able advocate for the cause which you supported, your sacrifice to truth and mature reflexion, adds much to your glory....

Tho' I see but very few persons, and have, since my misfortune[1] studiously declined all new acquaintances and never dine out of my own family, nor live at all in any of my usual societies, not even in those with which I was most closely connected, I shall certainly be as happy as I shall feel myself honoured by a visit from a distinguished person like you, whom I shall consider as an exception to my rule. I have no habitation in London, nor never go to that place but with great reluctance, and without suffering a great deal. Nothing but necessity calls me thither; but tho' I hardly dare to ask you to come so far, whenever it may suit you to visit this abode of sickness and infirmity, I shall be glad to see you....

... I have the honour to be Sir, with great respect and regard

Your most obedient and very much

obliged humble servant,

EDM BURKE.

[Mackintosh accepted Burke's invitation and spent some days with him at Beaconsfield. Mackintosh's recollections of their conversations at that time are of interest, none perhaps more so than this excoriating account of the innovating "new school" of philosophers:[2]]

Talking of the anti-moral paradoxes of certain philosophers of the new school, he (Burke) observed, with indignation, "They deserve no refutation but those of the common hangman.... Their arguments are, at best, miserable logomachies, base prostitutions of the gifts of reason and discourse, which God gave to man for

---

1 The death of his son Richard on 2 August 1794.

2 From *Memoirs of the Life of the Right Honourable Sir James Mackintosh, Edited by His Son, Robert James Mackintosh* (Edward Moxon, 1835), vol. I, pp. 93–94.

the purpose of exalting, not brutalising, his species. The wretches have not the doubtful merit of sincerity; for, if they really believed what they published, we should know how to work with them, by treating them as lunatics. No, sir, these opinions are put forth in the shape of books, for the sordid purpose of deriving a paltry gain from the natural fondness of mankind for pernicious novelties. As to the opinions themselves, they are those of pure defecated Atheism. Their object is to corrupt all that is good in man—to eradicate his immortal soul—to dethrone God from the universe. They are the brood of that putrid carcass, that mother of all evil, the French Revolution. I never think of that plague-spot in the history of mankind, without shuddering. It is an evil spirit that is always before me. There is not a mischief, by which the moral world can be afflicted, that it has not let loose upon it. It reminds me of the accursed things that crawled in and out of the mouth of the vile hag in Spenser's Cave of Error. Here he repeated that sublime but nauseous stanza.[1] You, Mr. Mackintosh, are in vigorous man-

---

1 The allusion is to Book I, Canto I, of Edmund Spenser's *The Faerie Queene*, in which the terrible monster Errour is detected in her Cave:

XV
And as she lay upon the durtie ground,
Her huge long taile her den all overspred,
Yet was in knots and many boughtes upwound,
Pointed with mortall sting. Of her there bred
A thousand yong ones, which she dayly fed,
Sucking upon her poisonous dugs, eachone
Of sundry shapes, yet all ill favored:
Soone as that uncouth light upon them shone,
Into her mouth they crept, and suddain all were gone.
...

XX
Therewith she spewd out of her filthy maw
A floud of poyson horrible and blacke,
Full of great lumpes of flesh and gobbets raw,
Which stunck so vildly, that it forst him slacke
His grasping hold, and from her turne him backe:
Her vomit full of bookes and papers was,
With loathly frogs and toades, which eyes did lacke,
And creeping sought way in the weedy gras:
Her filthy parbreake all the place defiled has.
(*continued*)

hood; your intellect is in its freshest prime, and you are a powerful writer; you shall be the faithful knight of the romance; the brightness of your sword will flash destruction on the filthy progeny."

In casting Mackintosh as the Redcrosse Knight of the poem, Burke appears to anoint him as his successor in the fight against Jacobinism and as the slayer of revolutionary error.

Appendix H: "Delivered Over to Infamy at the End of a Long Life"

1. **Selections from Burke's two speeches on the Quebec Bill (May 1791), in** *The Speeches of the Right Honourable Edmund Burke in the House of Commons and in Westminster-Hall* **(Longman, Hurst, Rees, Orme, and Brown, 1816), vol. IV, pp. 15–32**

[In the following selections, drawn from proceedings in the House of Commons in May 1791, a number of central themes in Burke's view of revolutionary politics come together: the preference for experience over innovation and theory; the reverence for the English Constitution and disdain for an experimental and blank-slate approach to constitution writing; abhorrence at the idea that the excesses of the French Revolution might be justified by some future and beneficial end result (the *theological* dimension to Burke's take on this is especially to be noted here); and visceral horror expressed toward the astonishing and sublime violence of the Jacobin beast ("a shapeless monster, born of hell and chaos"). Burke's defence of his consistency is a conspicuous theme in these speeches, which also illustrate the enormous personal toll that Burke's crusade against the Jacobins took on him: his alienation from the Whig Party, his consequent political isolation, and the loss of his long, cherished and politically productive friendship with Charles James Fox. The dramatic scene captured the imagination of caricaturists (see Fig. 3: *The Volcano of Opposition*, attributed to Frederick George Byron, in which a stream of wild invective—"The very dregs of infamy! Fiends of Hell! Pimps, Panders, Parasites, Devils!" etc.—vomits forth from Burke's mouth, while Fox weeps at the loss of friendship). The following selections commence after a speech by Fox, in which he had criticized Burke for using a debate on Canadian affairs to launch instead a discussion about France, marvelled at Burke's inconsistency, and declared that the French Revolution was "one of the most glorious events in the History of Mankind."]

... Mr. BURKE commenced his reply, in a grave and governed tone of voice, observing that although he had himself been called to order so many times, he had sat with perfect composure, and had heard the most disorderly speech that perhaps ever was delivered in that House. He had not pursued the conduct of which an example had been set him, but had heard, without the least interruption, that speech out to the end, irregular and disorderly as it had been. His words and his conduct throughout had been misrepresented, and a personal attack had been made upon him from a quarter he never could have expected, after a friendship and an intimacy of more than two-and-twenty years; and not only his public conduct, words, and writings, had been alluded to in the severest terms, but confidential conversations and private opinions had been brought forward, with a view of proving that he acted inconsistently.... He could not help thinking, that on the subject of the French revolution, he had met with great unfairness from the right honourable gentleman, who had accused him of speaking rashly, without information, and unsupported by facts to bear out his deductions, and that he had been treated in a manner that did little justice to his feelings, and had little appearance of decency on the part of the right honourable gentleman....

... He could not, however, be persuaded, from what the right honourable gentleman had urged, to give up his purpose of stating to the House, upon this occasion, his mind with regard to the French constitution, and the facts which led him to think as he did; and certainly in this he thought there could be nothing disorderly, especially when so much had been already introduced, not about the constitution of Quebec, but about the American constitution. He had asserted, that dangerous doctrines were encouraged in this country, and that dreadful consequences might ensue from them, which it was his sole wish and ambition to avert, by strenuously supporting the constitution of Great Britain as it is, which, in his mind, could better be done by preventing impending danger, than by any remedy that could afterwards be applied; and he thought himself justified in saying this, because he did know that there were people in this country avowedly endeavouring to disorder its constitution and government, and that in a very bold manner....

After what had been said, nobody could impute to him interested or personal motives for his conduct. Those with whom he had been constantly in habits of friendship and agreement, were all against him, and from the other side of the House he was not likely to have much support; yet, all he did, was no more than his duty. It was a struggle, not to support any man, or set of men, but a struggle to support the British constitution, in doing which he had incurred the displeasure of all about him, and those opposite to him; and, what was worst of all, he had induced the right honourable gentleman to rip up the whole course and tenor of his life, public and private, and that not without a considerable degree of asperity. His failings and imperfections had been keenly exposed, and, in short, without the chance of gaining one new friend, he had made enemies, it appeared malignant enemies, of his old friends; but, after all, he esteemed his duty far beyond any friendship, any fame, or any other consideration whatever. He had stated the danger which the British constitution was daily in, from the doctrines and conduct of particular persons; however, as neither side of the House supported him in this, but as both sides thought otherwise, he would not press that point upon them now in any stronger way than he had done; but he would still aver, that no assistance which could either be given or refused to him, would ever bias him against the excellence of the British constitution; nor lead him to think well of the French revolution, or the constitution, as it was named, that was formed in its place....

... The malignity with which the right honourable gentleman had spoken of his sentiments with regard to government, and the charge he had brought against him of inconsistency in his political life and opinions, were neither fair nor true; for he denied that he ever entertained any ideas of government different from those which he now entertained, and had upon many occasions stated. He laid it down as a maxim, that monarchy was the basis of all good government, and the nearer to monarchy any government approached, the more perfect it was, and *vice versa*; and he certainly, in his wildest moments, never had so far forgotten the nature of government, as to argue that we ought to wish for a constitution that we could alter at pleasure and change like a dirty shirt....

... It certainly was indiscretion, at any period, but especially at his time of life, to provoke enemies, or give his friends occasion to desert him; yet if his firm and steady adherence to the British constitution placed him in such a dilemma, he would risk all; and, as public duty and public prudence taught him, with his last words exclaim, "Fly from the French constitution." [*Mr. Fox here whispered, that there was no loss of friends.*] Mr. Burke said, *Yes, there was a loss of friends—he knew the price of his conduct—he*

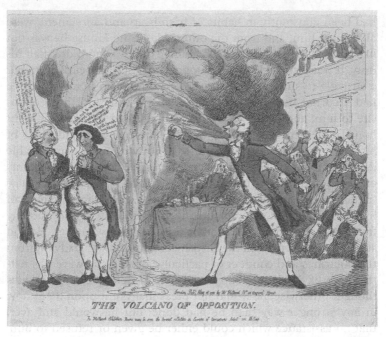

THE VOLCANO OF OPPOSITION.

Figure 3: *The Volcano of Opposition,* attributed to Frederick George Byron, 1791. Yale Center for British Art, Paul Mellon Collection.

had done his duty at the price of his friend—their friendship was at an end....

Before he sat down, he earnestly warned the two right honourable gentlemen[1] who were the great rivals in that House, that whether they hereafter moved in the political hemisphere as two flaming meteors, or walked together like brethren hand in hand, to preserve and cherish the British constitution, to guard against innovation, and to save it from the danger of those new theories. In a rapturous apostrophe to the infinite and unspeakable power of the Deity, who, with his arm, hurled a comet like a projectile out of its course—who enabled it to endure the sun's heat, and the pitchy darkness of the chilly night; he said, that to the Deity must be left the task of infinite perfection, while to us poor, weak, incapable mortals, there was no rule of conduct so safe as experience.[2] ...

1 Fox and Pitt.
2 In a different report of the debate, from the *Oracle* on 7 May 1791, Burke claimed it was inadmissible to claim that the French

Mr. Fox rose to reply, but his mind was so much agitated, and his heart so much affected by what had fallen from Mr. Burke, that it was some minutes before he could proceed. Tears trickled down his cheeks, and he strove in vain to give utterance to feelings that dignified and exalted his nature. The sensibility of every member present seemed to be uncommonly excited upon the occasion. Being at length recovered from the depression under which he had risen, Mr. Fox proceeded to answer the assertions which had caused it. When he had concluded,

Mr. BURKE again rose. He began with remarking, that the tenderness which had been displayed in the beginning and conclusion of Mr. Fox's speech, was quite obliterated by what had occurred in the middle part....

... The inconsistency of his book with his former writings and speeches, had been insinuated and assumed, but he challenged the proof by specific instances; and he also asserted, that there was not one step of his conduct, nor one syllable of his book, contrary to the principles of those men with whom our glorious revolution originated, and to whose principles, as a Whig, he declared an inviolable attachment. He was an old man, and seeing what was attempted to be introduced instead of the ancient temple of our constitution, could weep over the foundation of the new.

He again stated, still more particularly, the endeavours used in this country to supplant our own by the introduction of the new French constitution.... He observed, that Mr. Fox himself had termed the new French system a most stupendous and glorious fabric of human integrity.[1] He had really conceived, that the right honourable gentleman possessed a better taste in architecture, than to bestow so magnificent an epithet upon a building composed of untempered mortar. He considered it as the work of Goths and Vandals, where every thing was disjointed and inverted.

... The present state of France was ten times worse than a

Revolution would bring benefits to humanity despite its initial (violent) costs: "To do evil that good may arise from it was by no means the province of MAN, who may be very liable to err in his prophecy of events. This was the direct and incommunicable attribute of the DEITY.... The power therefore of committing present and positive evils for the chance of eventual benefit, could not be assumed by man without the utmost arrogance or presumption." Langford et al., vol. IV, 345n1.

1 On 15 April 1791, Fox had called the new French constitution a "stupendous fabric."

tyranny. The new constitution was said to be an experiment; but the assertion was not true. It had already been tried, and had been found to be only productive of evils. They would go on from tyranny to tyranny, from oppression to oppression, till at last the whole system would terminate in the destruction of that miserable and deluded people. He said that his opinion of the revolution in America did not at all militate with his opinion of the revolution of France. In that instance, he considered that the people had some reason for the conduct which they pursued.

Mr. Burke said, that he was sorry for the occurrence of that day. Sufficient for the day was the evil thereof.[1] Yet if the good were to many, he would willingly take the evil to himself. He sincerely hoped that no member of that House would ever barter the constitution of this country, the eternal jewel of their souls, for a wild and visionary system, which could only lead to confusion and disorder. With regard to pretences of friendship, he must own that he did not like them, where his character and public conduct, as in the present instance, had been so materially attacked and injured....

11 May 1791

... Mr. Burke resumed his argument, and contended that he had a right to be heard, while he endeavoured to clear himself from the foul conduct that had been imputed to him. Would the House, he asked, think he was a fit man to sit there while under the imputation he had described? If he had wished to attack the right honourable gentleman for his opinions respecting what had happened in France, he was free to do it any day he chose; as the right honourable gentleman had sufficiently often avowed those opinions in that House. Finding himself, without any cause, separated and excluded from his party, it was a loss which he severely felt; but while he felt it like a man, he would bear it like a man.... In the course of the conversation the other evening, the right honourable gentleman had said, that he had written a book which he had thought it seasonable and proper for him to go about and reprobate in all its essential parts and principles. [A cry of No! no! from the opposition benches.] He rose therefore to justify himself in the face of that House and of his country, and in the face of an adversary the most able, eloquent, and powerful that ever was encountered, and (he was sorry to

---

1 Matthew 6:34.

perceive) the most willing to rake up the whole of his opinions and conduct, in order to prove that they had been abandoned by him with the most shameless inconsistency. He avowed the book and all it contained. He said he had written it, in order to counteract the machinations of one of the most desperate and most malignant factions that ever existed in any age or country. He would still oppose the mischievous principles of such a faction, though he was unfortunate enough to stand alone, unprotected, supported with no great connexions, with no great abilities, and with no great fortune. And thus was he delivered over to infamy at the end of a long life, just like the Dervise[1] in the fable, who, after living till ninety in the supposed practice of every virtue, was tempted at last to the commission of a single error, when the devil spat in his face as a reward for all his actions![2] In order to support monarchy, had he said, the other evening, that it was right to abuse every republican government that ever existed? Had he abused America, or Athens, or Rome, or Sparta? But every thing had been remembered that he had ever said or written, in order to render it the ground of censure and of abuse. He declared that he could not caution the House too much against what had passed in France, but he had not called that country a republic; no, it was an anomaly in government, he knew not by what name to call it, nor in what terms to describe it:

"—————————————————————A shape,
If shape it might be called, that shape had none
Distinguishable in member, joint, or limb;
Or substance might be call'd that shadow seem'd,
For each seem'd either; black it stood as night,
Fierce as ten furies, terrible as hell,
And shook a dreadful dart; what seem'd his head,
The likeness of a kingly crown had on.
★ ★ ★ ★ ★ ★ ★ ★
A cry of hell-hounds never ceasing bark
With wide Cerberian mouths full loud, and rung
A hideous peal."[3]

It was, he added, "A shapeless monster, born of hell and chaos."

---

1 Dervish, a member of a Sufi religious order.
2 Burke is alluding to the Islamic story of the hermit Santon Barsisa and the Devil.
3 John Milton, *Paradise Lost*, Book II, 666–73, 654–56.

Works Cited and Select Bibliography

Burke's Works

There are many editions of Burke's works. The latest, and definitive, edition is

Langford, Paul, et al. *The Writings and Speeches of Edmund Burke.* 9 vols. Oxford UP, 1981–2015.

Also cited in the text are the following:

The Works and Correspondence of the Right Honourable Edmund Burke. 8 vols. Francis & John Rivington, 1852.
Hampsher-Monk, Iain, editor. *Burke: Revolutionary Writings.* Cambridge UP, 2014.

Among the unabridged editions of *Reflections on the Revolution in France,* the following editions are noteworthy, with illuminating introductions and notes by each editor: L.G. Mitchell (Oxford UP, 1993), Conor Cruise O'Brien (Penguin, 1968), and J.G.A. Pocock (Hackett, 1987). The text of each of those editions is based on the last (or "seventh") edition prepared by Burke himself. For a text utilizing the first edition (and with an extensive and authoritative critical apparatus), see J.C.D. Clark's edition (Stanford UP, 2001).

Correspondence

Copeland, Thomas W., et al. *The Correspondence of Edmund Burke.* 10 vols. U of Chicago P, 1958–78.

Biographies

Ayling, Stanley. *Edmund Burke: His Life and Opinions.* St. Martin's Press, 1988.
Bourke, Richard. *Empire and Revolution: The Political Life of Edmund Burke.* Princeton UP, 2015.

Bromwich, David. *The Intellectual Life of Edmund Burke: From the Sublime and Beautiful to American Independence.* Belknap Press, 2014.

Cone, Carl B. *Burke and the Nature of Politics.* 2 vols. U of Kentucky P, 1957–64.

Kramnick, Isaac. *The Rage of Edmund Burke.* Basic Books, 1977.

Lambert, Elizabeth R. *Edmund Burke of Beaconsfield.* U of Delaware P, 2003.

Lock, F.P. *Edmund Burke.* 2 vols. Oxford UP, 1998–2006.

Magnus, Philip. *Edmund Burke: A Life.* John Murray, 1939.

O'Brien, Conor Cruise. *The Great Melody: A Thematic Biography of Edmund Burke.* U of Chicago P, 1992.

Prior, James. *Memoir of the Life and Character of the Right Hon. Edmund Burke.* Ticknor, Reed, and Fields, 1854.

Studies and Surveys

Blakemore, Steven. *Edmund Burke and the Fall of Language: The French Revolution as Linguistic Event.* UP of New England, 1988.

Butler, Marilyn, editor. *Burke, Paine, Godwin, and the Revolution Controversy.* Cambridge UP, 1984.

Canavan, Francis. *Edmund Burke: Prescription and Providence.* Carolina Academic Press, 1987.

———. *The Political Reason of Edmund Burke.* Duke UP, 1960.

Cobban, Alfred. *Edmund Burke and the Revolt against the Eighteenth Century.* 2nd ed. George Allen & Unwin, 1960.

Collins, Gregory. *Commerce and Manners in Edmund Burke's Political Economy.* Cambridge UP, 2020.

Copeland, Thomas W. *Our Eminent Friend Edmund Burke.* Yale UP, 1949.

Dwan, David, and Christopher J. Insole. *The Cambridge Companion to Edmund Burke.* Cambridge UP, 2012.

Freeman, Michael. *Edmund Burke and the Critique of Political Radicalism.* U of Chicago P, 1980.

Jones, Emily. *Edmund Burke and the Invention of Modern Conservatism, 1830–1914: An Intellectual History.* Oxford UP, 2017.

Kirk, Russell. *Edmund Burke: A Genius Reconsidered.* Arlington House, 1967.

Lacey, Robert J. *Pragmatic Conservatism: Edmund Burke and His American Heirs.* Palgrave Macmillan, 2016.

Levin, Yuval. *The Great Debate: Edmund Burke, Thomas Paine, and the Birth of Right and Left.* Basic Books, 2014.

Lock, F.P. *Burke's Reflections on the Revolution in France.* George Allen & Unwin, 1985.

Maciag, Drew. *Edmund Burke in America: The Contested Career of the Father of Modern Conservatism.* Cornell UP, 2013.

Macpherson, C.B. *Burke.* Oxford UP, 1980.

Morley, John. *Burke.* Macmillan, 1888.

___. *Edmund Burke: A Historical Study.* Macmillan, 1867.

Norman, Jesse. *Edmund Burke: The First Conservative.* Harper-Collins, 2013.

O'Gorman, Frank. *Edmund Burke: His Political Philosophy.* George Allen & Unwin, 1973.

O'Keefe, Dennis. *Edmund Burke.* Bloomsbury, 2013.

Parkin, Charles. *The Moral Basis of Burke's Political Thought.* Russell & Russell, 1956.

Ritchie, Daniel, editor. *Edmund Burke: Appraisals and Applications.* Transaction, 1990.

Robinson, Nicholas K. *Edmund Burke: A Life in Caricature.* Yale UP, 1996.

Stanlis, Peter J. *Edmund Burke and the Natural Law.* U of Michigan P, 1965.

___. *Edmund Burke, the Enlightenment and Revolution.* Transaction, 1991.

Weiner, Greg. *Old Whigs: Burke, Lincoln and the Politics of Prudence.* Encounter Books, 2019.

Other Works Cited

Boswell, James. *Life of Johnson.* 1791. Oxford UP, 1990.

Buckle, Henry Thomas. *The History of Civilization in England.* John W. Parker & Son, 1857.

Depont, M. *Answer to the Reflections of the Right Hon. Edmund Burke.* P. Byrne, A. Grueber, R. White, W. Jones, 1791.

Halifax, Marquis of. *Miscellanies.* W. Rogers, 1704.

Johnson, Samuel. *A Dictionary of the English Language.* J. and P. Knapton et al., 1755.

___. *Works.* George Cowie and Co. 1825.

Kirk, Russell. *The Conservative Mind.* Regnery, 2001.

Laski, Harold. *Political Thought in England from Locke to Bentham.* Thornton Butterworth, 1930.

Marx, Karl. *Capital.* 1867. Oxford UP, 1999.

Moore, Thomas. *Memoirs of the Life of the Rt. Hon. Richard Brinsley Sheridan.* J.S. Redfield, 1858.

Paine, Thomas. *Common Sense.* 1776. H.D. Symonds, 1792.

_____. *Rights of Man: Being an Answer to Mr. Burke's Attack on the French Revolution*. J.S. Jordan, 1791.

Quinton, Anthony. *The Politics of Imperfection*. Faber & Faber, 1978.

Sabine, George H. *A History of Political Theory*. Henry Holt & Company, 1937.

Tocqueville, Alexis de. *The Ancien Régime and the French Revolution*. 1856. Cambridge UP, 2011.

Trevelyan, G.M. *The English Revolution 1688–1689*. Oxford UP, 1938.

Vannatta, Seth. *Conservatism and Pragmatism*. Palgrave Macmillan, 2014.

Wollstonecraft, Mary. *A Vindication of the Rights of Men*. J. Johnson, 1790.

From the Publisher

A name never says it all, but the word "Broadview" expresses a good deal of the philosophy behind our company. We are open to a broad range of academic approaches and political viewpoints. We pay attention to the broad impact book publishing and book printing has in the wider world; for some years now we have used 100% recycled paper for most titles. Our publishing program is internationally oriented and broad-ranging. Our individual titles often appeal to a broad readership too; many are of interest as much to general readers as to academics and students. Founded in 1985, Broadview remains a fully independent company owned by its shareholders—not an imprint or subsidiary of a larger multinational. For the most accurate information on our books (including information on pricing, editions, and formats) please visit our website at www.broadviewpress.com. Our print books and ebooks are also available for sale on our site.

broadview press
www.broadviewpress.com